A Bird-Finding Guide to Ontario

CLIVE E. GOODWIN

A Bird-Finding Guide to Ontario

UNIVERSITY OF TORONTO PRESS

Toronto Buffalo London

© University of Toronto Press 1982
Toronto Buffalo London
Printed in Canada
Reprinted 1984, 1992

ISBN 0-8020-6494-9

Canadian Cataloguing in Publication Data

Goodwin, Clive E.
A bird-finding guide to Ontario

Includes index.
ISBN 0-8020-6494-9

1. Bird watching – Ontario – Guide-books. I. Title.

QL685.5.05G66   598'.07'234713   C82-094717-2

Publication of this book has been assisted by the Ontario Arts
Council under its block grant program.

Contents

Maps

Preface

Ontario offers a host of exciting opportunities for the bird-watcher. Over 400 species of birds have been found and over 270 have nested in the province. There are natural areas that range from deciduous woodlands in the south to arctic coastline in the north. Yet without precise directions on where to go to find birds, the sheer size and diversity of the province can defeat the visitor.

A Naturalist's Guide to Ontario, published seventeen years ago, established the value of a finding guide. Subsequent years have seen a growing demand across North America for bird-finding guides in particular, and recognition of the need for precise information about locations. This book sets out to meet that need, and provides directions to the best-known localities for finding birds in Ontario.

No book of this kind can be complete. There are a multitude of good places to watch birds in Ontario; it is only possible to offer a selection of the most popular and productive localities. I have covered these in some detail, but also attempted to provide the birder with choices of locations that should yield good birding across the province.

By the same token no book of this kind could be written without the help of many people. Particular thanks are due to the following, who made major contributions to the sections indicated: A.D. Brewer (Guelph, Luther Marsh, and Mountsberg); C.A., D.L., and J.L. Campbell (Pelee Island, Cambridge, and Kitchener/Waterloo); D.H. Elder (Chapter 8); and R. Tozer (Algonquin Provincial Park). They and many others provided other valuable information and assistance in a variety of ways, especially R.F. Andrle, D. Asquith, M. Bain, G. Bennett, R. Bowles, A. Dawe, G.M. Hamilton, J.W. Johnson, A.H. Kelley, E.W. Lewis, C.J. MacFayden, R.D. McRae, A. Mills, J. Nicholson, B. Parker, S. Peruniak, A. Rider, D.C. Sadler, A. Sandilands, M. Scholz, M. Smout, J. Wallace, and R.D. Weir. I am sure to have missed someone who made a key contribution, and indeed much of the information has been gathered over many years, with the willing help throughout that time of birders across the province.

Thanks also to G.D. Boggs and T. Beechey of the Ministry of Natural Resources' Parks Planning Section for allowing access to their files, and to B. Hogarth of the Pollution Control Branch of the Ministry of the Environment for making available a tabulation of the major municipal sewage lagoons. The Maitland Valley, Ganaraska, and Lakehead Region Conservation Authorities provided useful information. J. and P. Satterly and G.K. Peck provided information initially for my *A Bird Finding Guide to the Toronto Region*, used again here. All the information supplied has been modified to harmonize with the rest of the text, and responsibility for any errors or omissions is mine alone.

Finally, this book is a joint effort in all but name. My wife, Joy, has been an active participant in the book's preparation at every stage, and only her natural modesty prevents her name from appearing as co-author. It would not have been written without her support and contributions.

Works of this kind date quickly, and there are bound to be mistakes. We urge and welcome suggestions for corrections, changes, and additions for a future revision.

CEG

A Bird-Finding Guide to Ontario

1 / How to Use This Book

This chapter presents the plan of the book. There are four main sections. The first gives general information on Ontario birds and their status in the province, the next (Chapters 3–8) contains the regional accounts and forms the major body of the text, and the last two contain information for visitors and systematic lists of species.

The regional descriptions successively cover southwestern Ontario and the Niagara Peninsula, then south-central, eastern, central, and northern Ontario, and Lake of the Woods. At the beginning of each chapter is a map of the region showing the areas covered, together with a short general account of the bird life there.

The selection and treatment of areas covered varies both within the regions and from one region to another. In general, the more important an area is, the greater the coverage it receives; the amount of detail provided also depends, however, on the need to provide more directions for some areas than others.

Except for northern Ontario and Lake of the Woods, areas are listed alphabetically within each chapter. All are communities that appear on provincial roadmaps and thus in their indexes. (To find the account for a particular park in the book, even a well-known one like Algonquin, look it up in the index.) Bold capitals are used for the names of the more important areas. All areas are numbered consecutively, the numbers corresponding to those on the key maps.

Selection of areas has been influenced by accessibility, particularly in the north. For this reason, the bulk of the northern chapter departs from the plan of the rest of the book to trace the routes of the two main legs of the Trans-Canada Highway. There are doubtless hundreds of good places elsewhere that deserve listing, but, whether known or not, are hard to reach.

In the detailed directions to birding spots I have assumed that the reader has access to a reasonably up-to-date provincial road-map. For provincial parks and Conservation Authority areas, which are usually well signposted on the highways, few directions are provided. Areas of relatively minor interest also receive only brief mention, but for sewage lagoons and other places that can be hard to find, more detailed directions are provided, which should be adequate to locate them from the book alone. In general, the localities mentioned are on public land unless noted otherwise; I have tried to avoid listing areas that are private property.

Sewage lagoons are an exception to this rule, although with a couple of exceptions only municipal lagoons are included. Most of these are at present posted against trespassing although bird-watchers are tolerated. The attitudes of the local ministry officials to this kind of use vary widely from active encouragement to tossing birders out, but such attitudes are changing, mostly in the direction of greater tolerance. Be that as it may, this book tells where the lagoons are, not whether one can get into them or not. That must be assessed at the time of one's visit; seek the necessary permission if in doubt. Also be warned that hunting may be going on in these areas, legally or illegally. The ministry postings are made partly because of this possible activity, but mainly because officials want to deter people from trying to use these places for swimming pools – they are deep, if nothing else! Whether bird-watchers continue to be tolerated depends increasingly on how everyone behaves, so do be responsible in visiting lagoons.

In using the book, first read Chapter 2. The first section gives a general picture of the province as a whole, the habitats it contains, and common breeding birds one can expect to encounter. The second section gives notes for each season on weather conditions, the kinds of birding that can be most productive, and the commoner birds that will be seen.

FINDING A PARTICULAR BIRD

To find a particular species, refer to the systematic lists in Chapter 10. These give an idea of the seasonal abundance. In using the lists, read the definitions of the abundance symbols first. Note that each symbol does not represent an assessment of absolute abundance, but rather reflects the likelihood of seeing a particular bird. For example, in absolute terms Ruby-throated Hummingbirds are common summer residents, but since it is not easy to find one and even local birders might be distressingly vague about where to look for one, they are listed as uncommon in that season.

Now refer to the index. If the bird is fairly common, it will likely be mentioned in only the general sections of the book. Less common species are often mentioned in the appropriate area accounts. These give locations where the species is known to occur with some regularity. If the bird that is being sought is not common and no locations are given for it, it is either thinly distributed in suitable habitat or does not appear consistently enough anywhere to warrant special mention. One's best bet then is to visit one of the better birding areas in the appropriate season and hope for the best. Chapter 2 gives more details on habitat types and seasonal movements, but the following summaries may help in the selection of a good area (italicized locations are judged best. The numbers correspond to those used for the areas in the text).

1 Breeding Season

Southern and deciduous forests: Arkona (3), Aylmer (4), *Blenheim* (7), Campbellville (69), *Grand Bend* (21), Kettle Point (26), Kingston (141), *Leamington* (28), Long Point (30), Pelee Island (36), Port Lambton (40), St Catharines (45)

Mixed forests: Angus (62), Bancroft (127), Brighton (129), Campbellville (69), Cloyne (133), Englehart (182), Grand Bend (21), *Huntsville* (167), *Kingston* (141), Lake Superior Provincial Park (203), Port Elgin (105), Quetico Provincial Park (194), Wiarton (121)

Boreal and coniferous forests: Bancroft (127), Cloyne (133), Hearst (187), *Huntsville* (167), Lake Superior Provincial Park

(203), Long Point (30), *Sibley Provincial Park* (192), Tobermory (116), Upsala (198), Uxbridge (119)

Swamp forests: Angus (62), Blenheim (Rondeau) (7), Freelton (19), Kincardine (86)

Bogs: Angus (62), Arthur (63), Cochrane (185), Moosonee (211), Ottawa (145), Port Colborne (38), Upsala (198), Sibley Provincial Park (192)

Marshes: *Arthur* (63), Atikokan (195), *Blenheim* (7), *Brighton* (129), *Chatham* (11), Cochrane (185), *Elmvale* (77), */Hamilton* (23), Kingston (141), Lake of the Woods (216), Leamington (28), *Long Point* (30), Midland (91), Pickering (103), *Port Lambton* (40)

Old Fields: *Ferndale* (80), Gore Bay (166), Kingston (141), Lake of the Woods (214), Newcastle (97), Palgrave (101), *Picton* (148), Rockton (43), *Sebright* (107), Wiarton (121)

2 Migration

Blenheim (7), *Brighton* (129), Gore Bay (166), Kettle Point (26), Lake of the Woods (216), *Leamington* (28), *Long Point* (30), Meldrum Bay (171), Moosonee (211), Ottawa (145), Pelee Island (36), *Picton* (148), Sarnia (49), Sault Ste Marie (207)

3 Winter

Bancroft (127), *Huntsville* (167), Ivy Lea (140), Kingston (141), Leamington (28), *Niagara Falls* (33), Toronto (117)

DECIDING WHERE TO GO

You may wish to select a suitable spot to find birds in your immediate locality. If so, check the key maps and select the numbers closest to you. Alternatively, you may wish to select a particularly good area for a trip. In this case check the above list and then refer to the accounts in the text for the areas listed, or look through the area accounts and pick the major areas (ie, those shown in bold capitals) and decide where to go. If there are limitations on time or area, the maps can be helpful to aid selection.

If only one place can be visited and you have some flexibility, visit Point Pelee in May (see Leamington). If there is time for two, from Pelee go on to Algonquin Provincial Park (Huntsville), where more northern species can be observed and warblers seen on their breeding grounds.

Chapter 9 notes some of the sorts of things a stranger to Ontario might wish to know.

NOMENCLATURE

Everyone has his own ideas about bird names. I have decided to be conservative and follow the 5th Edition of the American Ornithologists Union Check List (with supplements). The one exception is the marsh wrens: I have adopted the far better American Birding Association terminology of Sedge Wren for the Short-billed and Marsh Wren for the Long-billed Marsh Wren. In recognition of the fact that the AOU Check List is being revised and some present names may vanish, I have provided in the following list a cross-comparison between present terminology and names used in the Check List of the American Birding Association:

AOU	ABA
White Pelican	American White Pelican
Gannet	Northern Gannet
Anhinga	American Anhinga
Harcourt's Storm-Petrel	Band-rumped Storm Petrel
Black Duck	American Black Duck
Pintail	Common Pintail
European Wigeon	Eurasian Wigeon
Goshawk	Northern Goshawk
Marsh Hawk	Northern Harrier
Bobwhite	Common Bobwhite
Turkey	Wild Turkey
American Golden Plover	Lesser Golden Plover
Least Tern	Little Tern
Ground Dove	Common Ground Dove
Screech Owl	Common Screech Owl
Eastern Wood Pewee	Eastern Pewee
Common Raven	Northern Raven
Common Crow	American Crow
Mockingbird	Northern Mockingbird

AOU	ABA
Wheatear	Northern Wheatear
Starling	European Starling
Cardinal	Northern Cardinal
Dark-eyed Junco	Northern Junco
Tree Sparrow	American Tree Sparrow

2 / Ontario and Its Bird Life

The province of Ontario has an area of 1,068,587 square km (412,582 square miles), or over four times that of the United Kingdom and a third more than the state of Texas. It is not only huge in area but in extent: it is over 1600 km, or 1000 miles, from its western boundary to its eastern limit on the St Lawrence River, and also from north to south.

A region so enormous has a diversity of life forms to match. In the extreme south is the deciduous forest, which extends south to the Carolinas. In the far north is a tundra coastline at Cape Henrietta Maria. On the western boundary plants and animals more typical of prairies can be found. At last count 417 species of birds have occurred in the province, and at least 276 have nested.

For the travelling birder Ontario thus offers great opportunity, and for those who would cover it well great challenge. The greater part of the far north is inaccessible except by air and knowledge of its bird life is fragmentary. Even the south, away from the larger population centres and a few well-covered hotspots, is not known in detail by birders.

Forestlands

Before settlement, most of the province was forested, and three major forest areas have been identified. The Deciduous Forest Region (J.S. Rowe, *Forest Regions of Canada*, 1972) occupies the southernmost peninsula, east to Grand Bend on the Lake Huron shore, through the city of London to Toronto on Lake Ontario.

East of Toronto a narrow belt of deciduous forest continues along the lake to the Kingston region, although this lacks the more typical southern plants. The birds of this area are discussed in Chapter 3, on southwestern Ontario. North of this limited zone of hardwoods are the mixed forests of the Great Lakes–St Lawrence Forest Region. This is the characteristic forest cover over much of settled Ontario. Its northern limits extend to New Liskeard on the east and to Kenora on the west. It occupies the shorelines of lakes Huron and Superior, apart from the narrow strip of deciduous forest at the south end of Huron and the Superior shore between Thunder Bay and Lake Superior Provincial Park. It consists of stands of sugar maple, beech, and other hardwoods in company with white pine, balsam fir, and hemlock. To the north these hardwoods are gradually replaced by birch and aspen, and the pine by spruce. These trees are characteristic of the Boreal Forest, which is discussed more fully in Chapter 7, on northern Ontario. It extends to the shores of James and Hudson Bay, and is the predominant forest type over the largest area of the province. Along the north coast, around Cape Henrietta Maria, the forest gives way to open tundra.

The major forested areas in the south are associated with the Pre-Cambrian Shield and to a much lesser extent with the Niagara Escarpment. The characteristic countryside of the Shield is a rugged and scenic mixture of forest, rock, and small lakes. This occupies most of the land north of Lake Huron and extends south from there in a huge wedge – the Frontenac Axis – to Port Severn at the southeast end of Georgian Bay, and from there east roughly to Gananoque and Brockville. It then runs north almost to Arnprior, and parallels the Ottawa Valley before joining the river near Chalk River. This enormous area is covered predominantly in mixed forestland.

The Niagara Escarpment is a limestone escarpment that follows the north shore of Manitoulin Island and the east shoreline of the Bruce Peninsula. It continues close to the Georgian Bay shoreline almost to Collingwood and then runs south to Hamilton, after which it parallels the south shoreline of Lake Ontario to Niagara Falls. In places it becomes obscured, but associated with it are some of the largest and most continuous areas of woodland west of the Shield. In the southern sections deciduous forest predominates. Woodland and reforestation (usually with red pine) also occur in areas of infertile or poorly drained soils, as described more fully below under farmland.

Farming occurs in many places where suitable soils exist, and plants characteristics of one forest region can be found north or south of its limits where soils and topography combine to create the appropriate conditions. Many of the areas mentioned in this guide are of this kind: pockets of habitat different from their surroundings. Relatively few birds are uniformly distributed across a landscape of such diversity.

Following is a series of summaries of the more common species that are likely to be encountered by the bird-watcher in Ontario and the places they are most probably to be found in the breeding season. First, however, some cautions are in order. Distribution and habitat preferences differ from one species to another, and even the latter may change geographically. For example, we have heard Connecticut Warblers singing and apparently inhabiting territory in three distinctly different types of habitat in different parts of the province – but to date no one has succeeded in finding a Connecticut Warbler nest in Ontario, so there is no absolute proof the bird nests here! Furthermore, some species occur across several habitat types. Downy Woodpeckers and Black-capped Chickadees are more likely to be found in a wood-lot than in a field, but shrubby fields often will yield both species. Finally, birds are much less selective about habitat during migration; to use another example, Yellow-rumped Warblers almost qualify as open country birds in fall, when they can be found masquerading as pipits on shorelines and feeding across weedy fields by the dozen.

Remember, then, in using the following listings of birds most likely to be encountered in various habitats, that they will not always be found there, and that they might be found elsewhere as well. In general these species will not be mentioned again.

The typical species of the deciduous woodlands are discussed in Chapter 3, but many birds occur in summer throughout the more accessible forestlands of the province. (Species asterisked are permanent residents in most areas.) These are:

Ruffed Grouse*	Common Flicker
Great Horned Owl*	Pileated Woodpecker*
Ruby-throated Hummingbird	Hairy Woodpecker*

Downy Woodpecker*
Least Flycatcher
Blue Jay*
Black-capped Chickadee*
Brown Creeper
Red-eyed Vireo
Black-and-white Warbler
Black-throated Green Warbler

Chestnut-sided Warbler
Ovenbird
Mourning Warbler
American Redstart
Rose-breasted Grosbeak
Purple Finch
Chipping Sparrow

Several of the above are significantly less common in the south than farther north, and such species as Ruffed Grouse, Brown Creeper, and some warblers are very local or found only occasionally in summer in the extreme southwest.

A number of other species are even harder to find in the south, although common enough farther north. References in the text on southern Ontario to wooded areas having northern affinities or species imply that some of these birds can be expected. They are:

Yellow-bellied Sapsucker
Alder Flycatcher
Red-breasted Nuthatch
Winter Wren
Hermit Thrush
Swainson's Thrush
Golden-crowned Kinglet
Ruby-crowned Kinglet
Nashville Warbler

Magnolia Warbler
Yellow-rumped Warbler
Blackburnian Warbler
Northern Waterthrush
Canada Warbler
Pine Siskin (erratic)
Dark-eyed Junco
White-throated Sparrow

(Species with ranges that normally do not extend south of our central Ontario region are listed in Chapter 6.)

A number of other common woodland birds in southern and central Ontario become markedly less common or are wholly absent farther north. These species with southern affinities are:

American Woodcock
Whip-poor-will
Great Crested Flycatcher
Eastern Wood Pewee
White-breasted Nuthatch*
Wood Thrush

Veery
Yellow-throated Vireo (local)
Black-throated Blue Warbler
Northern Oriole
Scarlet Tanager
Indigo Bunting

Finally, as a group, the woodland raptors are elusive and difficult to locate, so their true breeding status is always difficult to establish, and most are more conveniently looked for in other seasons. The Red-shouldered Hawk often soars over farm woodlots in late spring, and its distinctive call can often act as a guide to it. The Broad-winged Hawk often sits on roadside wires in forest areas. The Screech Owl, which is the common owl of the populous south and a noisy little bird, is the easiest owl to find. Where the Barred occurs its distinctive hooting is characteristic, but it is local in distribution.

Most of the commoner species listed below under farmlands can also be found in the forested areas as well, occupying the edge habitats if not the woodland itself. The two species of cuckoo occur across the south in both woodland and thickets. The Yellow-billed is much less common to the north, and both species vary greatly in numbers from year to year and from place to place.

Farmlands

In regard to the agricultural south of Ontario, discussion about the natural forest cover is academic. Even those areas that are forested have been manipulated extensively by man. In the southwest only isolated groves and wood-lots remain in some parts, but elsewhere in the south a patchwork of fields and woodlands occurs in areas of poorer soil.

Farther north, large areas of agricultural land occur around Sudbury, on Manitoulin Island, and north and east of Sault Ste Marie, and farther north again, in the clay belts around New Liskeard and Cochrane, near Thunder Bay, and in the extreme west around Rainy River. Rainy River is discussed separately in Chapter 8.

The following breeding birds are commonly associated with farmlands, including the brush and scrub areas of field corners and old fields:

Red-tailed Hawk*	Common Nighthawk
American Kestrel*	Chimney Swift
Killdeer	Common Flicker
Rock Dove*	Eastern Kingbird

Eastern Phoebe
Horned Lark
Tree Swallow
Bank Swallow
Barn Swallow
Cliff Swallow (local)
Common Crow
American Robin
Cedar Waxwing
Starling*
Yellow Warbler

House Sparrow*
Bobolink
Eastern Meadowlark (Western
    from Thunder Bay west)
Red-winged Blackbird
Common Grackle
Brown-headed Cowbird
American Goldfinch
Savannah Sparrow
Vesper Sparrow
Chipping Sparrow
Song Sparrow

Several of these species, notably Chimney Swift, Eastern Phoebe, Bank Swallow, and Bobolink, become considerably more local in the north, and may be hard to find there. Several other species, some of them typical of brushy or edge habitats, fit the above category but are even rarer in the north. They reach their northern limits in the area defined as central Ontario in this book and along the north shore of Lake Huron, or are thinly distributed elsewhere:

Mourning Dove
Red-headed Woodpecker
Willow Flycatcher
Rough-winged Swallow
Purple Martin
House Wren

Gray Catbird
Brown Thrasher
Warbling Vireo
Northern Oriole
Rufous-sided Towhee
Field Sparrow

Mourning Doves are expanding their range at present and soon may become familiar to birders in the north. References in the text to farmland species with more southern affinities usually imply that some of these species occur.

The text includes numerous references to poor or marginal farmland, or old fields and the like. Broadly, there are three kinds of environment that create such conditions. In the north, where the growing season is short and the returns from agriculture low, there is much pastureland that is reverting to or at least partly occupied by willow and alder scrub. Drainage is often poor, resulting frequently in areas occupied by sedges and, sometimes, open water. Farther south such conditions more typically reflect poor soils. They occur among the agricultural pockets on the Pre-Cambrian shield, but more commonly on the thin soils of some of the limestone and moraine areas.

Limestones are most typical of Manitoulin Island and the Bruce Peninsula, the Carden plain east of Orillia, the Flamborough plain east of Cambridge, much of Prince Edward County, and other parts of eastern Ontario. Typically the limestone bedrock is close to the surface and the rocky pastures contain shrub roses, hawthorns, and white cedars; rail and stump fences are common; and, again, extensive poorly drained areas may have heavy sedge growth.

The hilly, rolling country associated with moraines occupies huge areas of the south, west of the Pre-Cambrian Shield. Soils are often pebbly with many large boulders, the hilltops are dry, and the hollows have small ponds and marshy areas. The landscape is not ideal for modern farming techniques, and again there is dry pasture with scattered scrub, patches of marsh, and ponds, albeit in a very different landscape. Reforestation is common in this country.

Similar but more localized conditions occur on the drumlin fields, which are as widespread as the moraines themselves. A drumlin sometimes represents a hill of poor, arid soil in an otherwise fertile area – or even overlying the limestones.

In addition to the typical farmland birds a group of rather local species can be found in these habitats. The most common are:

American Bittern	Sedge Wren
Marsh Hawk	Eastern Bluebird
Common Snipe	Loggerhead Shrike
Upland Sandpiper	Grasshopper Sparrow

Short-eared Owls, on their rare breeding attempts in the south, seem to have favoured this country. Clay-coloured Sparrows occur, chiefly in reforested areas before the pines have reached 3–4 metres in height. Henslow's Sparrows are very local breeding birds in the south only, and their numbers have declined in the last twenty years or so. They are commonest in these habitats, and seem to favour those parts of old fields where taller, denser vegetation has developed in some of the depressions, with goldenrod and aster mixed with tall grasses. By contrast,

Grasshopper Sparrows seem to favour thinner grass in the drier parts of the fields, and often use mullein stalks as song posts. To the north in the clay belts, with the exception of bittern, Marsh Hawk, and snipe, these species appear to be rare or are wholly absent.

Wetlands

Ontario probably has more shoreline than any comparable area in the world. The Great Lakes shores alone amount to over 3800 km, and the seacoast along Hudson Bay and James Bay represents another 1094 km. The patchwork quilt of smaller lakes and connecting streams across the north and the Shield in the south is best appreciated from the air: small wonder canoeing is a major recreational activity in the province!

The character of the Great Lakes shores varies: it is sandy, gravelly, or rocky depending on location. The beaches attract Spotted Sandpipers in summer, small flocks of shorebirds in migration, and patrolling gulls year round where open water occurs, but the absence of significant tidal movement means that in most places large feeding concentrations of birds do not occur. Marshes, the mud flats associated with rivers, and areas of algae deposition are the places birds gather. The last two develop frequently in autumn, when water levels drop and the green algae which have built up in the lakes over the summer are deposited in pungent masses.

The Great Lakes themselves are particularly noteworthy for wintering and migrant waterfowl, but the many offshore islands are nesting sites for herons, ducks, gulls, and terns that feed along the shore and in the waterfront marshes. The colonies of these species completely cover many of the smaller islands, most of which are designated nature reserves or wildlife sanctuaries. Several of these islands are well known and most are regularly visited by Canadian Wildlife Service biologists or by teams from local nature clubs to band birds and assess the status of their populations. These places are not usually listed in this guide because the breeding colonies are vulnerable to disturbance and should be left undisturbed if possible. In any case, access tends to be difficult and all of the species can be readily seen along the shores.

Species nesting on the islands include:

Double-crested Cormorant	Ring-billed Gull
Red-breasted Merganser	Common Tern
(local)	Caspian Tern (south only)
Herring Gull	

The marshlands associated with the mouths of rivers along the Great Lakes, and with lakes and other waterbodies mainly south of the Shield, have a rich array of breeding species. In these wetlands extensive stands of cat-tail (*Typha* spp.) and open, shallow water areas are characteristic, although brushy areas with alder and willow and wet sedgy fields often occur. Typical species that can be found in summer are:

Pied-billed Grebe	American Coot
Great Blue Heron	Spotted Sandpiper
Black-crowned Night Heron	Black Tern (local)
(local)	Belted Kingfisher
American Bittern	Marsh Wren
Mallard	Common Yellowthroat
Blue-winged Teal	Red-winged Blackbird
Virginia Rail	Swamp Sparrow
Sora	

Least Bittern and Common Gallinule occur only in the marshes of southern Ontario, where the former is secretive and local and the latter often conspicuous. Three other species – Mute Swan, Canada Goose, and Gadwall – are expanding their ranges and becoming increasingly common along Lakes Ontario and Erie, and thence gradually northward. The first two are from feral populations, as are large numbers of Mallards in the same area.

Swampy woodlands are often associated with the larger marshes, and there are some huge swamps in the south. In addition to the landbirds these support, the following waterbirds occur most commonly in wooded or partly wooded habitats:

Green Heron	Hooded Merganser
Wood Duck	American Woodcock

The development of flood control reservoirs and sewage lagoons has added important waterbird habitat. The lagoons in particular have become significant out of all proportion to their size: the fertile waters of these places can yield at different times marsh, mud flat for shorebirds, or open water for ducks (or nothing at all!) depending on their management. At Long Point, for example, it is possible to find the Port Rowan lagoons full of waterfowl when the huge marshes seem dead. Wilson's Phalaropes, which have expanded their range recently, are often associated with sewage lagoons.

Most of the species of ducks that occur in the province in migration must be added to the list of birds that can be found in marshes during the breeding season, even though there is no evidence they nest there commonly, or at all. Large numbers of waterfowl move through the region to breed farther west or north, but it is not unusual to find a few of these birds lingering in favoured localities and sometimes nesting. The more usual such species are:

Black Duck	Redhead
Pintail	Canvasback
Green-winged Teal	Lesser Scaup
Northern Shoveler	Bufflehead
American Wigeon	Ruddy Duck

The lakes of the Shield tend to be unproductive of waterbird habitat. They are relatively infertile and have steep, rocky shorelines. More productive wetland in these areas – and indeed in any of the forested country – often occurs in conjunction with beaver dams, where extensive flooding leads to the development of wet meadows and bogs. Breeding birds typical of this range of habitats include:

Common Loon	Common Merganser
Great Blue Heron	Common Snipe
American Bittern	Belted Kingfisher
Black Duck	Alder Flycatcher
Ring-necked Duck	Olive-sided Flycatcher
Common Goldeneye	Common Yellowthroat
Hooded Merganser	

Ospreys may also occur over larger water bodies. Canada Geese occur naturally in the north.

Urban Habitats

Urban areas resemble a patchwork of open country and edge habitats, sometimes with more extensive wooded areas in parks and river valleys. Rock Dove, Starling, and House Sparrow are the familiar city birds, but Common Nighthawks and American Kestrels are regular, and in the more natural areas most of the common species listed under farmlands and forestlands can be found.

SEASONAL CHANGES

The above picture of bird distribution is true for the breeding season, but is a very partial picture indeed when the year as a whole is considered. In Ontario birds are on the move in every month of the year, and migration is heavy for some six months. Only for a brief period in June is bird distribution fairly static; all the species enumerated above will then be found occupied with the business of rearing families, but even then unmated and non-breeding birds can wander, often far from their established breeding grounds.

Winter

Winter is the time when birds are in smallest numbers and is a convenient departure point for a review of seasonal changes. There is much less variation in the onset of winter across the province than in its departure. Even in the south the first snow usually falls in late October, though it quickly vanishes. Not until late November or early December does the snow stay. By then freeze-up is well established in the north, where things will stay frozen for well over four months. Some areas never freeze, however, and in these patches of open water and sheltered land, duck and other species that normally move farther south can survive. (See Chapter 7 for additional comments on the birds in northern Ontario in winter.)

In the south the characteristic pattern of alternating periods of colder and milder weather can result in substantial thaws and even in a total disappearance of snow on the ground for periods over the winter. The amount of snow is related less to temperature than to location: localities lying south and east of Georgian Bay, Lake Huron, and Lake Ontario (the 'snow belts') receive much more snow than do other areas, as the prevailing winds pick up moisture crossing the lakes.

Along the lower Great Lakes it is always rather a toss-up whether Christmas will be white or green, but by January the situation is usually less ambiguous and snow and ice prevail. (Temperatures can drop well below −20°C but more often range between 0° and −10°C.) Early March sees the return of warmer weather, but snow often lingers even here until late in the month, and early April blizzards are not infrequent, although rare enough to confuse road maintenance departments.

Bird distribution is far from static in winter. Even the species asterisked above as resident are often only questionably so. They are present year-round but also often migrate in numbers: who is to say that the starling at the feeder in December is the same one that nests in the garden in April?

The species that migrate annually to the south are relatively few. The common landbirds are Dark-eyed Junco and Tree Sparrow. Several other species, however, appear almost every year in varying numbers – sometimes they are almost absent and in other years (often on a regular cycle) large invasions may occur. These erratic species are:

Rough-legged Hawk	Bohemian Waxwing (rare)
Snowy Owl	Evening Grosbeak
Long-eared Owl	Purple Finch
Short-eared Owl	Pine Grosbeak
Black-backed Three-toed Woodpecker	Common Redpoll
	Pine Siskin
Northern Three-toed Woodpecker (rare)	White-winged Crossbill (rare)
Northern Shrike	Snow Bunting

In a similar class, but not usually annual in occurrence and appearing only in small numbers, are Gyrfalcon and Hawk, Great Gray, and Boreal Owls. Lapland Longspurs typically occur at this time of year as isolated, darker, and smaller-looking birds in Snow Bunting flocks.

Waterbird numbers depend on the prevalence of open water, which varies greatly from year to year and during the winter itself. In severe winters even most of the Great Lakes freeze. Often the lakes are frozen too far out from shore to allow good viewing of the open water that remains. The west end of Lake Ontario usually remains open, however, and the typical winter waterfowl are given in the Toronto account.

The annual Christmas bird counts give a good picture of early bird numbers. In the north the number of species present on the censuses rarely exceeds 30 and is usually much smaller, but southern counts can exceed 100, although totals of 25–30 are more typical for inland localities. Even the largest counts include many species that are unlikely either to survive or to remain as the winter progresses, although in the south it is not unusual to find such species as crows present in substantial numbers throughout the season, gradually declining in abundance to the north and east. The following species (other than duck and gulls) are the principal ones that regularly linger over winter in varying numbers:

Great Blue Heron (rare)
Mourning Dove
Belted Kingfisher
Common Flicker
Red-headed Woodpecker
  (rare)
Horned Lark
Common Crow
Red-breasted Nuthatch
Brown Creeper
Winter Wren
American Robin
Hermit Thrush
Golden-crowned Kinglet

Cedar Waxwing
Yellow-rumped Warbler
  (rare)
Red-winged Blackbird
Rusty Blackbird
Common Grackle
Brown-headed Cowbird
American Goldfinch
Rufous-sided Towhee
Field Sparrow
White-throated Sparrow
Swamp Sparrow
Song Sparrow

In addition, all three accipiters, and Red-shouldered and Marsh Hawks are usually present in small numbers, particularly in the south. Many other species can be found in favoured areas.

Winter birds tend to be concentrated in places where there is an abundance of food, and sheltered spots in mixed and evergreen woodlands are often the best natural areas in which to find birds at this time, especially if there is open water nearby. Man-made food sources are very important, and one should search newly manured fields (Horned Larks, meadowlarks, and Snow Buntings), feed-lots and corn cribs, especially in the southwest (blackbirds), dumps (crows and blackbirds in the south, ravens in the north), and, of course, feeding stations, which can yield almost anything.

This is often the best time of year to see rarer resident species such as Red-bellied Woodpeckers, Tufted Titmice, and House Finches, which visit feeders more regularly in winter than at other times. The London area is the most productive for Red-bellieds and Niagara for titmice; House Finches are expanding rapidly, and at present seem established at Niagara-on-the-Lake, St Catharines, St Thomas, Toronto, and Kingston – and doubtless, by the time this is being read, at several other places!

In regard to waterbirds, warm water outfalls from power plants and the like can concentrate duck and gulls. The characteristic winter birds tend to be nomadic, even juncos and Tree Sparrows moving freely, especially after storms.

Spring Migration

In the south spring migration begins in February with the movement of small flocks of Horned Larks across the frozen fields and of finches. Later in the month steady, high flights of crows scatter across the sky on mild days, and noisy flocks of immaculate Ring-billed Gulls appear along the lower Great Lakes.

In the north the first movements can be a month or more later, and the entire migration is telescoped into a much shorter period, mainly from late April onwards. The chronology that follows is more applicable to southern Ontario, although even here there can be significant variations – sometimes a week to two weeks – in the overall status of migration between west and east. In general migration is earliest in the southwest and along the shores of Lake Erie, and is progressively later as one moves east and north.

March and early April bring heavy waterfowl movement, birds appearing in open leads as soon as the ice breaks up. Very heavy concentrations can occur at these points. There can be enormous gatherings of duck at this time (see Long Point, Chatham). The weather in this period is stormy and unpredictable, and birds arrive in the pushes of warm air, often to move south again in prolonged wintery spells. Landbirds, especially blackbirds, move in numbers from late March on.

With April and May comes the major push of spring migration, slowly at first but with a flood of migrants in May, including virtually all the warblers. Now the north catches up – there is not much more than a week's difference between the average May warbler arrival dates at Toronto and those along the north shore of Lake Superior. The movements are still closely associated with warm weather systems, and can be stalled completely in cooler periods.

Migrants are less selective than breeding birds in their choice of habitat. Nevertheless, it still makes sense to look for waterbirds in wet areas and forestbirds in wood-lots. Consider the weather: on cold, windy days sheltered sunny places closer to the ground are favoured. Look also for places that will concentrate migrants: the shoreline is one such place, and groves of trees, sheltered ravines, and pockets of vegetation along the shore are often more productive than similar areas inland. Concentrate on habitat edges, where woodlands and fields meet: a greater diversity of birds can be expected there. Large tracts of woodland or open country are often less productive than islands of habitat, where birds have less opportunity to disperse. Along the shorelines, marshes and river mouths will yield dabbling duck, but also watch wet fields for these species and early shorebirds. Promontories into lakes are often especially productive.

Ontario springs have very variable weather: on 24 May I have used a parka in Toronto, but more often have felt too warm in shorts. The weather is changeable, so one can end up wearing both. Generally early May is quite cool everywhere, but by late May a light jacket often suffices even farther north.

The noteworthy widespread events in the spring migration include huge Canada Goose movements east of Oshawa and towards the west end of Lake Erie. These birds fly north, the main numbers in early April, when several thousands can be seen in a day in the Port Hope–Kingston areas. In late May – usually around 24 May – there is a heavy Whimbrel movement along Lakes Erie and Ontario, and about the same time Dunlin also move in large flocks with smaller numbers of Black-bellied Plover, Ruddy Turnstone, Red Knot, and Sanderling. Brant flights occur in late May and early June, and seem most regular in the Kingston area and north to Ottawa, although smaller numbers occur west to Toronto.

It is no accident that the shorelines of the lower Great Lakes – Erie and Ontario – are prominent in the above account. Point Pelee, Rondeau, and Long Point concentrate the migrants, but the entire shoreline from Kingston to Niagara and thence to Amherstburg can yield excellent birding. In spring other water-birds that can be expected include loons (mainly Common, but some Red-throated), grebes (mainly Horned, and Red-necked, but look for the rare Eared and the very rare Western), Double-crested Cormorants, Whistling Swans, all of the pond duck, and Redheads, Canvasback, Lesser Scaup, White-winged Scoter, and Red-breasted Merganser most commonly among the diving duck, in addition to the wintering species. Vagrant herons turn up, and shorebirds can often be found on wet fields back from the shore-line as well as along the shores themselves. Bonaparte's Gulls feature largely in heavy gull movements.

The sections on Grimsby and Vineland deal wth spring hawk flights. Farther north, see South Baymouth for a note on the Mani-toulin Island movements of Oldsquaw, White-winged Scoter, and Whimbrel.

By early June only a few landbirds are still moving in num-bers – Blackpoll and Mourning are the last warblers to arrive, with nighthawks, cuckoos, later flycatchers, and shorebirds. Usually by mid-June breeding populations are established and nesting is in full swing. Throughout the month, however, birds continue to move. Shorebirds in particular can be found roam-ing in the last two weeks – presumably either non-breeding birds or birds that have lost their nests or broods and started to move south immediately afterwards.

The Nesting Season

The nesting season starts in February and March with owls and Gray Jays, and is well under way in April and May for resident and early migrant species. Even along the Hudson Bay coastline nesting activities are progressing well by the end of June. A few species, notably the crossbills, seem to breed when conditions suit them. Rock Doves can be found in breeding condition throughout the year, and Mourning Doves have been found nesting from at least March to October.

In general, however, broods are out in early July and there is not much activity after mid-August. If one defines summer as June, July, and August, then at least half this period is occupied by fall migration!

Distribution in the breeding season is detailed above and requires no further elaboration.

Summer weather can be very warm – temperatures in the 30°C range are regular in southern Ontario – but less so in the north where there is overnight cooling (which you cannot depend on farther south!).

Fall Migration

The start of the fall shorebird migration usually seems to be under way by the beginning of July. Then such species as Lesser Yellowlegs and Semipalmated Sandpiper begin to appear in small numbers away from the breeding grounds. Momentum builds up during the month, with large swallow flights developing as well. By August the main shorebird passage is under way, and flycatchers, thrushes, and warblers are also in good numbers by month end. August is still very warm, the vegetation is lush, and the birds are very quiet, so it does not seem like a big migration month, but in fact some of the heaviest movement of the year occurs then.

September is fall's answer to May – almost anything can turn up and major hawk flights with the onset of brisk, cooler weather make mid-September a delight.

By October the landbird passage is past its peak and the water-fowl hunting season has begun (usually about 25 September). Away from favoured lakefront localities the countryside can seem very quiet and birds few. Sparrows are still widespread, however, and other species that are still moving in open country at this time include Horned Larks, Water Pipits, Yellow-rumped and Palm Warblers, American Goldfinches, and Lapland Long-spurs. Hawks continue to move, principally Red-tailed and Rough-legged Hawks, and this is the best time to see Golden

Eagles. Canada Geese move south over the same routes they used going north, but their movement is more prolonged so it tends to be less spectacular than in the spring. From the Bruce Peninsula south through London and Sarnia small flocks of Snow Geese may also be expected.

All movements described for October continue into November, but the month's real interest comes in the flights – always unpredictable – of winter species such as Northern Shrikes and finches. More predictable November migrants are Tree Sparrows and Snow Buntings, and diving duck build up in huge numbers in areas where hunting does not disturb them (see Toronto, Picton). The largest single concentration of waterbirds in this period is along the Niagara River (see Niagara Falls): it is one of the most outstanding birding spectacles in the province at any season. By early December, apart from a few final hawk and waterbird movements, migration is over.

In autumn, cold air triggers migration, warm weather stalls it. (This is easy to forget in October and November, when pleasant weather is often the product of warm fronts.) The northern shorelines of the Great Lakes are obstacles to southward movement: in prolonged periods of poor weather landbirds moving slowly south tend to concentrate in suitable habitats near the lake. The bird-watcher who waits for the rainy weather to end will be too late! By contrast, diurnal migrants move in good weather. For hawk flights, watch for cool, sunny days with moderate winds from the north or northwest.

Once again, the importance of the Great Lakes' shorelines emerges, particularly of the lower lakes. The huge swallow movements which occur there from July are most notable at Long Point, at Point Pelee, in the Niagara area, and at the east end of Lake Ontario. Early fall is a good time for southern herons to wander north, and they often end up in lakeshore marshes.

In September hawk flights develop along the north shores of the lakes (see Amherstburg, Port Stanley, Pickering, and Picton), but there are similar movements in the north around Marathon and north of Thunder Bay. Accipiters and falcons usually move singly, low, and directly over the tree-tops and close to the lakeshore – accipiters may even move out well over the lake – while buteos, Marsh Hawks, and Turkey Vultures soar, often in high, spiralling groups. The most spectacular movement is that of

Broad-winged Hawks, which move in huge milling flocks, sometimes with a hundred or more birds in each. Blue Jays and Monarch Butterflies are other features of the lower lakes at this time: the jays in long straggling flocks and the butterflies like huge dark snowflakes, all following the shore.

In late September and October large chickadee movements can occur, and most of the waterfowl listed for spring appear again, building up in large wintering flocks in November. However, hunting limits their distribution at this time. Less common species to be looked for include Sharp-tailed Sparrow in dense, short marsh vegetation – Beggar's Ticks' (*Bidens* spp.) beds are good – mostly in early October, and Purple Sandpiper, Red Phalarope, and King Eider in November.

In September and October the west end of Lake Ontario and the south end of Lake Huron are noted for some pelagic species not normally expected away from the ocean. Jaegers (mainly Parasitic, but with Pomarine later), Sabine's Gull, Black-legged Kittiwake, and phalaropes are the species usually seen. They are sometimes visible from shore (see Sarnia, Kettle Point, Hamilton, and Toronto) as well as on offshore boat trips that are sometimes arranged by local birders at Hamilton, Toronto, and Kingston.

Autumn, like spring, has changeable weather. In September, temperature ranges are similar to those in May, but by October and November it is usually cool, and often cold, raw, and windy.

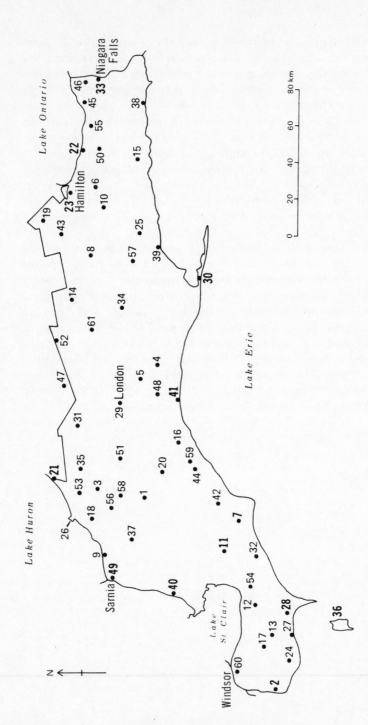

MAP 1 Southwestern Ontario

3 / Southwestern Ontario and the Niagara Peninsula

This chapter includes the counties of Middlesex, Oxford, and Brant and the Regional Municipality of Hamilton-Wentworth and all the area south of them. Together they make up much of the Deciduous Forest Region in the province.

This part of Ontario includes some of the best-known birding localities in the province and many larger centres of population. There is relatively little 'natural' forest left, although apart from the counties of Essex, Kent, and Lambton farm wood-lots and wooded river valleys are widespread. Here and there are pockets of more northern vegetation, and along the northern edge of this region mixed forest communities begin to appear. The natural forest cover, where it remains, is rich and diverse, with oaks and hickories joining the maples and beeches of the forests farther north. The three westernmost counties are heavily agricultural and there are flat plains in some sections that may never have been forested. The land along the Lake Erie shoreline continues generally flat, although more rolling country develops to the north, and between the Hamilton area and Niagara Falls the steep north-facing ridge of the Niagara Escarpment follows roughly the southern shoreline of Lake Ontario, with a narrow zone of orchard land between it and the lake. Some of Canada's richest farmland occurs in the region, although on the sandy soils of western Haldimand-Norfolk extensive reforestation with pine occurs.

The region is of particular interest both because it is the stronghold of southern species that occur only rarely elsewhere, and because its location as a peninsular tip to the rest of the province channels migrants and creates concentrations of species and rarities that have become internationally famous.

Several species occur more commonly in this region in summer than in other parts of Ontario, although most are still rare and local. They are:

Great Egret	Mockingbird*
Bobwhite*	Blue-gray Gnatcatcher
King Rail	White-eyed Vireo
Forster's Tern	Prothonotary Warbler
Barn Owl*	Louisiana Waterthrush
Red-bellied Woodpecker*	Yellow-breasted Chat
Acadian Flycatcher	Hooded Warbler
Tufted Titmouse*	Orchard Oriole
Carolina Wren*	Cardinal*

Three other species – Golden and Blue-winged Warblers and Cerulean Warblers – although also southern, are probably more readily found in breeding season in the larger wooded areas just northeast of the region than here, although in migration all three occur regularly in some numbers on Point Pelee and the other Lake Erie spits. A small number of Bald Eagles occur along the Lake Erie shore, part of a population that was once far commoner and more widespread.

Two introduced gamebirds, the Gray Partridge and Ring-necked Pheasant, fall into a separate category as their distribution is uneven, but the pheasant is commoner in parts of this region (notably Pelee Island) than elsewhere, and Gray Partridge are apparently widespread in the eastern parts.

Deservedly the best-known birding locality in Ontario, and probably in Canada, is Point Pelee (see Leamington). Its fame rests on the numbers of both birds and species that occur there during migration, and over the years more rarities have appeared there than in any other locality in the province. The other Lake Erie spits of Rondeau and Long Point, although lacking Pelee's almost ideal blend of topography and location for concentrating landbird migrants, represent major concentration points in themselves (see Blenheim for Rondeau).

For gulls and other waterfowl the mouth of the St Clair River at Sarnia, Kettle Point on Lake Huron, and the Niagara River all have well-earned reputations as well. Both Long Point and the marshes along Lake St Clair are outstanding in spring. For raptors, Holiday Beach Provincial Park and Hawk Cliff near Port Stanley are important in fall, and Beamer Point at Grimsby in spring.

The Niagara River between Fort Erie and Niagara-on-the-Lake (it is all included under Niagara Falls below) is particularly note-worthy for many southern birds in the colder months, and it is still good then for waterfowl as well.

Exceptional though this region is, naturalists elsewhere should take heart and recognize that it is much the most heavily covered part of the province. More thorough coverage of spots elsewhere could probably identify other important concentration points, as work at Prince Edward Point and Mississagi Light has shown. Indeed, in the region itself it is only in recent years that the full significance of the Sarnia–Kettle Point area has been recognized, and parts of Pelee Island have the potential to be a second Point Pelee, though they are less easy to reach.

(1) **Alvinston** – The A.W. Campbell Conservation Area north of Alvinston (3 km east of Highway 79 on Brooke Concession 6–7) is in an attractive natural area with hardwoods, bottomlands, river, and ponds. There is an entry fee.

(2) **AMHERSTBURG** – Highway 18, which follows the Detroit River from Windsor to south of Amherstburg, can be very pro-ductive of waterbirds. One noteworthy area is the mouth of the *Canard River* approximately 9 km north of Amherstburg. Here there are extensive marshes on both sides of the road and duck gather off the river mouth, especially large flocks of Canvasback in the fall. Depending on water levels, shorebirds can be numer-ous here in the autumn as well. It is also possible to reach the river a little higher up: County Road 1, just north of the high-way bridge, runs east to follow the river for a short distance, and if the next bridge upriver is crossed, the sideroad to the right does the same going west.

South of River Canard is the small community of *Edgewater Beach* – the first houses are only about ½ km south of the point where the highway turns right after crossing the marshes. There is a sewage lagoon here, opposite the third sidestreet running right (Foam Street, which is no more than 0.2 km from the first street). Turn left and drive ½ km to the lagoon gate.

Holiday Beach Provincial Park is some 15 km southeast of Amherstburg and 2 km south of the community of Malden Centre on County Road 50. It is principally known as a hawk observation point, but borders the extensive Big Creek marshes and Lake Erie itself, and so is a good place for waterbirds as well. Highway 18 also crosses Big Creek some 3 km west of Malden Centre. The marshes usually have readily visible Great Egrets and other herons in the warmer weather. A baited waterfowl feeding area is 1.2 km east of the park on County Road 50. There is hunting at Holiday Beach.

The hawk movements here in fall are heavier than at any other Ontario station. In September Broad-winged and Sharp-shinned Hawks and American Kestrels in that order predominate, with Sharp-shinneds, Red-taileds, and Turkey Vultures in October and Red-taileds in November. Well over 30,000 Broad-wingeds can be seen in a single day, and in all 15 species of raptor occur regularly, although Goshawks, eagles, Ospreys, Peregrine Falcons, and Merlins are usually only in small numbers. Often the soaring hawks are extremely high, and viewing can be better at Hawk Cliff (see Port Stanley), although on any day when there is heavy movement some birds are usually low enough to be seen easily.

(3) **Arkona** – The Ausable River valley north of Arkona is an exceptionally rich area of hardwoods and bottomland. Several Carolinian bird species have been recorded in summer including Hooded Warbler and Louisiana Waterthrush and species rare in the southwest, such as Veery and Chestnut-sided Warbler. However, access is difficult, the only area in public ownership being Rock Glen Conservation Area just north of Arkona (2 km east). There is a hiking trail open *only* to members of the Lambton Wildlife Trust on the east (Middlesex County) side. Highway 7 crosses this valley just east of the Highway 82 intersection.

(4) **Aylmer** – Lake Whittaker Conservation Area (entry fee) is a small lake associated with an extensive hardwood forest. It is

14.3 km north of Aylmer on Highway 73, and 4.3 km east on County Road 37 (gravelled).

A much more important area is *Springwater Conservation Area* west of Aylmer. From the intersection of Highways 73 and 3 drive west 4.2 km to Orwell and turn south. The area is 2.8 km down this road, and the fine Carolinian wood-lot just ½ km east on the sideroad there. This has been one of Ontario's most reliable stations for Hooded Warblers.

Another key Aylmer location is the sewage lagoons. Drive west from the town as above, but go 2.2 km to the first sideroad north. This is easy to miss. It is unmarked, just past Roger's Sideroad on the south (which is marked) and immediately on the other side of a green barn on the corner – at least at the time of writing. The lagoons are on the left 1.2 km up this road. Controlled shooting occurs there, but at other times they have been most productive.

Aylmer also has a Wildlife Management Area with feeding ponds that are good for waterfowl, particularly Whistling Swans, in early spring (March). To reach these drive north from town on Highway 73 one concession to County Road 32, signposted to Ontario Police College. Drive east one concession and turn south, following the yellow signs to Aylmer Wildlife Swan Viewing.

(5) **Belmont** – The sewage lagoon is 0.8 km south on Highway 74, from its intersection at the south end of town with County Road 34. Turn right on Yarmouth Concession 15 and drive 1 km west to the lagoon gates over the tracks.

(6) **Binbrook** – The Conservation Area (entry fee) here includes a medium-sized lake. Drive south to the 7th Concession and follow the signs.

(7) **BLENHEIM** – There are three areas of note here.
   The sewage lagoons can be most productive. To reach them, from the junction of Highways 40 and 3 in Blenheim, drive west 2.9 km on Highway 3 to Harwich Concession 3 just outside town. Turn north and drive 1 km crossing the tracks; the lagoons are on the right.

The Erieau Road (Kent Road 12) is 1.4 km west again on Highway 3. Turn south. *Erieau Harbour* is approximately 8 km away at the end of the road. At 7½ km, just outside the village, on the right is a pond and marsh (*McGeachy Pond*), which is good for ducks, gulls, and, under the right conditions, shorebirds. The low-lying fields on the way down can also yield migrant shorebirds, and Brewer's Blackbirds have bred there. The harbour (3½ km from the pond) gives fine views of the lake and bay to the north, and there are usually herons, ducks, and gulls. Occasionally a Bald Eagle may fly over, and shorebirds can be seen on the shoreline to the northeast or even on the pier itself.

Rondeau Provincial Park is east of Blenheim, south from Highway 3 via Highway 51. However, you can cut across to Rondeau from the Erieau road.

Returning northward, 3 km from the end of McGeachy Pond turn east on Bisnett Road (which is unmarked at this end). Drive 3 km east to the road end at a T-intersection, and turn right on Concession 2 WCR. This goes south some 2 km before turning east at Shrewsbury as Cathcart Street and joining (at a stop street) with County Road 11, which continues east to join Highway 51 (8 km) running south to Rondeau.

This route passes many marshy spots and more are accessible down the sidestreets of the village of Shrewsbury. The road is all hardtop at present except for 3½ km in the middle.

County Road 11 joins Highway 51 some 2.2 km from Highway 3, and south 2.8 km the highway bears west to enter the park. Just before this turn it crosses the marshes at the north end of Rondeau Bay, which can yield marsh birds and (again depending on water levels) shorebirds.

The peninsula occupied by the park is shaped like a huge comma with the tail pointing north. On the inner, bay side are extensive marshes which can be viewed from an 8 km walking trail leading across them. Little Gulls occur in summer and many rare waterbirds turn up here. Whistling Swans gather in the bay in March, and a pair of Bald Eagles nests along the edge of the marsh. In fall there is waterfowl hunting and the area loses its appeal.

The main area of the park is covered by probably the finest remaining stand of Carolinian hardwoods in southern Ontario, with a rich flora and fauna. Cerulean Warblers are regular, and Acadian Flycatchers nest along the South Point Trail and Prothonotary Warblers in the wet, wooded sloughs at the south end. This is the only accessible Ontario breeding station that has been occupied consistently by the latter two species. Other southerners, such as Red-bellied Woodpecker and Tufted Titmouse, occur but are less predictable. Some forest species uncommon in southwestern Ontario, such as Pileated Woodpecker, Brown Creeper, and Veery, can also be found in summer. Recently Chuck-wills-widow and White-eyed Vireo have occurred as well, the vireo nesting.

In migration the park can teem with migrants, but its extensive woodlands and general configuration makes it less easy to cover and it concentrates birds much less than Point Pelee, some 70 km farther west. The beach areas have cottages and are heavily used for recreation, but are excellent for watching gull, duck, and shorebird movements.

There is an entrance fee, a good interpretive program, a large campground, and lots of trails. Be sure to get bird and plant lists, and ask the naturalists for help in locating wanted species – there is usually at least one highly competent birder on staff. The nearest motels are in Blenheim.

(8) Brantford – At *Cainsville* on the eastern outskirts of the city, the sewage lagoons are on the east side of Shaver Street, which is on the south of Highway 2 just 0.9 km east of the major intersection of Highways 2, 53, 54, and 403.

West of this intersection 4 km, and in Brantford itself, is *Mohawk Park*. This is at the foot of Lynnwood Drive and 0.3 km south of Colborne Street, the name of Highway 2 at this point. The park is a large city park with mixed woodlands, and a lake that can be productive in migration times.

(9) Bright's Grove – The sewage lagoons are south off Lakeshore Road (County Road 7) 1.2 km east of the Waterworks Road – driving west just past Errol Sideroad. The lagoons are not visible from the road; cross the tracks and walk south to the line of trees. These lagoons have been productive of both migrants and breeding waterfowl, such species as American Wigeon, Green-winged Teal, and Ruddy Duck occurring in summer.

(10) Caledonia – Roads parallel both sides of the Grand River from Brantford almost continuously through to Dunnville. The major roads occupy the northeast bank, and Highway 54 in particular passes through excellent habitat – woods, riverside fields, and marshes – close to the river from north of Caledonia down to Cayuga. This area can be very productive of landbirds, particularly in winter, and in migration periods enormous concentrations of swallows can occur over the river in cool spells.

(11) **CHATHAM** – The east shoreline of Lake St Clair between Walpole Island and the mouth of the Thames River is a flat plain drained by an extensive network of ditches and dykes, and intensively farmed. There are few trees except groves of willows which attract migrant landbirds along the higher areas of the shores and dykes, and there are extensive marshes. The open farmland attracts enormous flocks of blackbirds in late summer and fall; Horned Larks, Lapland Longspurs, and Snow Buntings in later fall; and waterfowl especially in early spring when huge numbers of Whistling Swans and Canada Geese gather on the corn stubble. The Lake St Clair area is reputed to be the most important gathering area for waterfowl south of James Bay. Shorebirds can be found on wet fields, and plover are regular in migration.

The area lies northwest of Chatham and south of Wallaceburg, roughly between the villages of Mitchell Bay and Prairie Siding. From the north take Highway 40 south from Wallaceburg to the *Mitchell Bay* sideroad (County Road 42). The village is some 10 km southwest, and its waterfront affords views of the southeast end of the Walpole Island marshes and of the lake. East of town 1.7 km, on the north of the County Road, is the village sewage lagoon.

The Mitchell-Dover Townline (County Road 34, but it is unmarked) is 1 km east, and it runs southeast through the village of Grande Pointe. The first sideroad west past the village (7 km from County Road 42) is the 8th Concession Dover; it runs 7.6 km to end at Klein's Camp, where you should make a turn south on to a gravel road (West Townline Road), which runs alongside a wide drainage canal. Over the canal to the west are marshes which themselves are closed to hunting, and there are several opportunities for viewing these from the road.

After 1 km you pass the headquarters of the *St Clair National Wildlife Area* on the other side of the dyke; 1.4 km farther on turn right on a bridge across the Canal, on Dover Concession 4. This road runs along the south side of the National Wildlife Area before ending at 1.8 km. It is possible, with discretion, to stop to view the marsh (although there is no parking allowed). Now return to the bridge – do not cross it, but turn left (north) to drive up the west side of the canal. At 1 km is a parking lot where one can walk along a dyke (5 km return) which runs diagonally across the marsh to the west corner. The marsh is managed for waterfowl and consists of extensive areas of cattails with open reaches and patches of wet meadow.

These marshes have all the usual marshland species in summer and can be very productive in early spring, with large numbers of migrant waterfowl – the peak Whistling Swan concentrations are usually in late March – and shorebirds later if water levels are suitable.

This National Wildlife Area promises to replace in part in birding interest the extensive *Bradley's Marshes* farther west, much of which have been drained in recent years. After viewing this area, cross the bridge to rejoin the West Township Road and continue south. After 3.7 km the road turns left on a dyke running along the north bank of the Thames, but about ½ km before this point it crosses an east-west road on a 'Yield' sign. By turning right there one can drive to the Bradley Farms on the north bank of the Thames near its mouth. Ask permission to visit the marsh; you will be charged a small fee, given a permit, and directed to a northbound gravel road that ends at the Lake. There is excellent landbirding along the willow groves here and the marshes, though much smaller than formerly, continue to be most productive. Bradley's is closed during certain times of the year.

Whether you visit Bradley's or not, if you wish to go south you can leave via the road east along the Thames dyke. This continues 3.4 km to a stop street. Turn right and cross the bridge into *Prairie Siding*. The road joins Kent County Road 36 and a left turn leads to Chatham. For Point Pelee turn right and drive 2.5 km to County Road 1 on your left just across a bridge. Turn south to go to Tilbury and Wheatley. When coming from the south or east, reverse all the directions.

If you continue straight ahead instead of turning left to Tilbury you will find yourself on County Road 2. It runs some 14 km west to the village of *Stoney Point*. Here it intersects with County Road 35, itself another route to and from Point Pelee, as it becomes Highway 77 south to Leamington when it meets Highway 401.

By turning right at County Road 35 (or continuing north straight ahead if you have driven up 35) you arrive at the shoreline of Lake St Clair. The road to the right is sometimes good, especially in years when the water level is high and the lawns and fields flood. This road continues east some 2½ km to dead-end at an overgrown marsh. To the south, down a lane and across the tracks, is the sewage lagoon.

(12) **Comber** – For the Comber sewage lagoons, turn east on County Road 44 from Highway 77. Drive 0.2 km to Windsor Avenue on the south and turn; the lagoon gates are 0.3 km ahead.

(13) **Cottam** – The sewage lagoon is east on County Road 27 from the intersection with Highway 3. Drive 0.2 km to the lagoon driveway on the right.

(14) **Drumbo** – West of here 4.8 km on Oxford County Road 29, and also west of Highway 401 Exit 250, is *Chesley Conservation Area*. This includes a sphagnum bog and white cedar–tamarack swamp; and more northern birds can be found.

Two sideroads north, east along Blenheim Township Concession 9 and west of Highway 401, is the large *Black River Swamp*, another area with northern affinities. Balsam fir and black spruce occur, and again more northern birds can be expected.

(15) **Dunnville** – This town has a number of interesting areas close by, the nearest being the extensive marshes along the Grand River west of town. These extend for some distance north from the Dunnville bridges across the Grand, and southwards

almost to the river mouth. There are a variety of vantage points, from the bridges themselves and sideroads on both sides.

The road crossing the bridges is Regional Road 3, and the west bank of the river at *Port Maitland* is accessible from Regional Road 11, which turns south off Road 3 just after the second bridge. Drive 6 km south to a stop street and turn into the village. This road runs 1 km to the river mouth, the last half along the river. There are excellent views to the north, and of the piers and lake to the south.

Straight ahead from the above stop street the road bears right as Lakeshore Road and parallels the shore for some 2 km. This is *Grant Point*. The shoreline here can yield shorebirds, gulls, and duck.

Returning to Regional Road 3, about 1 km west of the bridge Road 20 bears off to the right. At this point is *Byng Island Conservation Area* (entry fee), with river access and hardwoods along the bank.

There is a small sewage lagoon 11½ km northeast of Dunnville associated with *Oswego Park* housing development. Turn north opposite the hospital on John Street; drive to its end in Jarrett Place, turn right and then left on Diltz Road. The lagoon is past the community and across the tracks on the right.

Rock Point Provincial Park is 11 km southeast of town via Regional Road 3 (not Highway 3). The park is noted for its shorebirds, which can occur in outstanding numbers and variety in the autumn and which also can be numerous in spring. Its attractiveness depends on lake levels and the amount of algae built up along the shoreline.

Regional Road 3 continues east, eventually joining the shoreline of Lake Erie at *Lowbanks*. Another good vantage point, *Mohawk Point*, is 2 km west along the shoreline from here on a small sideroad. From Lowbanks east good opportunities for lake viewing exist along the shoreline roads almost continuously to Port Colborne.

(16) Dutton – For the sewage lagoons, turn left on Shakleton just after crossing the tracks northbound on County Road 15 (County

Road 13 eastbound is almost opposite Shakleton). Drive 0.4 km to the end of the street; the lagoon drive runs ahead beside the tracks.

One of the finest wood-lots along the Thames is on the property of Mr Dougald Murray, in South Ekfrid Township. Mr Murray's woods have been one of the few consitently good places in Ontario to see Red-bellied Woodpeckers, and are also good for other woodpecker species, as well as Wood Ducks. To reach them drive north from Highway 401 on the Dutton sideroad (Elgin County Road 8) 8½ km to the Thames River, then take the first sideroad east (1½ km, Ekfrid 3R-S) and drive about 2½ km to the first sideroad running south. Mr Murray's farm is 1.5 km along on the right, opposite a sideroad running east. Entry to the woods is by permission from Mr Murray.

Many of the roads running south from Highway 3 to the lake in this area provide lake viewing. One particularly pleasant spot is near Tyrconnell, 9 km south of Dutton, where the small *John Pierce Provincial Park* is located 1 km east in a deciduous woodland with ravines to the east and west. There is usually a good assortment of the landbirds typical of the southwest.

(17) Essex – There are two separate sets of sewage lagoons at Essex. The larger southwest complex is on the south of Highway 3 just west of the North Malden Road intersection, which is 2.2 km west of the intersection with Essex Road 23. The drive is 0.1 km south on the North Malden Road, on the right.

For the northeast lagoons turn north on Essex Road 23 and proceed 2.9 km to Essex Road 8. (To do so, cross Talbot Street on the stop light and bear right at a stop street immediately after.) Drive east 0.8 km and the lagoon drive is on the left.

(18) Forest – The sewage lagoons are southwest of town. From the light in town where Highway 21 turns south, continue on the highway 2.4 km to Plympton Concession 12 on the right. Turn and drive west 2 km to a gravel (later clay) road on the right. The lagoon gate is 1.4 km north on the right.

(19) Freelton – There are several interesting areas south and west of this community at the corners of Highways 6, 97, and Regional

Road 4. West on Highway 97 the road passes through the north end of Beverly Swamp and at 9 km arrives at the *Valens Conservation Area* (entrance fee). From the west the area is some 14 km east of Galt. It consists of a large lake with marshy edges, which are attractive to waterbirds in migration. It is heavily used for recreation in summer, and there is controlled hunting in autumn.

Beverly Swamp lies south of Highway 97 and east of Regional Road 4 (Brock Road). Drive 2 km south from 97 on County Road 4 to the hamlet of Strabane (coming north from Highway 5 it is 10.6 km). Turn west on the Eighth Concession West. The swamp begins some 4 km west of here, but the most extensive area is west of Westover Road, in the 2½ km stretch to the Valens Road. There is more north along the latter road and a section 4½ km east of Valens on Highway 97. The Seventh Concession has an access area to the Beverly Swamp Reserve on the north 1 km east of Valens Road.

The swamp is heavily wooded and excellent for warblers and other woodland species. Whip-poor-will, Winter Wren, Northern Waterthrush, and White-throated Sparrow breed regularly. Turkeys have been released in this area and man-made ponds attract shorebirds.

West of the intersection of Regional Road 4 and Highway 5 is *Christie Conservation Area*, another large artificial lake that is heavily used for recreation in summer. It is drained down later in the year, but can have interesting waterfowl. There are extensive woodlands as well (entry fee).

(20) Glencoe – For Glencoe sewage lagoons, drive south on Highway 80 from the tracks across the road at the south side of town 2.4 km to Ekfrid 2nd Range N road, and turn left. The lagoons are 1 km along on the north.

(21) GRAND BEND – This is the nearest community to the Pinery, and it also has sewage lagoons. For the latter, drive 1.1 km east on Highway 81 to Stephen Concession 22 on the right. Turn, and the lagoons (visible from the road) are 2.2 km along on the right.

The *Pinery Provincial Park* (entry fee) is 9 km southwest of town on Highway 21. It is an excellent birding park as well as being most important botanically. There are deciduous woodlands along the Ausable River, extensive oak–pine woodlands, and a fine dune system along the shore of Lake Huron. The deciduous woodlands along the river have nesting Blue-gray Gnatcatchers, Cerulean Warblers, and other southern species. The pines attract more northern species such as Magnolia Warbler, and Prairie Warblers nest very locally at the rear of the primary dunes. This is one of only two sites for this warbler in Ontario that are easily accessible by road, but in neither is the species doing well. In winter finches occur in the pines. In migration the whole area can be particularly rich in spring for landbirds, while in autumn it shares some of the character of Kettle Point farther west as a vantage point for observing waterbird migration. Large loon movements occur.

There are several large camping areas, and this park has the most extended season of any in the province. There is a good interpretive program, and usually at least one knowledgeable birder on staff.

(22) GRIMSBY – Grimsby is best known for *Beamer Point*, a major observation point for spring hawk migration. Leave the Queen Elizabeth Way on Christie Street south, which continues south up the escarpment as Mountain Street. At the top turn right opposite the church on Regional Road 89. Follow this road around west 1.7 km to the entrance to the Beamer Point Conservation Area, north along Quarry Road. Turn right and drive down to the entrance of the area on the right. The best observing is from the parking lot itself, although the woods and fields adjacent can have interesting passerines at this time.

Unlike autumn hawk migration, the spring movement tends to be associated with the movement of warm air into the province. The principal species observed are Sharp-shinned Hawks (April and early May), Red-tailed Hawks (March and April), and Broad-winged Hawks (late April–early May). Substantial numbers of Turkey Vultures also occur, and in March Red-shouldered Hawks are common. This is the best place in Ontario to see the latter species, although all the movements are closely related to weather. In all some 15 species are regular, but as in fall Goshawks, eagles, Ospreys, Peregrine Falcons, and Merlins are never seen in any numbers. The count totals do not equal those recorded at the autumn hawk stations, and an entire season's totals may only equal the thousands of Broad-winged Hawks alone that can occur on big days in fall at Hawk Cliff or Amherstburg. Nevertheless, the movement can be very exciting and the birds are often agreeably low, moving over at tree-top height in many cases.

Grimsby also has a sewage lagoon. It is north of the Queen Elizabeth Way and west of town, off Oakes Road. This road crosses the QEW; the lagoon is ½ km west along the first sideroad north of the bridge. From the QEW there is no exit at Oakes Road, so one must either get off at Grimsby (if driving west) or at 50 Road (if eastbound) and follow the north serviceroad.

50 Road leads to *Fifty Point*, with lake viewing, and the conservation area to the east has a small lake.

(23) **HAMILTON** – This city, situated at the westernmost end of Lake Ontario and at the point the Niagara Escarpment bends along the south shore of the lake, has an abundance of fine birding areas. There are excellent marshes and varied exposures along the escarpment providing shelter for landbirds, which also concentrate along the beach and around the bay on migration.

You can cover Hamilton Bay quite well without entering the city itself, and Dundas Marsh is accessible with only minimal city driving. Take Highway 403 to the exit for Highway 6 north. At the first traffic light north of the interchange (about ½ km) turn right, following the signs for Highway 2 and Plains Road. This road runs south 0.8 km over 403 again, and joins Highway 2 (Plains Road) at a T-intersection. Here a right turn will take you towards Dundas Marsh and a left turn to the areas around Hamilton Bay itself.

To cover *Dundas Marsh*, turn right (south) and drive 1 km to the Guelph Road, which is past the Rock Garden and is signposted to the Royal Botanical Gardens Arboretum. Turn right on this road, drive down the hill, and go 0.8 km to the arboretum entrance on your left. It is a good idea to pick up a map of the RBG properties at the Interpretive Centre here if it is open (there is one posted outside if not). This shows all the areas described below. From the parking area there is an extensive network of trails that leads down to the marsh (Cootes Paradise) and runs some 3 km along the wooded north shore.

Reaching the south shore and west end is more complicated. Return to the Plains Road and turn right to continue south across the high level bridge. This can be a good vantage point for hawk migration in autumn. At 1.9 km bear right on Dundurn Street North and continue 0.6 km to King Street West. Turn right here and continue straight ahead on King Street at 0.9 km when the main flow of traffic angles left. The next light (0.2 km) is Longwood Road. Turn right here, and drive to its end. Then bear left into a parking area which gives access to Princess Point at the southeastern end of Cootes Paradise, and to one end of the network of walking trails along the south shore, which is also heavily wooded.

Other access points are from the foot of Marion and Forsythe Avenues. To reach these return to King Street West and continue west about ½ km to Marion Street. At the foot of this street and 0.2 km farther west on the cross street here (Oak Knoll Drive) is parking and access to the Westdale Ravine Trails. For Forsythe, return to King and continue west to the next light at Sterling Street. Turn right here and drive 0.8 km to the stop street at Forsythe. Turn right. There is no parking on this street (although people do so) but sometimes one can enter the university grounds and park there. From this street one can reach the southwestern end of the trails.

The west end of the marsh is accessible via Cootes Drive, which turns off Main Street West west of the McMaster University complex. Main Street is the first main artery south of King Street and the areas just described. Cootes Drive leads to Dundas, and a description of Spencer's Falls there is given at the end of this Hamilton account. Bear right on Cootes Drive. The road crosses Spencer Creek 1.3 km from the turn; this is the entrance to the South Shore Trail (it is signposted), which leads to vantage points for viewing the west end of the marsh. There is limited parking along the road. Continue 0.8 km on Cootes Drive to Olympic Drive, the first road on the right. Turn and drive to the Hydro Station (0.2 km), where it is possible to turn sharp right and drive back down a section of old road to the canal. Park here and walk east along a narrow spit of land that runs between the canal and the marsh on your left. A little farther along Olympic Drive (0.5 km) is parking for the sports complex and one can walk over to the north side of this same area.

The marsh has the usual assortment of breeding species, including a small colony of Black-crowned Night Herons, but is even more interesting in migration. Large numbers of duck and a few Whistling Swans are often present in March, and in autumn, depending on water levels, the area can abound in shorebirds.

Continue on Olympic 1.9 km to Valley Road and the parking lot for *Borer's Falls Conservation Area* to the north. Valley Road itself leads 1.3 km to Rockchapel Road, where a left turn leads to the Botanical Gardens' Rock Chapel Sanctuary (1.1 km). All these areas have the mixed woodlands and deep ravines characteristic of this section of the Niagara Escarpment.

To return to the starting point, continue east on Olympic Drive (now York Road), which leads back to Highway 6 just 0.6 km north of the original turn-off to Plains Road.

It will be recalled that to cover *Hamilton Bay* one should turn left on to Plains Road after leaving Highway 6. On the left at 0.8 km is a drive in to parking for the Botanical Gardens Rose Garden and the Cherry Hill Gate, which leads to 4–5 km of walking trails in the wooded *Hendrie Valley*. Just past this entrance on the right of Plains Road is a sideroad signposted to the Royal Botanical Gardens' Headquarters and Woodlawn Cemetery. Bear right here and drive to Spring Garden Road. Turn right again and *Woodlawn Cemetery*, which provides good views of the west end of Hamilton Bay, is on the left. Spring Garden Road itself leads down to the water and up the other side (as Valley Inn Road) to rejoin Plains Road. The section of road just described is quite narrow, and there is a low bridge en route. In addition to waterbirds, berry-eating species, attracted by the shrub plantings around the formal gardens here, can be found in autumn and winter.

The back part of the *Holy Sepulchre Cemetery*, 0.8 km farther east on Plains Road from the Woodlawn Cemetery turn-off, also provides views of the harbour. From here continue another 2.1 km east to LaSalle Park Road, and turn right again. At 0.4 km is a stop street: continue straight ahead down the hill to the car park on an old loading dock. Here there are excellent views of Hamilton Bay both east and west. *LaSalle Park* itself, just east of this spot, can yield migrant landbirds, and continuing east on North Shore Boulevard there are periodic views of the Bay (Burlington Golf and Country Club at 1.6 km and some of the dead-end streets on the right after the road merges onto King Road at 1.6 km can be particularly good) and eventually one reaches the Queen Elizabeth Way.

Hamilton Bay is busy and polluted. However, it concentrates waterfowl in early spring and autumn, when sizeable flocks of Canvasback and some scoters usually occur, as well as the more usual wintering species described for the lakeshore. In winter, any open leads or other water areas will usually yield birds as well.

If you continue on east under the QEW you will enter the town of Burlington and can cover the lakeshore east to Toronto (qv), or turn right at the stop light just past the hospital to cover the beach strip which separates Lake Ontario from Hamilton Bay. Coverage of this area is easier starting at the other (south) end and accordingly it is so described below.

The *Burlington–Hamilton Beach* strip concentrates migrant landbird flocks moving along the lakeshore, and because it is the extreme west end of Lake Ontario it can provide a vantage point for seeing offshore water birds, especially in periods of easterly gales. Jaegers often can be seen close to shore in such periods, and it is a good place for rarer gulls and waterfowl. At other times the usual mix of migrant and wintering ducks and gulls occurs (see the description of the western lakeshore under Toronto), but there is not much to be expected in summer.

The area is between the Queen Elizabeth Way and the lakeshore. The south end access is from Highway 20 east of the QEW. The highway terminates in Confederation Drive northbound, and this road in turn curves round to become Van Wagner's Beach Road, with lake viewing on the right and some small (but often productive) patches of marsh on the left, between it and the QEW. At 1.5 km the road joins Beach Boulevard. Turn right to proceed along the strip.

First, however, a left turn takes one under the QEW bridges on Woodward Avenue, and immediately under the bridges on the right is a dirt road leading to an area of landfill which has some pools and views of the waters of the heavily industrialized southeast end of Hamilton Bay. This is an excellent spot for waterfowl in migration and in winter, and the pools can also yield shorebirds and herons. The entire area is changing as landfill proceeds, and I suppose will eventually vanish. The same spot can also be reached from a drive-off (the old toll booth area) at the south end of the QEW Burlington Skyway bridge. This is only accessible to southbound traffic, and is about 1½ km past the end of the Skyway proper.

Turning right along the beach strip from the Van Wagner's Beach light, one passes a series of short dead-end streets on the lakeside, most of which can provide access to the beach. At 4 km there is parking on the right by an abandoned amusement pavilion. Walk up and over the tracks to view the beach just south of the Burlington ship canal. On the left of the road here drive down to the bay side of the canal and view that. The north side is accessible from a road on the left just over the bridge, or 0.2 km farther on, via the entrance to the Canada Centre for Inland Waters. Park on the north side of the canal and walk along the wall out to the lake. This whole area can be very good for loons, grebes, ducks, and larids.

The QEW beach exits and access at the north end are 0.8 km farther along from the Canada Centre for Inland Waters, and 1.2 km farther again brings you to Lakeshore Road in the town of Burlington itself, and the lakeshore Spencer Smith Park on the right just past the lights. For an account of these areas and the Lakeshore eastwards, see Toronto.

By continuing into the town of Dundas from Cootes Drive after covering the west end of Dundas Marsh one joins Highway 8 westbound. Leaving Dundas the highway climbs the escarpment, passing under a railroad bridge en route. At the top of the hill it curves into the village of Bullock's Corners, where Brock Road enters from the north. At the intersection turn *sharp* right on to Falls View Road. Cross the bridge and turn right to drive 0.4 km to *Spencer Gorge Wilderness Area*. This very attractive area overlooks Webster's Falls. The gorge below is a heavily wooded, sheltered area where Louisiana Waterthrush has bred and which is attractive to landbirds in all seasons. The gorge is accessible by steps down from the falls, and also from a sideroad beside the railroad tracks. This runs off to the left from Highway 8 just before the railroad bridge as one goes down the hill to Dundas.

(24) Harrow – The sewage lagoons here are one of the few places in southern Ontario where Yellow-headed Blackbirds have summered (and presumably nested). To reach them drive west on Highway 18 from McAffee Street in the centre of town 0.7 km to Roseborough Street on the right. Turn north, go 1.2 km to the next road (Concession 3), and turn left there. The lagoon drive is 1.5 km along south of this road.

(25) Jarvis – The sewage lagoons are south off Highway 3 down a dirt road at the back of the lane in to the car wash, opposite Walpole Street and 0.3 km east of the intersection of Highways 3 and 6.

(26) KETTLE POINT – Kettle Point is an Indian reservation village that occupies a small promontory into the south end of Lake Huron. As such it is a particularly good place for watching autumn waterfowl movements, which come closer to shore here than elsewhere on the lake.

Kettle Point is west off Highway 21 at the point the highway curves south towards Forest, 10 km south. Lambton Road 7 continues west here, and West Ipperwash Road turns north almost immediately from it. Turn on to West Ipperwash Road, and then left 0.2 km ahead at a sign to Kettle Point Park. This road runs west to the shore (2.5 km) and then curves to follow the shoreline north. At 4 km farther are the Kettle Point Concretions, with a historic site sign, and then the shoreroad turns sharp right 0.7 km ahead.

Interesting waterbirds can be seen all along here, but the best spots for watching migration are from the area of the concretions up to the point the road turns. Here in autumn loons, duck, and gulls moving down Lake Huron are visible from the shore, particularly in periods of strong northwest winds. The species seen at the mouth of the St Clair River (see Sarnia) can be expected here too, and large flights of loons occur, including the occasional Red-throateds and (very rarely) an Arctic.

Migrant landbirds follow the shoreline spring and autumn, and in spring considerable concentrations can occur. In the breeding season the extensive swampy woodlands of the Indian reservation can yield species rare in the southwest, such as Marsh Hawk, Whip-poor-will, Sedge Wren, and Northern Water-thrush, as well as southern species such as Blue-gray Gnatcatcher and Golden-winged Warbler.

(27) **Kingsville** – To the west of Leamington several areas around Kingsville can be worth a visit. The town itself is some 12 km west on Highway 18. Drive west through it to the intersection of Essex Road 50, which joins Highway 18 from the south a short distance past the creek bridge. Just 0.8 km west of this intersection on Highway 18 is the long, narrow drive which leads over the fields to the north to the sewage lagoon.

Otherwise Road 50 is much the more interesting road. Turn south on it and drive towards the shore. At 1.7 km is a narrow dead-end road on the left which actually runs along the shore, but generally this is not worth the trouble as less than 1 km farther on 50 itself turns down along the shoreline. Other points of interest are (distances from point to point):

3.4 km	(from Highway 18) a small marsh along Wigle Creek.
0.9 km	McCain Sideroad stop street. Turn left.
0.5 km	Cedar Creek mouth. From here to
1.8 km	the end of Cedar Creek marshes, there is marsh viewing on your right.
1.5 km	The lawns on the left along here sometimes have standing water, and hence shorebirds, in spring.
0.7 km	Turn north on Essex Road 23.
2.1 km	Cedar Creek crossings. Herons and egrets are usual.
1.0 km	Another arm of Cedar Creek.
0.6 km	Highway 18. Cross this and continue north.
4.1 km	Turn right on Gosfield South Concession 3.
5.7 km	The feeding area of Miner's sanctuary on the right. Scan the flocks of Canada Geese present in spring and fall for other species. Snows and White-fronteds are possible.
0.7 km	Ponds on the right can have shorebirds and duck.
0.7 km	Highway 29. Turn right to return (3 km) to Kingsville main street and a return (left) to Leamington if you have come from Point Pelee.

A pair of Bald Eagles nests in this area, and this route can also often yield geese, egrets, and shorebirds that may be absent around Point Pelee itself.

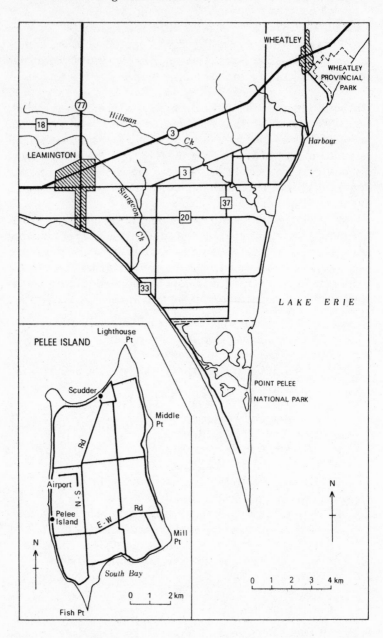

MAP 2 Point Pelee and Pelee Island

(28) **LEAMINGTON** – Southeast of this town, which lies at the intersection of Highways 3 and 77, is *Point Pelee National Park.*

Point Pelee is a birding legend. In spring visitors from all over the world congregate on the point to view the restless tide of birds pouring north, to seek rare waifs from other parts of the continent, and to capture the excitement of watching migration actually in progress. But although visitors in early May sometimes seem to outnumber the birds, Pelee is of great interest year-round.

On the second week-end in May nowadays it is not unusual for the loop road on the point to be closed by 8:00 AM because the large parking lot at the Interpretive Centre is full. Drive down in October, however, and you could be the only birder in the park! While it is true that the peak spring warbler numbers occur usually around the second week-end in May, Pelee is a fascinating place in any season. In early May you can find the point cold, windswept, and almost empty of migrants. It is undoubtedly at its best when migration is at full flood, but there can be heavy movement from the first waterfowl in March through to the last stragglers in December. Late April–early May is the best time to observe southern rarities overshooting, and late May can be good both for shorebirds if suitable habitat exists – which usually means standing water on the onion fields – and for later landbird migrants such as cuckoos or Mourning and Connecticut Warblers (the park is one of the best places to see the latter). In July heavy swallow movement begins, which continues, with autumn shorebirds, into August. In September accipiter passage is heavy, together with other hawks and landbirds. October and November yield waterfowl including Whistling Swans; however (incredibly for a national park), hunting is allowed at present.

The park is much less noteworthy for breeding birds than Rondeau (see Blenheim) but many southerners have bred, including Chuck-wills-widow and (long ago) Bewick's Wren. It is the best place to see Carolina Wren (now scarce), Blue-gray Gnatcatcher, Yellow-breasted Chat, White-eyed Vireo, and Orchard Oriole in the breeding season.

In spring many of these species are easier to find, together with such species as Little Gull, Forster's Tern, Golden and Blue-winged Warblers, Northern Parula, Cerulean and Prairie

Warblers, and Grasshopper Sparrow. The following birds are rarer, but occur quite regularly in spring: Cattle Egret, Glossy Ibis, Red-bellied Woodpecker, Acadian Flycatcher, Bewick's Wren, Mockingbird, Prothonotary, Worm-eating, Kentucky and Hooded Warblers, Louisiana Waterthrush, Summer Tanager, Blue Grosbeak and Dickcissel (both rare), Henslow's, LeConte's, and (rarely) Sharp-tailed Sparrows. Remember these are just the more likely species – at Pelee no rarity, no matter how improbable, should be dismissed.

Rarities are less predictable in autumn, but migrant numbers can be higher than in spring. The heavy vegetation and relatively light coverage in autumn both undoubtedly influence the rarities located in this period.

A feature of the migration in both seasons is the spectacle of birds leaving the tip. In spring this reverse migration occurs even in favourable weather, and large flocks of blackbirds and other species move rapidly south along the point, either to head off the tip, or to mill aimlessly above the bushes at the end. In autumn this movement is, of course, heavier and there is a greater sense of urgency as small passerines often try to fight their way out over the water into adverse winds.

In winter there are often stragglers present, and further rarities such as Mountain Bluebird have turned up. At these times the red cedars in the old orchard areas and along the roads provide important shelter for landbirds, together with the low areas between the old beach ridges.

The park is a spit of land jutting out into Lake Erie south of Leamington, but the traditional Pelee birding area includes the entire area south of Highway 3 from Leamington, to Wheatley on the east. It includes the shoreline and Wheatley harbour, dyked arable land, and the marshes along Hillman Creek as well as the point itself. The entire area can be very productive.

The park proper is roughly triangular in shape. Its narrow side joins the reclaimed farmland to the north. Its east and west sides are long, gently curving sand and gravel beaches which finally meet in a slender sand spit. This tip – the southernmost part of Canada's mainland – alters from year to year, and the character of the entire park changes with the water level of the lake and under the impact of severe storms. In high-water years many areas can be flooded.

A wooded dune ridge backs the West Beach, and the road runs down the east side of this ridge. The rest of the north end of the park is occupied by a large marsh, which narrows as the point itself narrows, and finally is replaced by deciduous woodlands. More open field areas mark the sites of former farming and cottage developments. The road finally divides to form a loop which terminates at the Interpretive Centre. From here a free train service will take the visitor the remaining 2.3 km to the tip.

To reach Point Pelee take Exit 48 from Highway 401 and proceed south on Highway 77 through Leamington, following the signs to the park. Turn left (east) at the lights at Seacliffe Drive (County Road 20), and bear diagonally right (southeast) on County Road 33. This passes the golf course and crosses a bridge over Sturgeon Creek, and then follows the shoreline to the park gates.

Obtain a park map and bird check list at the gate, and check with the Interpretive Centre staff for directions to any unusual birds. Noteworthy areas within the park include the tip for huge flocks of Red-breasted Mergansers in spring and autumn, gulls and shorebirds on the tip itself, migrant landbirds in the bushes at the end, and views of birds flying off the point. (Birders should refrain from walking out far beyond the last line of bushes, as birds on the tip often do not return once they have been alarmed.) The road between the tip and the centre, the nature trail that starts from the centre, and the trail through Tilden's Woods northeast of the centre are all excellent for migrant landbirds, and the marsh boardwalk can be good for marsh birds. The Sparrow Field near the tip and other old field areas can yield the elusive field sparrows such as LeConte's, Henslow's, Grasshopper, and Sharp-tailed in season. Woodcock and Whip-poor-will are regular in the woods north of the group campground in spring. There really are no 'best' places for watching birds in the park – it is all superb.

The onion fields and Hillman (Stein's) Marsh form important parts of the Pelee area, providing habitat for open field, marsh, and shorebirds less available within the park itself.

Essex County Road 20 (which you will recall you turned off diagonally en route to the park to follow County Road 33) runs east to join the east beach of the point, winding along the south side of Hillman Marsh for its last 2 km or so. South of this road lies a grid of roads criss-crossing the low-lying fields, most of them bounded by deep drainage ditches, while the roads themselves follow the tops of the dyke system. All of these roads are worth covering, as the fields attract shorebirds, gulls, and open country species. The ditches often yield heron and duck. Pools of standing water can be particularly productive.

One route is to turn east just outside the park gate on Mersea Township Road E. This road gives access to points overlooking the north side of the large Pelee marsh. The road ends in 3 km at Township Road 19. Turn north, and continue 3.4 km north to Township Road C. The ditches along this stretch can be particularly productive, as can the fields to the east, where gulls often gather in large numbers. Turn east on Township Road C, which goes to Marentette Beach (private) and then continues northwards along the beachline as the East Beach Road. Periodic views of the lake are possible, the trees along here can yield migrants, and the wires are particularly good for swallows. Finally the road curves east along the south shore of Hillman Marsh, now as County Road 20. (A ½ km dead end road which continues along the beach yields good overlooks of the marsh.) Follow the south shore of the marsh, where the road permits periodic stops to view the wetland from the dykes. Continue 0.3 km past the junction with Township Road 19 and take the first right (County Road 37). Drive 1.5 km to the next intersection and turn right again, to cross Hillman Creek and (0.3 km) turn right once more on a road which now runs 2½ km to the east shoreline again. It follows the north side of Hillman Marsh and there are many points of interest along it: the wet areas and marsh both west and east of the bridge crossing half-way down, any wet areas behind the houses just past here to the south, and after passing Township Road 21, the wood-lot to the south and the fields to the north (by a house painted, from time almost beyond recall, purple), and then the marshy areas on both sides of the road past here. At the end is a small parking lot on the right. From here there are views of the shoreline and lake, and it is possible to walk south along the barrier beach.

The rarities these areas have yielded over the years are legion. The wood-lot and marsh by the purple house have been good for Prothonotary Warbler, the wet areas running to the marsh itself for King Rails, and one can usually be sure of all the more common marshbirds in season.

Just before the road ends (0.2 km) a sideroad runs to the north through the cottages. This road parallels the shore for some 3 km (it becomes Pulley Road) and turns left (Milo Road) to run along the south side of Wheatley harbour, where the gulls can be interesting. It ends at Township Road 4. Opposite is a small marsh, sometimes good for duck and Black-crowned Night Herons. A right turn leads to the other side of the harbour or north to Wheatley itself (3 km), while a left turn ends up eventually in Leamington.

East of Wheatley is *Wheatley Provincial Park,* 2 km south on the shore. The hardwoods here are attractive, the lagoons along the shore and creek can yield waterbirds, and there may be duck and gulls on the lake. There is even a small but good sewage lagoon in the campground. (The whole place would probably rate much more highly as a birding spot if it were not so close to Pelee!)

Township Road 4 is not a particularly interesting one for birds, as most of the best places are south of it. However, if one turns left on it (ie, headed back to Leamington) the first 4 km can be worth while. It jogs left and then right, becoming County Road 3 in the process; a small creek crossing just west of the second jog may have waterbirds. Then it is usually better to take the first left to join County Road 37, which leads back to the roads around Hillman Marsh and the onion fields.

The route just described is merely one of many, and birders without a car (or without the inclination to drive around dusty backroads) can spend the days very profitably without leaving the park itself. Going on about Pelee's quality is superfluous: suffice it to say that if you can visit only one place in Ontario, visit Pelee. For the tyro birder, however, one caution is in order. You may well leave more frustrated than when you arrived! The sheer volume of birds on a good day can be bewildering and overwhelming.

There are several motels in Leamington, and private campgrounds there and off the road to the park itself (Sturgeon Woods Trailer Park), and at Wheatley Provincial Park. In busier times there is a small food concession in the national park, but otherwise the nearest restaurants are in Leamington, Wheatley, and along County Road 33. There are several good picnic areas in the park, and numerous washrooms (but none between the interpretive centre and tip terminal of the train).

(29) London – This city has a number of fine parks, especially along the banks of the Thames River, which are good for migrant landbirds: Springbank Park is north of Commissioners Road and Springbank Drive in the west of the city, and Gibbons Park is west of Richmond Street and north of Oxford Street in the north.

Fanshawe Lake, northeast of London, is another large Conservation Authority project. From the intersection of Highbury Avenue northbound (the continuation of Highway 126) and Highway 22, turn right on Fanshawe Park Road, which is County Road 31. Drive 2.4 km east to Clarke Road. Turn right for the dam area, which is in the grounds of the conservation area 2 km south, and which gives access to extensive parkland along the west shoreline. Alternatively, turn north and drive 1.4 km to Concession 6, which dead-ends 1 km to the west. Park, and walk straight ahead and to the left around the crest of the bank. There are excellent views of the lake, and landbirds along the fields and woods. In migration periods waterfowl and gulls often gather in numbers on the waters here, and the area has produced many interesting records.

The *Westminster Ponds* are a group of small lakes surrounded by woodland south of London. The Walker Ponds are southeast of the Wellington Street south–Commissioners' Road intersection, and the Pond Mills area is farther east near Highway 126. The property is part-public, part-private, but much of it is visible from the roads. The sheltered ponds attract Pied-billed Grebes and pond duck, and the woodlands and old field areas landbirds. Collectively they form one of the best birding areas around London.

Access to this area is via Pond Mills Road south from Commissioners' Road (the first major intersection west of Highway 126). Follow Pond Mills to Southdale Road, when the ponds at Pond Mills are on the left. Southdale runs west (2½ km) to Wellington, with the Walker Ponds on the right. North on

Wellington there is more area on the right south of the hospital grounds. More effective coverage can be achieved with a city roadmap, but the above is enough to locate the areas generally.

Dorchester Swamp, east of London, is the large area of wet woodland around the intersection of Highways 73 and 401 (Exit 203). It is privately owned and access is by permission of the local landowners. However, you can do some productive birding from the roads themselves. Louisiana Waterthrush and Hooded Warbler have occured here.

The *Delaware-Komoka* areas along the Thames River constitute some of the more interesting birding locales west of London. From Highway 2 at Delaware turn north on County Road 3. This road passes through excellent birding country south of the river, and there is ready riverbank access at the County Road 16 bridge (3.2 km) and again 1.2 km farther along. When 3 ends at County Road 14 turn left and drive towards Komoka. There is more river access at 1.6 km, and 3.4 km from there are flooded gravel pits along both sides of the road for 2 km. These are excellent for migrant waterfowl. At the 2 km point there is natural woodland along Komoka Creek, and 6.2 km farther on the road joins Highway 81 at Mount Bridges.

Parts of these areas are private property and as usual, although the public is tolerated in some areas, discretion should be used and permission sought if there is any question.

(30) LONG POINT – Long Point is one of the finest birding areas in the province. It is a migrant concentration point second only to Point Pelee and a major staging area for waterfowl – in terms of readily accessible, visible waterfowl numbers, the best in Ontario.

On the map, Long Point is the most impressive landform along the Lake Erie shoreline – it is an enormous sandspit that juts eastwards out into the lake. Along the southerly lake side are long beaches backed by high sand dunes (Piping Plover occur and formerly bred). On the north side, where the point creates a large bay, extensive marshes have formed, and between the dunes and the marshes are varying amounts of woodland, much of it coniferous reforestation, interspersed with open grassy areas.

The marshes have a rich avifauna, including both the usual marsh species in the extensive areas of cat-tail and grass marsh species such as Common Snipe and Sedge Wren in the short grassy sections. Forster's Terns nest and Little Gulls probably do, although the nesting areas are not readily accessible. However, the terns range widely, and this is the best area to see this species during the nesting season. Woodcock occur in the wooded areas, which form islands of vegetation which concentrate landbird migrants. The huge area of the point – most of it inaccessible except by boat or on foot – precludes the kind of intensive coverage that Point Pelee receives, and also means that birds are not concentrated to the same extent. The mix of migrants, however, seems to be similar, and the Pelee listings provide a reasonable guide to the rarities that can be expected.

Waterfowl concentrations towards the end of March and in early April are spectacular. Birds move in as soon as any open water can be found, and enormous numbers are usually present by late March. Traditionally the point used to be noted as *the* place to see Whistling Swans at this time, but in recent years the birds tend to be more dispersed, the Lake St Clair area (see Chatham) yielding much larger numbers of these beautiful birds.

Good birding places around Long Point are not confined to the point alone. There are both deciduous woodlands and extensive areas of pine reforestation, as well as good waterfowl viewing locations, along the shoreline both east and west. As many of these as possible should be covered if best advantage is to be taken of a visit. But let us start with the point itself. It is at the foot of Highway 59, and only the bottom quarter or so is readily accessible without a boat; however, there is enough to keep one busy for several hours.

The last intersection north of the point is with Haldimand-Norfolk Road 42. South (0.7 km) of here the highway crosses the marsh on a causeway, and there is a small pull-off from which the marshes on both sides of the road can be scanned. The road continues 0.7 km to Big Creek bridge where you can pull off again, and it then continues with the bay on the left and Big Creek Marsh and National Wildlife Area on the right. There is a viewing stand on the left at 2 km. In early spring the bay can be filled with large flocks of waterfowl – mainly Redheads, Canvasbacks, American Wigeon, and Coot, but with smaller numbers of scaup, Buffleheads, and Ruddy Duck. Puddle ducks and Ring-necked Ducks gather mainly to the west in the marsh. Whistling Swans can turn up anywhere in the marshes or along the shoreline.

After crossing the Big Creek marshes the Highway curves east to follow the line of the point itself. Turn right here on Hastings Drive, which runs in the opposite direction west along the shoreline with the Big Creek Marsh to the north. Flocks of Red-breasted Mergansers can be seen on the lake in early spring and in fall, more ducks in the marsh, and landbirds along the beach strip. Sometimes in early spring Hastings Drive washes out, but by driving to the end (3 km) one can park and continue westwards through the line of trees and dense shrubbery along the shoreline.

Returning to the highway, drive east some 5 km to the road's end at *Long Point Provincial Park*. This drive passes through the cottage community of Long Point, most of which is of no interest, but the eastern section of the cottage road that parallels the highway on the lake side can have a good variety of landbirds in migration (it is called Woodstock Drive; the choice part is east from Norfolk Avenue). On the left, Bay side of the highway the bottom of Teal Drive at 1.1 km from the turn can have good views over the marshes; and farther east the marshes and scrubby evergreens along the road itself can be good for viewing birds. At 2.5 km from Teal Drive is Old Cut Road, Turn here and drive to a Y-intersection (0.5 km) where Rogers Avenue turns right. Both streets dead-end at the bay and both are of interest: by bearing right one ends up at some boat-houses with good views out over the bay and the outer sections of the marshes. By bearing left one will have good marsh viewing and – usually – excellent landbirding along the lawns and in the scattered trees of the cottages.

Continuing east on the highway, at 0.1 km is Lighthouse Crescent, leading to some thickets of evergreen, and in the park immediately ahead evergreen (mostly pine) reforestation plots alternate with grassy and marshy sections, and areas of open dune. These evergreen tangles can be alive with small landbirds. The marshes continue on the bay side, and at the park's eastern limit stretch away to the horizon. From here on these marshes are only accessible by foot along the beach or by boat, and large areas are privately owned by the Long Point Company.

There is a controlled hunt on the point, but since much of the area north of the park and the Big Creek Marsh is a sanctuary, waterfowl viewing opportunities still exist.

To visit some of the areas on the adjacent mainland return to County Road 42 and turn west (left). This leads to the village of Port Royal; noteworthy spots include the cemetery on the right at 2.5 km, with views of Big Creek, the Creek itself at 0.4 km, *Port Royal Waterfowl Sanctuary* ('Lee Brown's') on the left at 1.6 km, and the small parking lot on the south at 2.0 km with more marsh access. West of here the marshes narrow and become swamp woodland (Prothonotary Warblers have been recorded) but are more difficult to get to, and end altogether in about ½ km. Swans and other waterfowl may be seen in the fields in spring all the way to Port Burwell and indeed along the entire Lake Erie shoreline. However, Lee Brown's always provides good viewing, and there may be Snows or White-fronteds with the geese here.

The best lake viewing between Long Point and Port Stanley is from the mouths of the major streams. *Port Burwell* has a stream, small harbour, and access to wooded hillsides and a stream valley. Coming from Long Point, you can turn left at the T-intersection to view the lake east of the harbour, and then return to continue north and cross the river. On the right at the top of the hill is the conservation area, running north along the west bank of Otter Creek, and a left turn leads down to *Iroquois Beach Provincial Park* on the right, with a wooded ridge along the shore and dune vegetation lower down; straight ahead can be seen the west side of the harbour, which can be good for gulls. Farther west again, *Port Bruce* has a small harbour and beach.

North on Highway 59 from Long Point and the County Road 42 intersection some of the sideroads east and west can be productive. Notable are Concession 2 of South Walsingham (4 km), and *Backus Mill Conservation Area*, the entrance of which is reached by going east on Concession 2 (also accessible from County Road 42 where it turns east north of Port Rowan). The area has a small pond which can yield the occasional shorebird or Hooded Merganser, and the feeder can have good landbirds.

The old house here is the headquarters of the internationally known Long Point Bird Observatory, which operates banding stations on the point and has a wide range of research activities. Its staffing is limited and it is not in a position to be able to provide help to visiting birders (otherwise little else would get done!).

Farther north on 59 (3 km) Concession 4 to the east becomes a sand road of uncertain quality after the first ½ km or so, but at about 1 km you come to Backus Woods on the right, a fine deciduous wood-lot with a trail running south through it. Landbirds here include Ruffed Grouse and Pileated Woodpeckers.

Concession 6 (3 km, the first sideroad north of Highway 24) runs 3.7 km east before becoming a sand road, This road can be productive farther on – yielding Red-shouldered Hawk and Pine Warbler, as well as other warblers – and the open areas in the reforestation to the south just before the end of the pavement have in the past had Prairie Warblers, but the colony has virtually vanished.

By driving south to Highway 24 and continuing east one comes to *St Williams Forestry Station* headquarters, with a public fishing area and picnic area which can yield good birding. This extensive area of large evergreens has created a huge island of habitat absent elsewhere in the region, and has attracted many species with more northern ranges. Some noteworthy breeding records have been recorded, including a couple of Ontario's few Lark Sparrow nestings.

Just east of here Highway 24 crosses Regional Road 16. Turn south to the village of St Williams and (4.5 km from the turn) to the road running along the shore to Normandale, described below.

County Road 42 east of Highway 59, which you will recall is just north of the Long Point causeway, passes a cemetery on the right (0.3 km) which can produce landbirds, and at 0.7 km is Mill Road on the left. The sewage lagoons are 0.7 km along on the right, and can have waterfowl in plenty when the Long Point marshes seem to be empty.

Continue into Port Rowan. The first road to the right on rounding the corner to go north on the main street leads east along the shoreline and has lake viewpoints. It enters the St Williams road immediately south of the Normandale sideroad referred to above. An alternative route is County Road 42 itself, which runs north and east to St Williams. It has some wet spots en route. At St Williams turn south to the Normandale Road.

The latter also follows the shore, and at 4.4 km can be seen the large *Turkey Point* marshes on the right. At 0.6 km farther on, past the top of the hill, is a good overview area for these marshes; 2.3 km farther still is a small creek and ponds on the left, which are sometimes good for landbirds. A further 0.7 km brings one to the Turkey Point road. I have never found it very productive, but you can drive down and along the pier at the end (some 3 km) with lake viewing all the way, and there are swampy woods to the right at the bottom of the hill on the way in.

By turning north on the Turkey Point road one comes to the provincial park entrance (0.3 km) and then at 1.5 km to the entrance to the *Fish Hatchery*. There is a large pond there which almost always has a good assortment of ducks in migration time. There is a trail around it through the woods, which is not usually worth walking the whole way round, although the south side can be good for landbirds and the wet areas at the beginning of the north side can have woodcock.

The Normandale Road crosses the Turkey Point road and is interesting in itself. There is lake viewing from the Van Norman Public Fishing Area on the right entering Normandale and, if you continue east, again at Port Ryerse. The narrow valleys these communities occupy, as well as Fisher Glen, often attract landbirds in winter and in cold periods in migration.

Tourist facilities in the Long Point area are few. There is camping at Long Point and Turkey Point Provincial Parks and again at Backus Conservation Area. The towns of Simcoe and Port Dover to the east have motels and hotels, and Port Rowan has some limited facilities as well.

(31) **Lucan** – To reach the sewage lagoons, turn north on County Road 13, which is the first street on the right after crossing the tracks on Highway 4 westbound entering town. Turn right, then

(0.4 km) left on County Road 47, the Fourth Concession. Continue 1.5 km to the point 47 turns right, and turn left. The lagoons are on the left 1.1 km ahead.

(32) **Merlin** – This village, 5½ km north of Highway 3 on County Road 7, has a sewage lagoon located on the north side of County Road 8. The driveway – leading over a large field – is 0.9 km east of the junction in the village of the two county roads.

(33) **NIAGARA FALLS** – The Niagara River and its vicinity are chiefly noted for their autumn and winter birds, particularly gulls and duck along the river itself. It is over 70 km from Fort Erie, where the river leaves Lake Erie, to the mouth at Niagara-on-the-Lake, and the Niagara Parkway runs beside or close to the river for almost the entire distance. A day or even more can be spent covering the area at peak periods, as enormous numbers of gulls and large flocks of duck can occur, particularly in late fall. Fourteen species of gulls have been recorded, most of them annually.

The peak periods are in October through early December, when there are huge flocks of Bonaparte's Gulls, usually accompanied by scattered birds of rarer species – Little, Franklin's, and Black-headed Gulls and Black-legged Kittiwake are the most usual. Later most of these smaller gulls move out and Glaucous, Iceland, and a few Thayer's Gulls join the thousands of Herring and Ring-billed Gulls. There are small numbers of Great Black-backed Gulls through most of this period, and Lesser Black-backed Gulls have been seen with increasing frequency in recent years.

Duck numbers build up in November. The principal species are Canvasback, scaup, Common Goldeneye, Bufflehead, Old-squaw, and Common Merganser, but there are smaller numbers of Mallard, Black Duck, Gadwall, and American Wigeon. The rarer species that can be expected include Barrow's Goldeneye, all three scoters, and Harlequin Duck, with scattered loons and grebes (Eared are rare but regular). Scattered shorebirds along the rocks around the falls regularly include Purple Sandpipers, which are then sometimes present well into winter.

Good numbers of all waterbirds continue over the winter, but of particular interest at this season are the resident landbirds –

Mockingbird, Tufted Titmouse, Carolina Wren, and House Finch are the most noteworthy. Many other wintering species occur in sheltered areas and at feeders. Barn Owls are generally distributed on the peninsula, but unless you have access to a nesting site you are unlikely to see them.

The Niagara River is less noteworthy at other times, and some movements (such as the main fall hawk flights) by-pass the peninsula completely. However, there are large movements of Common Nighthawks and Purple Martins in early autumn, and interesting waterfowl can turn up at any time.

In the route described below the most productive areas are around Niagara Falls itself, and to a lesser extent at Fort Erie and around Queenston, although there will be birds visible along the entire length of the river. Watch the ornamental plantings along the route for berry-bearing trees that can attract waxwings and other fruit-eaters.

It is easier to cover the river from south to north, and you can omit the southern section altogether if time is limited. The account will start from the Lake Erie shoreline just west of Old Fort Erie. This point is some 3 km along Lakeshore Road from the Peace Bridge (the bridge to the United Sates), which is also the end of the Queen Elizabeth Way and Highway 3. The kilometreages that follow are from point to point. The route begins at Bardol Street, where Lakeshore Road begins, and assumes you will drive east and north following the shoreline and river bank. The name of this road varies: it is variously called Niagara Boulevard, Lake Shore Road, River Road, and perhaps other names I have never noticed. The main thing is to stick to the main road closest to the river.

0 km   Bardol Street. The rocks along this stretch of waterfront often have shorebirds, as do the lawns a little farther on. The waters in this section are good for scoters.

3.3 km The Peace Bridge. Look for duck, gulls, possible phalarope. Several vantage points follow in parking lots and drive-offs along the Fort Erie waterfront.

1.5 km Gilmore Road. This drive-off usually seems to conclude the most interesting sections around Fort Erie. From here to the control dam north of Chippawa (24 km) the duck and gulls gradually thin out, but interesting finds are still possible.

7.2 km The marina waters concentrate duck when the neighbouring river is frozen.

1.4 km A marshy area, good for pond duck.

15.2 km The control structures at the mouth of the Welland River at Chippawa. Gulls and terns loiter on them.

0.8 km Keep right over the Chippawa bridge, and right again to continue along the parkway.

1.3 km A large parking lot near the high gates and control dam on the river. A major stop for gulls, terns, and waterfowl generally.

0.5 km The road forks here into north- and south-bound lanes. There is no parking, but a stop at the south end of the fork is usually possible – and worth while! You can view gulls and duck below the dam.

0.4 km There is nowhere to park, but the enclosed waters on your right often attract the odd rarer duck.

0.3–0.5 km Small parking areas. Walk over the lawn to the river, which is often very productive here, because less disturbed than elsewhere. Gulls and duck loiter. The woods of Dufferin Islands opposite yield common landbirds, and the entrance to the loop road around these islands and their associated ponds starts to the left just between the two parking lots. Pied-billed Grebe, herons, and puddle duck may be here prior to freeze-up.

0.4 km From the start of the Dufferin Islands loop is a small parking lot just north of the old power plant building on the right. This is perhaps the best single spot in the entire route. Gulls and duck are everywhere, possible shorebirds on the rocks, and a colony of Black-crowned Night Herons in the willows on the small islands.

0.6 km A bus parking lot usually open to anyone later in the season. From here take a short walk upstream to a low stone wall overlook, which is a good place to view Table Rock and the other rocks and rapids above the Horseshoe Falls. Also, look down into the gorge near the top of the falls.

1.0 km Street parking starts here. Walk upstream to view the gorge if not covered at the last stop, and also look downstream at the whole area, particularly about the power plant outlet in the gorge below the restaurant. Downstream from here is a belvedere (gazebo) at the edge of the gorge where a good view of the area is possible, particularly the waterfowl upstream from the *Maid of the Mist* dock.

0.7 km   The Princess Elizabeth Building (with a small restaurant and souvenir shop, and the only rest-rooms we have found open consistently in the colder months). Behind is the private road down to the *Maid of the Mist*. Walk down if your heart's in good shape, and cover the river as far south as possible. You can also 'scope the area from the road gate, if you cannot get down for some reason. Many rarities have been found here, and it is one of the places King Eiders can turn up.

0.5 km   The Rainbow Bridge parking lots. More views of the gorge.

6.4 km   Niagara Glen Nature Area, despite its name, has never yielded much in the bird line for us. Not worth stopping.

0.7 km   Niagara School of Horticulture. Park on the right and walk over to the grounds. There usually are active feeders: it is a good place for Mockingbird and other landbirds.

1.4 km   A parking area on the right at the Sir Adam Beck generating station. Look down on the gulls here: good for white gulls.

1.2 km   The entrance to the bridge to the USA, on left.

0.7 km   The entrance to Highway 405 west to Toronto, on left.

0.2 km   A T-intersection. Turn right, but note that the berry-bearing trees and evergreens around the Brock Monument may have landbirds.

0.9 km   At the bottom of the hill is an intersection with York Street. Ahead is Queenston. Left on York leads to St Davids (qv). Turn right and then bear left on Front Street.

0.4 km   A turn-off to the right (opposite Dumfries Street) leads down to parking areas where one can check gulls again – this area is particularly good for the smaller gulls – and walk upriver to cover the woodland for landbirds. One can also walk (or drive) north down the hill to the dock and view the river from there. Continue north on Front, which finally turns onto Walnut, and right again on Queenston Street.

0.4 km A small drive down to a park area on the right, the other end of the narrow dirt road that goes north from the dock. There is more river access here. Queenston joins the Parkway a little to the north. Continue on it. There usually is not much new on the river along this stretch.

8.8 km The road forks here. Bear right, but first check the large oaks here and along John Street to the west for Red-headed Woodpeckers and Common Flickers, present year-round. This is called Paradise Grove.

1.2 km One is now entering Niagara-on-the-Lake. Stop at the parks administration building for a view of the river. The well-grown gardens from here on are good for wintering landbirds. One is now on Ricardo Street.

0.6 km The marina may have open leads with interesting duck in winter.

0.2 km Turn right on Melville, then left at the Customs House, and check the river again. The road curves to join north-bound Delater Street, and when it too curves there is viewing of birds around the mouth of the river.

0.7 km Turn right on Front Street. The streets to the left were Ontario's first breeding station for House Finches. They are still there, and a drive around looking at gardens and feeders may yield both these and other Niagara area regulars such as Tufted Titmouse or Carolina Wren. Front finally curves west at Simcoe Street.

1.0 km Turn right on Queen Street and, 0.8 km along, check the river mouth and lake again.

This terminates the river drive. One is now at Lake Ontario, and can continue west along Niagara Boulevard, which curves around through well-grown gardens and, at 0.7 km, crosses a small creek that can be productive of landbirds. The road then turns south and joins Lake Shore Road (Niagara Regional Road 87) after about 1 km. A right turn 0.7 km from the corner leads to the sewage lagoons on the right, some of which are visible from the road. Road 87 continues west some 10 km to Port Weller (see St Catharines).

(34) **Norwich** – The drive to Norwich sewage lagoon is to the east of Highway 59, just before the railroad tracks cross the highway, 1 km south of its intersection with Main Street.

Main Street, Norwich, is County Road 3, and 9 km east of town on it there is quite an extensive tract of Conservation Authority woodlands along Big Otter Creek.

(35) **Parkhill** – *Parkhill Reservoir* is just northeast of town to the east of Highway 81. A good viewpoint of the water area is provided 2.2 km north of the Highways 7 and 81 junction. The entrance to the Conservation Area itself is to the east; it can yield waterfowl, especially during migration.

Just before this viewpoint County Road 18 intersects from the west. If you turn west here the woodlands of Parkhill Creek are to your right for ½ km, and 1 km from the intersection the sewage lagoon gate is on the right.

(36) **PELEE ISLAND** – Pelee Island is located roughly 13½ km south and east of the tip of Point Pelee, and is reached by ferries from Leamington and Kingsville, a 22-km journey. There are usually about two sailings daily between mid-March and mid-December, and it is quite expensive. (For map, see p 50.)

Ferry information can be obtained from Ontario Travel Offices or by calling (519) 724-2115. These ferries arrive at Scudder. During the crossing watch the many gulls, terns, and other waterbirds en route, and as you come in look for Great Black-backed Gulls off Scudder Dock.

First head northeast from Scudder. After some 1.5 km *Lighthouse Point Provincial Nature Reserve* is passed to the north. A large new colony of Double-crested Cormorants is the chief attraction here, in dead trees standing in Lake Henry, and some Herring Gulls occasionally nest as well. Rafts of loons, grebes, and diving duck occasionally congregate offshore in Lake Erie. Lake Henry is a favoured foraging area for herons and Great Egrets.

Later in the season shorebirds and Caspian Terns congregate here, especially if there are mud flats. Sharp-tailed Sparrows have been recorded along the south side of Lake Henry in September, when numerous raptors, especially accipiters, fly past the point.

Upland areas of Lighthouse Point, particularly the fine oak-hickory, blue ash savannah, and shrub tangles, have Carolina Wren, Blue-gray Gnatcatcher, White-eyed Vireo, and Orchard Oriole in summer.

Continue southeast approximately 2½ km from Lighthouse Point to *Brown's Point*. This is a splendid privately owned bottomland woods with many oaks and hickories. Look for Carolinian species here.

The *Airport*, a small grassed tract near the west centre of the island, is most easily reached via the North-South Road south from Scudder (some 4 km). Here Upland Sandpipers and Bobolinks (formerly Dickcissels) occur and Western and hybrid Meadowlarks should be watched for.

Farther south (about 7 km from Scudder) the *East-West Road*, a main road which traverses the island from Vincent Barrie Park on the east to West Dock Town, passes through some excellent oak-hickory and red cedar savannah, deserving of more attention from birders. Whip-poor-wills and a Chuck-will's-widow have occurred in summer, and in the scrub along the road a distinctive song type of Willow Flycatcher, sounding almost like an Acadian Flycatcher, occurs.

At the southeast end of this road, and of the island, are *Stone Road* and *Mill Point*, the latter directly accessible from South Bay of Lake Erie via Dick's Marina.

This is an extensive undisturbed tract of open savannah, with prairie elements, which usually has several pairs of Yellow-breasted Chats. Song and other sparrows, normally difficult to find on the island, occur here.

The southernmost extremity of the island, some 9 km from Scudder via the North-South Road, is *Fish Point Provincial Park Reserve* including Fox Pond and Mosquito Bay. The swamp forests here are of outstanding maturity and were formerly the site of one of the largest heronries in Canada. Great and Cattle Egrets, Black-crowned and Yellow-crowned Night Herons, King Rails, and Common Gallinules have all been recorded about the lagoon (Fox Pond).

Great Horned Owls, Red-bellied Woodpeckers, Winter and Carolina Wrens, Blue-gray Gnatcatchers, and Prothonotary Warblers occur in the breeding season. Offshore and on the extreme southern spit, Double-crested Cormorants, Great Black-backed Gulls, and Caspian Terns occur regularly. Herring Gulls may breed here, and Piping Plovers formerly did so.

Wet meadows at the northwest base of Fish Point have interesting shorebirds, and the low-lying fields farther north produce plovers and Marsh Hawks. Waterfowl may mass off the point, and hawks and warblers funnel through it in migration. More upland areas have harboured Yellow-breasted Chats and Orchard Orioles during the breeding season.

Bald Eagles formerly nested at several sites on the island but are scarcely seen now. Ring-necked Pheasants are probably more numerous than elsewhere in Ontario, but have greatly declined, and Yellow-billed Cuckoos seem more numerous than anywhere else in Canada. Barn Owls have been recorded (search old churches and barns), and Screech Owls are still fairly plentiful. Red-headed Woodpeckers, Carolina Wrens, and Eastern Bluebirds remain scattered but regular breeders, as do Orchard Orioles and Grasshopper Sparrows. Brewer's Blackbird was seen in 1980.

During migration the entire area provides marvellous birding and many rarities have occurred (Virginia's Warbler in 1974).

Pelee Island is technically an archipelago which includes the provincial nature reserves of East Sister and and Middle Islands; however, these should not be visited during the breeding season without permission from the Ministry of Natural Resources.

(37) **Petrolia** – At Petrolia the lagoon complex is not readily accessible, but can be viewed to the west of the road at a distance from King Street (the first sideroad west of Highway 21) and about 3 km south of Main Street.

The Petrolia Conservation Area is 1.2 km from the highway west along Main Street, and provides access to Bear Creek, which also crosses the highway about 2½ km north of town. There are old field habitats and some hardwoods along the stream.

South of Petrolia on 21 Oil City has a small but inaccessible lagoon northwest of the village, and south again is *Oil Springs*, with a larger one. To reach this turn east on Main Street and drive 1 km to Frederick Street on the north; the lagoon gate is 0.2 km ahead.

Another lagoon in this area is west of *Brigden*, itself west of Highway 21 along Highway 80. From the Moore-Brigden Road in the village drive west 2 km to Moore Road 9–10. Turn south and the lagoons are ½ km along on the left.

Western Meadowlarks have become very scarce in the province following the very cold winters of the late 1970s. The fields of Lambton County were a stronghold for these birds (and hybrids) and they should be listened for.

(38) **Port Colborne** – There are several interesting areas near Port Colborne. The remaining sections of *Wainfleet Bog*, a massive peat bog now much reduced by drainage and development, can be reached from two points.

Taking the intersection of Highways 58 and 3 west of town as a departure point, drive north on 58 1.4 km to Barrick Road on the west. Turn and drive 1.3 km to the point the road dead-ends at a peat farm, currently called F.A.Y. Farm. Ask for permission at the office to go in and drive north across a small bridge about 1 km on a dirt-peat road to a small parking drive-off on the left side near some dense shrubs. A trail starts here and runs north, eventually into open untouched bog.

Be sure to mark or otherwise note the point you enter the open bog, as it is easy to lose track of your position. Marsh Hawk, Short-eared Owl, and Lincoln's Sparrow have all occurred in this area.

To reach the second access point drive west on Highway 3 from the 58 intersection 5.4 km to Wilson Road, which crosses the bog to the north. On the east side of Wilson there is a trail which runs through the poplar-willow woodland. After several hundred metres this comes out into mostly open bog and eventually comes to untouched areas of bog. This trail has to be watched for as it grows over. It runs east off Wilson near the only dirt road that comes in from the west. Whip-poor-wills breed adjacent to Wilson, and the species noted above also can be found here.

Just 0.8 km west of Wilson Road is the intersection of Highway 3 and Regional Road 30. To visit *Morgan's Point* turn south on 30 and drive 3.1 km (the road turns and runs west) to Morgan's Point Road on the south. The point at the end (1.6 km) attracts shorebirds and other waterfowl, and the scrub and woods to the west concentrate migrants.

To reach *Mud Lake* return to the Highway 58 intersection and continue east almost 1 km to the light at Elm Street (Regional Road 80). Turn north here and drive 3.5 km to a small parking lot on the east side of the road. From this drive-off are two paths, one up to the top of the dyke to connect with a trail along it and around the lake, and the other along the south side of the dyke to connect with a boardwalk and trail running around the east side of the lake and into the cat-tail marsh. The lake is noteworthy for all the usual marsh species in summer and breeding records of several species of duck, including Ruddy. There is a controlled hunt here.

East of Port Colborne (some 14 km east of the Highway 58 intersection) is the Point Abino road. This runs south some 6 km to *Point Abino*, a privately owned point with wooded hills which have some Carolinian species in summer (Acadian Flycatcher is regular in woods at Abino Hills west of the point, reached from Holloway Bay Road) and which concentrates migrants. Access to the point road is uncertain – permission may or may not be given at the gate – and parking is difficult, but the area is a significant one.

(39) Port Dover – The Harbour (on the east of Highway 6 at the point it turns west at the bottom of the hill from the bridge) sometimes has interesting gulls and provides good views of the lake. Farther west St Andrew Street (1.5 km) and Mill Street (0.4 km) give access to points around the pond along the river behind the town.

Some 6 km north of Port Dover on Highway 6 is the intersection of Regional Road 3. Eastbound, this leads to Nanticoke and areas around the industrial developments there. Just past the intersection on 3 (1.8 km) is an excellent view of a Great Blue heronry to the north.

By continuing east some 6 km and continuing straight ahead when the county road turns left one will come to the village of *Nanticoke*. Turn left into the village and at 0.9 km turn right and drive to the shore, scanning the marshes along the creek on the right. Returning, farther east again there is lake-viewing west of the power plant at the foot of Regional Road 55 (0.8 km; there is a light at the corner) and east of the plant at 0.9 km. The Peacock Point road is at 4.4 km, and Selkirk Provincial Park at 2.5 km. All

of these have lake views, and the park has marshes along San-
dusky Creek.

(40) PORT LAMBTON – North of this village on the St Clair
Parkway the river can have duck and gulls, particularly in winter. The best area is at *Sombra*, and the four kilometres or so
between Lambton Road 2 and the bridge to the south of that
village tend to be best.

Both Sombra and Port Lambton have lagoons. For the one at
Sombra continue south on the Parkway 0.7 km from the street to
the ferry to the United States. Sombra Road 11 is to your left and
the lagoon gate is on the right just over the tracks, 0.3 km down
this road. Port Lambton lagoons are at the back of a field off
County Road 1, which joins the Parkway just past the ferry dock
entrance. Drive 0.8 km east on County Road 1 to the track to the
lagoon, which is on the right almost opposite the fire hall.

Just south of Port Lambton the road starts to follow the eastern
side of *Walpole Island*, with extensive marshes along the shore,
and some 8 km south the highway turns east and Kent Road 32
goes west over a bridge on to the island. It is an Indian reserve
with most of the habitation north of Road 32, which runs west
across to the far shore. There are five islands in all, and the bulk
of the 24,000 hectares lies to the south of the main road. Here
there is a network of dirt roads, but much of the area is remote
and relatively inaccessible. The extensive marshes along the
Lake St Clair shoreline occupy the south end. Here many nesting
species rare in both the region and Ontario as a whole have been
found, including Canvasback, Redhead, Ruddy Duck, Marsh
Hawk, Little Gull, and Forster's Tern. King Rails also occur.
There is a heronry of Black-crowned Night Herons and Great
Egrets, and the extensive wooded areas include sections of oak
savannah. Deciduous woodland species are present, and Brewer's Blackbird has been reported on the farming areas, but landbirds are less well known than waterfowl. For more extensive
excursions into the marshes permission should be obtained from
the Indian band.

(41) PORT STANLEY – This town is best known for its proximity to Hawk Cliff, but there are several other points of interest.
If you drive to town on Highway 4 you can continue (crossing

the river and bearing left) to the point where the highway turns right at the beach on the west of town. Drive straight ahead to the point the street ends. Cover the beach and the harbour from here.

To get to the east side of the harbour return on 4, crossing the river again, and turn right on Main Street, which ends ½ km ahead at a loading terminal. Turn left just before this and drive ahead to Little Beach, where you can view the lake east of the harbour.

Hawk Cliff is east of town and is a fine hawk observation and banding locale in fall but it is also a good place to view other migrants (both landbirds and waterbirds) moving along the shore of Lake Erie.

The same hawk species occur as at Holiday Beach (see Amherstburg), and as the birds are often easier to see the area has become known as the premier locale for watching fall hawk flights. Flights tend to be heaviest in periods with northwest winds and light cumulus clouds, and do not develop on rainy days or when the winds are southerly.

To reach Hawk Cliff from Port Stanley, at the point Highway 4 turns off Main Street in town to cross the river, turn east and drive diagonally up the hill on Joseph Street. This is County Road 23 and it turns left at the top of the hill to lead (1.6 km) to an intersection on the right with County Road 24. (Note that if you continue straight ahead you end up on Highway 4 again: coming south on the highway you can by-pass town by turning at this point.) Turn east on County Road 24 and drive 3 km, where the Hawk Cliff road is on the south opposite the intersection of County Road 22 going north. The road dead-ends at the lake.

For Port Stanley sewage lagoon, follow Highway 4 to the river bridge, drive west across it, and turn north on County Road 20. At 1.4 km is the intersection of County Road 21 on the right. Turn left on a road winding up a hill and go 1.1 km to a gravel road on the right. Turn here again and the lagoons are 1.1 km along on the left.

Returning to Country Road 20 again, it leads 10½ km north and west to the village of Fingal. Here a left turn on County Road 16 leads 3.1 km west to *Fingal Wildlife Management Area*. It is managed for Bobwhites among other species, and 1.2 km along one can drive down the west boundary to a small waterfowl feeding area with an observation tower. The sideroad crossing the south end can be interesting as well.

(42) **Ridgetown** – The sewage lagoons are north of town. From the junction of Highway 21 and Main Street in town (highway turns right) drive ahead on Erie Street and continue 1.4 km to Palmer Street, just before Erie Street crosses the tracks and turns right. Turn left on Palmer; the lagoons are 0.3 km along on the south.

(43) **Rockton** – North on Highway 52 from this community at the intersection with Highway 8, the area south of Kirkwall has many old fields. There are Christmas tree farms and reforestation here, and the resultant mix has created conditions suitable for Grasshopper, Henslow's, and Clay-coloured Sparrow, as well as Upland Sandpipers. Given the successional nature of these habitats, identifying specific areas is probably not worth while, but a search in the breeding season for these species could be productive. Henslow's seem to prefer sections of old fields where there is heavy growth of perennial forbs such as asters and goldenrods but with more open areas nearby; Grasshopper Sparrows prefer the thin grass in the drier, more infertile areas and often use small shrubs or mullein stalks as song perches; and Clay-coloureds seem to favour young evergreens of up to 4 metres in height.

(44) **Rodney** – For the sewage lagoons, drive south on County Road 3 1 km from the point it crosses the railroad in town, to County Road 2 (Back Street) on the left. Turn, and the lagoon gates are 0.7 km along on the north.

(45) **St Catharines** – The area around St Catharines is of interest for both the waterbirds along the Lake Ontario shoreline and for the woods and reservoirs on the Niagara Escarpment.

Port Weller, the entry to the Welland Canal, is northeast of the city and the canal piers are north of Regional Road 87. On the west side of the bridge over the canal on this road is Canal Road, leading to the beach at the west, and to the east is Broadway, which runs north to the other side. It is about 2 km to the open woods near the marina there. The whole area can be good for waterbirds.

Farther west *Port Dalhousie* is at the mouth of Twelve Mile Creek. Continue west on Regional Road 87 (Lakeshore Road) about 5½ km from the Port Weller bridge. Here Michigan Avenue on the right leads to the east side of the creek mouth. On the left is Martindale Pond, with an overview from Lock Street, to the right just ahead, and this leads to a large parking lot on the beach. Both the pond and the creek mouth are good for waterbirds. Continuing west on Main Street, the road to Henley Island (1.7 km) and Regional Road 38 (a further 0.6 km) are both to the left (south) and provide further views of the Pond. Road 38 is Martindale Road, which leads (1.8 km) south to the Queen Elizabeth Way intersection.

The areas around the escarpment can be reached form Highway 406, the controlled access road linking St Catharines and Thorold, and Welland to the south. The account below assumes a start at the intersection of this highway and Beaverdams Road. If one turns east on Beaverdams Road one will cross *Gibson Lake*, part of a power reservoir complex that extends east and west of here. At 1.9 km along is Decew Road, and a left turn here will lead 5.6 km west to Pelham Road. This route passes the reservoir complex to *Decew Falls* and the wooded areas on the public lands on both sides of the road. The route is good for both landbirds and waterbirds. West on Pelham Road from Decew Road is one entrance to the proposed Short Hills Provincial Park, on the left.

If one turns west on Beaverdams Road from Highway 406 one comes almost immediately to the Merrittville Road. Turn left here, and 2.6 km from 406 turn right (west) on Roland (or Holland) Road. This road leads to Hollow Road (2.4 km) on the left, and the *St Johns Conservation Area* with fine Carolinian hardwoods. Continuing west it winds through the beautiful rolling country south of the proposed *Short Hills Provincial Park*, with a day-use entry at 2.8 km. It then joins the Effingham Road 0.6 km farther on, and you can drive south to Highway 20. Another fine wooded area in this vicinity is the Hamilton Naturalist's *Short Hills* area. To reach it drive 3.8 km south on the Effingham Road to Mepler Road, and then 1.3 km west to Centre Street, where the reserve is on the northeast corner.

(46) St Davids – At St Davids there are some private sewage lagoons which can be visited with permission. The village is 3.9 km west on Regional Road 81 (York Road) from its intersection in Queenston with the Niagara Parkway. Coming from Queenston, turn right (north) on Regional Road 100 (Creek Road). At 0.4 km there is a cannery on the right with a lagoon behind it. The other lagoons are 1.3 km farther north. Turn left here on a dead-end gravel road opposite a gas station. The lagoons are 0.7 km along on the right.

To gain access to the ponds permission *must* be obtained from the manager at the cannery. Failure to do so could result in withdrawal of the privileges for everyone.

(47) St Marys – This town is in Perth County and hence in the south-central region, but it is also the nearest community to *Wildwood Reservoir*, which is mostly in Oxford County. This reservoir is on Highway 7 some 14 km southwest of Stratford and just 2 km east of the junction with Highway 19 southbound. The west end (the widest and most interesting for waterfowl) is readily visible from the highway, which is the dam causeway, and sideroads to the east and south lead to other viewing points. The reservoir attracts large numbers of Mallards and Black Ducks in spring and fall, and other species should be looked for in these flocks. East 1 km from the dam itself and opposite Perth Road 28 is the entrance to the Conservation Area, and 0.9 km along this road is the entrance to the *Dr R.S. Murray Forest*, a large area of mixed woodlands and pine plantations on the east shore of the lake. This tract can be good for landbirds.

(48) St Thomas – There are a couple of interesting town parks here. Travelling on Highway 4 south, from the junction of Talbot Street continue 2.6 km to a railroad crossing and turn left on Elm Street. Drive 0.6 km to *Pinafore Park* on the right, which has a pond and natural woodlands.

Waterworks Park is north of town. From the Highway 3 by-pass take the First Avenue exit north 0.5 km to South Edgeware Road, and turn left. This road leads west 1.2 km down the hill into the park, which has a fair-sized water impoundment and natural woodlands.

(49) **SARNIA** – The mouth of the St Clair River is probably the best place in Ontario to see such pelagic birds as jaegers and Sabine's Gulls close to shore in season. These birds and large numbers of other waterbirds move down Lake Huron in late autumn mainly during periods when the winds are northerly, and tend to appear around the mouth of the river at Sarnia, or to move down it.

Point Edward is the section of Sarnia here; to reach it drive west on Highway 402 and take the last exit to the right just before the International Bridge to the USA. The turn-off is about ½ km east of the customs stations, and leads directly to St Clair Street. Turn left and drive to the end at Victoria Avenue (1 km), then turn left again. Follow this road 0.3 km to Fort Street and turn right. Just before the water treatment building a road (0.2 km) runs left. Follow this around to a parking area overlooking the lake and river mouth. Walk east or west for additional viewing points. Many landbirds, and hawks also, move along the shoreline in fall and concentrate along the shore in spring migration.

If you wish to try some landbirding for a change, visit Canatara Park less than 1 km to the east. Return to Victoria Avenue, turn left and drive to Alfred Street (0.6 km), and turn left on Alfred. This road leads into the park, winding along the shoreline to emerge 1½ km later, as Lake Chipican Road, on to Christina Street North, which leads (turn left) into Lakeshore Drive and out towards Bright's Grove and Kettle Point (qv).

This park has wilder natural areas to the south, more lake viewing to the north, a small lake which attracts waterfowl and marshbirds to the east, open water in winter, and the usual city park facilities including washrooms. It is good for landbirds in spring.

The St Clair Parkway (County Road 33) follows the river south from the outskirts of Sarnia – just south of the intersection of Highways 40A and 40B – to Walpole Island, and can be a good birding road, particularly from late autumn to early spring, when duck and gulls congregate on open water.

Points of particular interest are Willow Park at the Lambton Generating Station just south of Courtright (usually a good place to view gulls) and farther south at Sombra (see Port Lambton) where the river is often very good for waterfowl.

(50) **Smithville** – The sewage lagoons are on the east side of town. From the railroad bridge crossing Highway 20 drive east 0.8 km to Regional Road 614 on the right. Turn and drive 0.3 km, crossing the stream. The long drive into the lagoons is on the left. They have been most productive.

(51) **Strathroy** – These sewage lagoons are very well known and have been the source of many noteworthy records. They are off County Road 39 west of town. From the main intersection in town of this road (Albert Street) and Highway 81 turn west. Note that the road bears diagonally right just past the intersection. Drive 2.7 km to a sideroad on the left, with a sign 'Waterfowl Viewing Area.' Drive south 1 km, crossing the busy railroad tracks with care, and the lagoons are on the left. There is a viewing tower, and a wide variety of waterfowl and shorebirds, as well as Bobwhites, have been recorded.

(52) **Tavistock** – The Tavistock sewage lagoons are at the back of the playing field, but perhaps an easier route to them is to drive north on Highway 59 to Hope Street East in the centre of town (this is County Road 24). Turn right on Hope Street and drive 0.4 km to Wellington Street. Right again, and the lagoons are clearly visible (and accessible) across the tracks ahead at the point this street (0.2 km) turns left.

(53) **Thedford** – The sewage lagoons are on the right, driving west on Highway 82, just ½ km after the long curve to the left leaving the village.

(54) **Tilbury** – Tilbury lagoons are west of County Road 1 and north of Highway 401. They are probably best viewed from the westbound lanes of Highway 401 between the two Tilbury interchanges (ie, get on at Number 63 and leave at Number 56).

(55) **Vineland** – For Vineland, exit from the Queen Elizabeth Way at the Victoria Avenue (Regional Road 24) exit and turn north. Just past the service roads is the entrance, to the west, of the *Vineland Agricultural Research Station*. The grounds here are

fine for migrant landbirds, and farther north (0.9 km) when the road turns along the shore there is a vantage point for viewing the lake. Accipiters follow the shoreline in spring, and heavy flights of waterfowl (Red-breasted and Common Merganser, scaup, and, in spring, Pintail) occur.

Jordan Harbour is east of here: return to the Queen Elizabeth Way and cross it to drive east on the South Service Road. The road turns south 1.5 km east, and views of the harbour can be obtained from the marina road directly ahead, and along the road to the south, especially at 0.7 km.

Ball's Falls Conservation Area, with more escarpment forest, is some 5.6 km south along Regional Road 24.

(56) Warwick – *Warwick Conservation Area*, in the village along Highway 7, has a small lake, bottomlands, and hardwoods.

(57) Waterford – At Waterford there has been extensive gravel extraction just east of Highway 24 and many ponds have been created. County Road 9, which runs east to the south end of town, passes several of these on both sides of the road. The Waterford Conservation Area South 0.6 km from 24 has mixed woods associated with some of the ponds.

North 1.3 km on 24 another road runs east to Waterford. This is Mechanics Road, and 1.8 km along it is the *Waterford Conservation Area* on the south, and at 0.8 km parking for the *Waterford Ponds Wildlife Management Area* to the north. The ponds here are much more extensive with a fair amount of marshland along the edges and some swampy areas with tamarack.

Waterford sewage lagoons are surrounded by a high fence – their entrance is south of Deer Park Road 1.3 km east of its intersection with Old Main Street, and 2.8 km due east of Waterford Ponds Wildlife Management Area above.

(58) Watford – There are sewage lagoons here, but they are down an extremely long drive. From the railroad bridge in town, drive 1.7 km south on Highway 79, and turn right on Brooke-Warwick Townline. The gate is 1 km along on the right, but one can hardly see the lagoons from there!

(59) **West Lorne** – The sewage lagoons are 2.7 km south on Highway 76 from its intersection with Elgin Road 2 in town. Turn west on Aldborough Concession 11 and drive 0.6 km; the lagoon drive is on the right.

One interesting spot along Highway 401 is off the eastbound lanes between the West Lorne and Dutton interchanges. Just west of the picnic area at the service centre here are some ponds which can be good spots for shorebirds, and occasionally have a few duck as well.

(60) **Windsor** – There are views of the Detroit River along the Windsor waterfront and south along Highway 18 (see Amherstburg). Waterfowl can be seen in migration periods and over winter.

At the southeast end of town along Ojibway Parkway (which becomes Highway 18) is *Ojibway Park*, a city park that has produced interesting stragglers on occasion. It is very interesting botanically, as is the Windsor Prairie reserve just east of here along Matchette Road. This, believe it or not, is the best remaining fragment of long-grass prairie in Canada.

(61) **Woodstock** – The *Pittock Dam and Conservation Area* is east off Highway 59 just north of town. The Pittock Park Road is the second road on the east after crossing the bridge over the railroad. The park gate is 1.5 km ahead, and the north bank parkland provides excellent views of a large lake. Like other reservoirs, it is heavily used for recreation, but waterfowl gather in spring and autumn, mainly Mallards, Black Duck, and Common Merganser. For some reason this lake seems less appealing to birds than does either Wildwood or Conestoga reservoir.

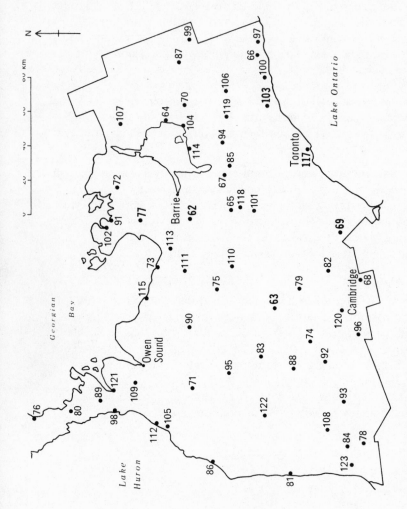

MAP 3 South-Central Ontario

4 / South-Central Ontario

Central Ontario means different things to different people, and there has been some tradition among field workers to use the term to refer to that part of the province occupied by the Boreal Forest south of the Hudson Bay Lowlands. The term is not so used here, where south-central Ontario refers to all the counties north and east of Middlesex, Oxford, and Brant together with the Regional Municipality of Hamilton-Wentworth; east to and including Simcoe, Victoria, and Durham counties. Bruce County is in, but Manitoulin Island is not.

This area is classified primarily as a zone of mixed forest, but sugar maple and beech predominate, with heavy conifer cover only in the more poorly drained or northern sections. Unlike in the areas to the southwest there are some considerable stands of woodland, particularly along the Niagara Escarpment, in the Bruce Peninsula, and in the three easternmost counties. Much of the countryside is hilly, the product of glaciation, but significant plains occur in the Bruce Peninsula and the Carden plain east of Orillia, the high country in the west of Dufferin and Wellington counties, and along Lake Ontario east to Toronto. Agriculture still is the major land use, although along Lake Ontario the city is taking over.

In this region many of the more southern species enumerated in the last chapter can still be found although in some cases only as scattered individuals. The bush and woodlands of the escarpment can provide strongholds for the following species:

Turkey Vulture   Blue-winged Warbler
Yellow-throated Vireo   Cerulean Warbler
Golden-winged Warbler

Ring-necked Pheasants and Cardinals are also common birds in
the south.

The Lake Ontario shoreline is both a major barrier to and a
pathway for migrants, and it is a rich area for birding in migration times although it lacks concentration points of the quality of
those farther east and west. The potential of the Lake Huron and
Georgian Bay shorelines has not been fully explored, but some
points at the north end of the Bruce Peninsula and areas around
Nottawasaga Bay have already been shown to concentrate both
landbird and waterbird migrants. Inland, several reservoirs and
three major wetlands – Luther, Wye, and Tiny marshes – are
also excellent for waterfowl passage.

The Lake Ontario waterfront between Toronto and Hamilton
attracts large numbers of wintering waterfowl, and the abandoned farmland around the urban areas hawks and owls in
winter. Toronto in particular, because of its size, acts as a heat
island in the cold weather, and the urban zone along the lake
often yields wintering birds that normally move farther south.

(62) **ANGUS** – Northeast of this village on Highway 90 lies
Minesing Swamp, an exceptional area for both birds and botany.
Here some southern species occur close to more northern ones,
as hackberry forest and black spruce bog exist almost side by
side. The swamp has several access points. Westbound from Barrie on Highway 90 drive to the intersection with Simcoe County
Road 28. Go north on 28 for 7½ km; the next half kilometre or so
crosses the eastern (Willow Creek) part of the swamp. Golden-
winged Warblers have occurred in the bushy areas at the beginning of this section, near the railway track.

Farther along Highway 90, Concession Roads 11 and 12 of
Vespra (the first two west of County Road 28) lead north into a
black spruce section of the swamp, with an abundance of warblers. Farther west again, and on the eastern edge of the village
of Angus itself, Sunnidale Concession 21–22 leads north into the
swamp, this time to end at Iron Bridge. There is canoe access

here to the Nottawasaga River north into the area, and the levees have southern plants such as hackberry, with Blue-gray Gnatcatchers and Yellow-throated Vireos occurring. In spring the flooded fields west of the lower stretch of this sideroad teem with waterfowl, with thousands of Pintail and other ducks. Canoe access from the north is at the Nottawasaga River crossing at Edenvale on Highway 26. The swamp is upstream from here, and many noteworthy features – a large heronry of Great Blues, and Cerulean Warblers and Yellow-throated Vireos nesting near the junction of the Nottawasaga and Willow Creek – are accessible only by canoe.

(63) **ARTHUR** – The sewage lagoons are just north of the railroad tracks and east of County Road 14. From the intersection of Highways 6 and 9 drive north 0.8 km on 6 to the lights at Frederick Street. This is County Road 14. Turn right and then follow the road left as it turns on Eliza Street. The tracks are 1.2 km from the lights, and the lagoons can be seen behind the houses at this point.

Some 6 km east of Arthur lies *Luther Marsh*, a huge area of some 6500 hectares created by the impoundment of the headwaters of the Grand River. The lake lies between Highways 9 and 89, and west of 25. It is only accessible by gravel roads, and there are several access points.

The marsh has three main, large areas of interest. These are: the actual lake and various islands and bogs therein, the northern woods, and Wylde Lake, which is an unusual raised bog of a very boreal character southeast of the main lake.

The lake is noted as a waterfowl breeding area. Fifteen species of ducks have been proved to nest, although not all do so annually. Very roughly in order of abundance these are Mallard, Gadwall, American Wigeon, Blue-winged Teal, Lesser Scaup, Redhead, Ring-necked Duck, Black Duck, Ruddy Duck, Green-winged Teal, Pintail, Wood Duck, Hooded Merganser, Canvasback, and Northern Shoveler. Most of these species nest on the islands and around the north bog. The best areas are around Big Island, the north bog, and Windmill Island: examine secluded coves.

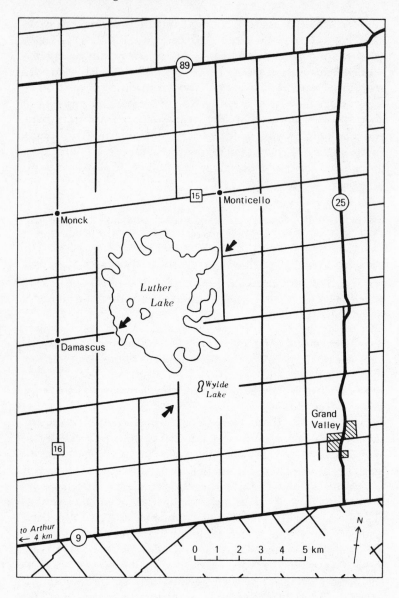

MAP 4 Luther Marsh

All the typical marsh species nest, as well as one or two pairs of Common Loons, Red-necked Grebes (rare), Wilson's Phalaropes, and three or four pairs of Ospreys.

In fall there are large areas of mud as the lake is drawn down, both around the edges and as semi-floating bogs scattered through the lake. These are very productive of shorebirds. The floating bogs are essentially bottomless and should not be walked upon.

The northern woods have typical woodland birds, including some more northern species, and Wylde Lake is noted for nesting Lincoln's Sparrows.

To reach the east side of the marsh from the east side, drive some 8½ km north from Highway 9 on Highway 25 through Grand Valley, to East Luther Concession 6–7 on the west. Turn here and drive west and then, as the road turns, north some 9 km in all to the well-marked entrance to the parking lot of the dam area on the left.

Coming from the west, drive 14.7 km east on Highway 9 from its intersection with Highway 6 at Arthur, to an unmarked road (it is some 2 km past a microwave tower) on the north. Go 8.2 km north, turn left (west) onto the unmarked gravel road which is Concession 6–7, and travel west and then north 6.9 km to the entrance as above. There is a Purple Martin colony here.

Good overviews may be had of the lake from here and, especially, from an observation tower located 1½ km south of the dam, on an internal road open to private vehicles, leading off from the parking lot.

From the dam an internal road, not open to vehicles, curves through the northern part of the area, roughly paralleling the shore, for 7 to 8 km. This road gives access to the large area of woodland on the north shore. Access to the other end of this road can be had via Concession 8–9 of West Luther Township. About 2½ km from the dam a look-out tower gives a good overview of the lake. About 5½ km from the dam, a trail, signposted 'Esker Trail,' leads in 1 km to another observation tower, which gives a good view over a willow swamp.

The dam is on Sideroad 20–21, and Monticello is located 2.2 km north of here. A road runs westwards from the village 7.5 km to Monck; west of Monticello 2.5 km this road passes through some good habitat. An open, wet, sedgy field on the northern side of the road has consistently yielded breeding Sedge Wrens for several years.

At Monck turn south on Wellington County Road 16 to Damascus, for access to the west side of the lake. This county road runs north from Highway 9, some 13 km west of the Highway 25 intersection and 5.8 km east of Arthur. From 9, drive 8.2 km to Damascus General Store. Turn east, go 2.7 km, crossing one unmarked crossroad, to the lake. This road, which disappears into the lake, is known locally as the Bootlegger's Road. It offers excellent views of the lake to the east and north.

Wylde Lake is also east of the Damascus road. Along Highway 9 the access road is 7.3 km from Highway 25 and 11.5 km from Arthur. It is the county line between Wellington and Dufferin counties – watch for the sign.

Go 5.3 km north until the road takes a sharp left-hand turn. From here, walk eastwards through an area of scattered tamarack and wet sphagnum bog; the lake itself is a little less than 1½ km in. The most interesting area is not the lake but the surroundings; Lincoln's Sparrows can usually be heard from the bend in the road itself. Note that on a dull day it is very easy to get lost in the Wylde Lake region, which is several square kilometres in extent. Take a compass.

Much the best way of seeing the lake and its birds is by canoe. Access is best from either the dam or the Bootlegger's Road (preferable in a west wind, because of shelter). A special permit is required.

A good route from the Bootlegger's Road is north, passing west of Big Island, then along the north bog to Esker Island, east to Windmill Island; if calm, south to Prairie Island, back west to Heron Island, and back along the east shore of Big Island to the Bootlegger's. An important caution is that the lake can become rough very quickly in the event of a wind springing up. There have been two fatalities in recent years; do not be the third.

Up until 31 July each year a permit is required to put any boat, including a canoe, on the lake. These are issued at the superintendent's house at the dam; contact the Grand River Conservation Authority, 400 Clyde Road, Cambridge ([519] 621-2761) for details. Outboard motors are not allowed.

Even with a permit, certain areas are prohibited of access during the breeding season. These include the vicinity of the heronry, several islands including Windmill and Prairie islands, and areas around active Osprey nests. These restrictions are purely for the good of the birds, and responsible naturalists will abide by them meticulously; failure to do so will in any case result in prosecution under the Conservation Authorities Act.

In autumn (mid-September) the entire area is used intensively for hunting, and birding is not recommended in this period.

(64) Beaverton – The sewage lagoons here are 1.4 km south on Osborne Street (County Road 23) from the intersection of County Road 15. Turn west on the Fifth Line of Thorah Township (it is marked 'Cedar Beach'), and the lagoons are ½ km along on the right.

(65) Beeton – The sewage lagoon is off the first street north entering town from the east (Patterson Street), which is 1.1 km from the railroad crossing at the west end of town. Turn north, drive 1.5 km to Lilly Street, and turn east; the lagoon gate is 0.6 km along on the left.

(66) Bowmanville – This town has several fine marshes to the south along Lake Ontario. Take Liberty Street exit (No. 432) from Highway 401, turning east on the Base Line and then south on Bert Street. Drive 0.3 km and turn sharply left just past the railroad tracks. This road leads to the east side of the river at Port Darlington (1.7 km), but a turn west on West Beach Road at 1 km makes it possible to cover extensive marsh from here to the beach (1.5 km).

Farther west a second marsh can be visited by returning to the Base Line and heading west, or leaving 401 at the Waverley Street exit (No. 431). Either way, turn south on Durham County Road 57 and drive 1.4 km south to the shore. A large marsh lies over a field to the east, and more marsh is along the cottage road that runs east at the shore. Where the southbound road reaches the shore view the lake and piers of the St Mary's Cement plant to the west for waterfowl and gulls.

(67) Bradford – The southern end of Lake Simcoe has been one of the few readily accessible places where birders could hope to find Yellow Rails. Typically the rails prefer 'grassy' marshes with shorter vegetation, and quite shallow water levels. Unfortunately this kind of marsh is readily drained for agriculture, and this has been the fate of most of the suitable ones around Lake Simcoe. Most productive in recent years has been a marsh north of Bradford at the east end of the 13th Line of West Gwillimbury Township. From the intersection of Highways 88 and 11 in Bradford (where 11 turns north) drive 8.5 km to the above sideroad and turn east. Drive 4.6 km, where a marsh opens out on the north. This has been suitable for rails, but at the time of writing, new drainage ditches are being constructed and its future suitability is in some doubt. By driving to the extreme end of the 13th Line you can gain access to the dyke system along the Holland River, and, by walking south here 1–2 km, other areas where the rails have occurred may be visited. Their presence in any event depends on water levels and sometimes all these areas can be dried out and unsuitable for them.

The marshes also yield the customary marshbirds including Sedge Wren, and in the past LeConte's Sparrows have nested in the Yellow Rail sections.

(68) **Cambridge** – From the intersection of Highway 24 and Regional Road 97 in Cambridge (Galt) drive on 97 west 4.6 km to Regional Road 71. Turn north and drive to the next intersection, or Regional Road 46. The area both along 71 and just east of the intersection, known as *Orr's Lake*, has small lakes with a good mix of woodland and swamp habitats right along the road. The lands themselves are signposted against trespassing and are also under heavy developmental pressure. From this intersection 4 km west on 46 is the *Roseville Swamp*, on both sides of the road and continuing north and south. It has Northern Waterthrush and Mourning and Canada Warblers in summer, as well as small choruses of Winter Wrens and White-throated Sparrows.

Northwest of Galt, and running along the Grand River to Blair, is Regional Road 42. This follows the Grand River. Between the river and the road is *Cruickston Park Farm*, a tract of natural land owned by the University of Guelph. The river rapids near the junction of the Speed attract concentrations of duck and gulls. Ruffed Grouse, Yellow-billed Cuckoo, Winter Wren, and Orchard Oriole have bred here.

There are several good areas between Cambridge and Paris, mainly accessible by Highway 24A (or Regional Road 75). *Spottis-*

wood is east on South Dumfries Concession 5 some 7 km north of Paris, or 10 km south of Cambridge. This is an area of deciduous woodland where southern species have occurred. Most of the property, however, is private, and permission should be sought if you wish to enter from the road.

Pinehurst Conservation Area is a further 2 km north, and again southern species occur, Blue-gray Gnatcatcher and Cerulean Warbler having been recorded in summer.

About 2 km farther on 24A the Brant County Line Road runs west (from the Despond Lake Trailer Park); the *Dickson Wilderness Area* is some 1½ km along it. Yellow-throated Vireos and Cerulean Warblers have occurred here, and the feeders attract interesting wintering species including Red-bellied Woodpeckers.

North again about 1 km, at the intersection of 24A and Regional Road 49, are *Bannister* and *Wrigley lakes*. There are extensive hiking trails among the rolling woodland around these lakes and an excellent mix of habitats including marshland. Turn west on 49 for access to these points.

The first sideroad east just north of this intersection passes through an excellent mixture of woodland and wetland habitats. Species present in summer usually include Red-shouldered Hawk, Red-bellied Woodpecker, Willow Flycatcher, Yellow-throated Vireo, and several warblers including Golden-winged, Blue-winged, Cerulean, Mourning, and Northern Waterthrush. Acadian Flycatcher has occurred here.

Some 2 km along this sideroad, at the first intersection, another sideroad running southeast passes through good marsh and bog habitats. About 3 km farther east again the road ends at the West River Road (Glen Morris Street, running south from the intersection of Highways 97 and 24A in Galt). This road follows the scenic Galt ridge both north and south, and has excellent birding along the entire route. If one drives south one eventually arrives at the Spottiswood area described above.

The *Alps Woods* are on Concession 10 of North Dumfries west of 24A and just east of Regional Road 47, which runs north from Regional Road 49 at Bannister Lake. These are fine mixed woodlands, part of the Regional Forest in this area, and again deciduous forest and associated species occur – Blue-gray Gnatcatcher,

Yellow-throated Vireo, and Cerulean Warbler have bred, but seem to have disappeared following drastic forest management.

Southeast of Cambridge (Galt) on Highway 8 the historic *Cheese Factory* Road runs south through rolling woodland, scrub, and ponded terrain. Willow Flycatcher, Eastern Bluebird, Pine Warbler, and (rarely) Yellow-breasted Chats have occurred. The road is the first concession west of the intersection of Regional Road 43 and Highway 8 (Elgin Street south).

(69) CAMPBELLVILLE – West of this village *Mountsberg Conservation Area* is significant because it often contains waterbirds – particularly shorebirds – at times of the year when other areas are unproductive. It is rewarding at other times too, however, with woodland birds along the trails and good numbers of waterfowl on the 200-hectare lake in early spring and later fall. Hooded Mergansers nest in boxes and often in Pileated Woodpecker holes, but are difficult to see.

In autumn the lake is drawn down, exposing mud flats at various areas. The location of these varies from year to year, but at present the best areas are at the eastern side of the lake, on either side of the railway tracks. The mud flats are very good for shorebirds, and thirty-one species have been recorded.

To reach the area from Campbellville, which is just south of the Campbellville exit off Highway 401 (No. 312), turn right (west) before the railroad crossing. Pass the Community Pond on the left; 1.6 km farther on is a cedar bog on the south side of the road, which is good for woodcock. Go a further 2.4 km to the Town Line and turn north. Continue along this road past the main entrance to Mountsberg (entry fee) some 500 metres, to the top of a small rise in the road. Here tracks lead off to both the left and right (there are gates at the entrance of each).

Walking along the left track takes you through several hundred metres of wet and dry woodland; the track terminates at the lake with a look-out tower. Good trails lead in both directions; access to these is also via the main entrance.

The right-hand track goes through a good variety of woodland. Trails are marked.

Continue on the gravel road as it curves west and then curves down a hill to enter a long causeway crossing an area of open water and marshland. There is a viewing tower here at the east end, and the entire causeway gives excellent views of the extensive area of wetlands to the south.

Coming on Highway 401 from the west you do not need to go as far as Campbellville as it is more direct to drive south from Exit 299, signposted to Hamilton. Drive some 3 km, through Morriston to the second sideroad east (Puslinch Line 35), and drive east about 4½ km, where the lake and look-out tower appear on the right.

After covering this area carefully, continue west and take the first sideroad south. Follow this road around to the next intersection on the east. Turn left and drive to the end of the road at the water, where there is a parking area and another viewing tower to the southeast, all giving further views of this very extensive man-made lake. Return to the intersection and turn south. The road leads back to the Campbellville road again. A left turn will lead there.

The Halton Region Conservation Authority, which owns and operates the site, conducts a vigorous outdoor education program at Mountsberg, involving numerous aspects of nature interpretation. A bird-banding program has also been carried out for several years; public demonstrations are given on a regular basis.

Farther up the Bronte Creek from Mountsberg is the *Badenoch Marsh* (also known as the Moffat Marsh). This is reached by turning north (right) on Concession 10, which is the first sideroad west of the causeway across the lake (ie, the opposite direction to the dam). Cross Highway 401 and turn right some 600 metres north of 401 at the ball park. The swamp is about ½ km east. It is an extensive area of cat-tails, willows, and woodlands. Breeding birds include yellowthroat, Marsh Hawk, and Swamp Sparrow.

Northeast of Campbellville lie the extensive woodlands of *Halton Regional Forest* and *Hilton Falls Conservation Area*. The area is divided into a number of tracts, of which the Turner Tract is best known. The forest's character is changing owing to both natural processes as it matures and to the Ministry of Natural Resources' management practices. The area is of prime interest for its exceptional wealth of breeding birds. At least 111 species have been reported as breeding, including 14 species of warblers.

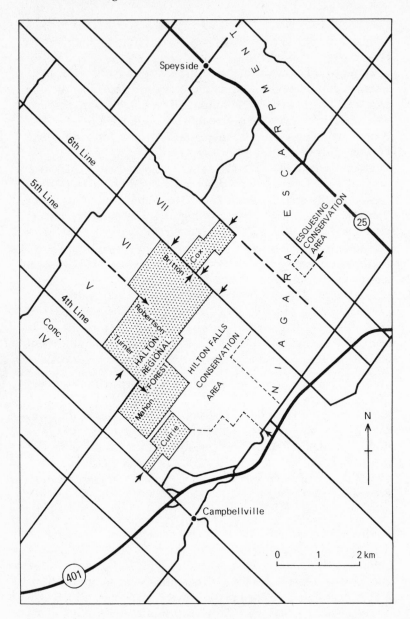

MAP 5 Halton Regional Forest

The terrain is heavily wooded over much of the area, with almost pure deciduous stands, many mixed stands, and six large plantations of conifers. Many beaver dams are present, and as a result there are extensive flooded areas containing dead trees and marsh vegetation. On the eastern side of the area the Niagara Escarpment runs due north from Highway 401 to Speyside. As a result of this diversity, most of the landbird species listed as occurring in summer in the region can be expected here. Other breeders include Goshawk, Blue-gray Gnatcatcher, Yellow-throated Vireo, Golden-winged, Blue-winged (and hybrids), Nashville, Cerulean, and Chestnut-sided Warblers, and Purple Finch. The area can also be good for winter finches in late autumn through early spring. There are several access points. What follows assumes a start at the Campbellville 401 interchange, but from the east an exit at Milton (No. 320) interchange is more direct. Distances below are point to point.

Going north from the Campbellville interchange on Regional Road 1, the first point is the entrance to the small Currie tract opposite the racetrack at about 1 km. Next, turn right on Sideroad 10 (1.1 km) and drive 1.3 km to the point the road turns north. There is entry here to the Turner and Mahon tracts, and 0.5 km farther north, another entry leading to the Robertson tract. Continue north (now on the 4th Line) to Sideroad 15 (about 3 km) and turn right again.

At 1.4 km the 5th Line runs south to dead-end in 1.4 km; walk south from here into the Robertson tract (parking is rather unsatisfactory). The 6th Line, another 1.4 km east, has many good access points. The first, 2.0 km south, is west of the road, leading into the Britton tract, then 0.3 km farther east to the Cox tract, another to the Britton tract west at 0.3 km, and then 0.5 km west again for pedestrian entry to the northeast end of Hilton Falls Conservation Area. Here you are 2.9 km north of Sideroad 5, for return to Campbellville or Milton.

Farther east on Sideroad 10, the next sideroad on the south (Milton Townline Road) runs 2.4 km south to an entry to the east side of the Cox tract. The road itself dead-ends farther on.

From the corner of the 6th Line and Sideroad 5 (which is also Regional Road 9, and is so called farther east and west) you can turn west and drive 1.6 km to the main entrance (fee) to the Hilton Falls Conservation Area. You can get a map of the trail system here and view the lake above the dam. This is 4½ km east of Campbellville, and Sideroad 5 leads back there.

East from the 6th Line at 1.9 km turn north on the Milton First Line and drive about 1.4 km to the mixed wood-lot of the Esquesing Conservation Area, or go straight ahead 1.3 km to the junction of Highway 25, where a right turn leads to the Milton interchange of Highway 401 (1.6 km).

(70) **Cannington** – This village, east of Highway 12 and north of 7, has rather inaccessible lagoons to the northeast. They are partly visible along the railroad track just east of the village.

(71) **Chesley** – The farmland along County Road 10 north of Chesley is very flat and open, and attractive to open country birds and hawks in autumn. In spring *Grimston Flats* along the Sauble River can attract waterfowl. For these drive north on County Road 10 (Main Street in Chesley) 10.7 km from the bridge over the river in town. This is Dobbinton Corners. Turn right on County Road 4, drive 2.4 km to a T-intersection and turn left (north). For the next 7 km or so the Sauble River criss-crosses this road (the Grey-Bruce County Line) and the fields are subject to flooding in spring.

The Chesley sewage lagoons are off Fourth Street West, which is 0.4 km south of the river bridge. If one turns west on this street, the lagoons are 0.7 km along it, associated with the town dump west of the street at the point it turns north.

(72) **Coldwater** – Northwest of here, near Fesserton along Highway 12 and along Highway 69 north to the area of Port Severn, there are extensive marshes along Matchedash Bay. These are relatively unexplored, but there is a huge blackbird roost here and there have been interesting waterbird reports from time to time. The network of sideroads from the two main highways gives ready access.

(73) **Collingwood** – The waterfront has several areas of interest. From the main intersection of Highways 24 north and 26, turn east and drive 0.3 km, and turn left after the highway crosses the first set of tracks. This road leads to the elevator, and provides views of the harbour on the west and a small bay to the east.

Look for gulls and duck, and shorebirds and open country species along the bay.

Returning to the highway, continue east 0.7 km to the point the highway turns right. Huron Street turns left here, and leads to Sunset Point Park on the beach. The road runs a short way both east and west. The park itself is manicured, but the adjacent cedars and trees south of the road can concentrate landbirds, and there are excellent views out over the water, which should be particularly interesting in autumn when there are storms from the north.

Going west from the main highway intersection, Birch Street at 0.5 km and Hickory Street at 1.0 km both lead to natural areas west of the harbour and further views over the water.

Some 12 km farther west, at *Craiglieth*, there is excellent lake viewing between the provincial park to the west and the intersection of Grey County Road 19 (Blue Mountain Park Road) on the east. By turning on to the County Road, then right at 0.3 km on to a sideroad signposted to the Alpine Ski Club, one can drive into a sheltered wooded area which is good for landbirds yearround. Farther west on Highway 26 the Arrowhead Road leads back towards the club. This intersection is 0.2 km east of the provincial park entrance, and by turning south here one can observe Clay-coloured Sparrows and other edge species in the old fields.

(74) **Dorking** – At this community, on Highway 86 some 40 km northwest of Kitchener-Waterloo, is the sideroad to the *Conestoga Reservoir and Conservation Area*. Turn northeast on County Road 11 and follow it around 5 km to the conservation area. The most accessible vistas of the waterbody are farther up this road. A half kilometre ahead is the dam itself, with gulls foraging at its base and excellent views of the large water area on the left. Another excellent vista is 1.5 km farther on again, where the widest part of the lake (which is roughly L-shaped) is visible beside the road. Other vistas are possible both from the county road and from sideroads around the lake to the north, south, and west.

This area is heavily used for recreation, but waterfowl gather in spring and autumn; in addition to Mallards, Black Ducks, and Common Merganser, loons, geese, and other ducks occur, and shorebirds are possible depending on the state and date of the drawdown. The area has been good for herons.

There are also old fields around the lake that can yield the interesting mix of species typical of such areas, and Short-eared Owls have bred here.

(75) **Dundalk** – The sewage lagoons are south on the first sideroad west of town. Turn west off Highway 10 on to County Road 9, drive 2.5 km to Proton Range SWT Sideroad 2, and turn south; the lagoons are 1.5 km on the left.

(76) **Dyer Bay** – This community at the northeast side of the Bruce Peninsula is accessible from Highway 6 via a sideroad which is hardtopped for most of its 10 km or so. Some 7.5 km from the highway is an area of wet fields that, depending on water levels, can yield ducks, rails, and shorebirds.

North of the village the shoreroad runs under the escarpment face for about 10 km to *Cabot Head* lighthouse and Wingfield Basin, an area of heavy woodlands, marsh, and open land that can be very good for migrants. Because of the configuration of the peninsula this represents its northeastern extremity, and hence acts as a trap for landbirds. The crystal-clear waters of Dyer Bay offshore have small flocks of Common Loons in summer, but I cannot recall ever having seen a duck here!

(77) **ELMVALE** – This village is close to several points of interest. For the sewage lagoons, proceed north 1.5 km on Highway 27 from its intersection with Highway 92 in town, and then turn east on Flos Concession 10. The lagoon gate is 0.7 km along on the north – but drive a little farther and view them readily from the road itself.

From the lagoons continue north on Highway 27 to the point at which it takes a long curve east. Turn west here on the Tiny-Flos Townline, and drive 200 metres to County Road 6, going north. One access point to the east side of *Tiny Marsh* is 1.5 km up this road, where a westbound sideroad dead-ends at the marsh. The main access route, however, is by continuing west along the Townline 3.6 km to the causeway, Interpretive Centre, and Observation Tower north of the road. This 567-hectare marsh is managed by the Ontario Ministry of Natural Resources and Ducks Unlimited primarily for waterfowl production, but it is an excellent place for shorebirds and other species. Even a Snow Bunting spent one summer along the north-south causeway.

Other access points to the area are from County Road 29, 2.5 km farther west. North on this road at 1.5 km is a sideroad to the east which dead-ends in the marsh, and 1.5 km farther again the eastbound sideroad will take you to the north end of the causeway. And from this corner you are only about 1 km from the road to Spratt Point.

Spratt Point is a small point of land on the east shoreline of Nottawasaga Bay which has proved to be a good vantage point for watching migrant loons, ducks, and gulls. To reach it continue north on County Road 29 from Tiny Marsh to Concession Road 4 (it is 4.1 km from the Tiny-Flos Townline that leads to the Tiny Marsh Interpretive Centre). Turn west, and bear left on the hardtop road 1.4 km from the turn. At Edmore Beach, 1.1 km farther, turn right on Balmoral Avenue. This gravelled road parallels the shore and has water access at several points, particularly 0.5 km along, which is Spratt Point. Immediately past here it rejoins the main road and one can return to County Road 29.

(78) Exeter – The sewage lagoons are west of town south of Highway 83. From the intersection with Highway 4, drive 2 km west to Stephen Concession 2–3. The lagoons are on the left 0.8 km south on this road. They have been one of the more productive lagoons in this part of the region.

Just the other side of Highway 4 on Highway 83 here is the *Morrison Dam Conservation Area*. Drive 2 km east to Usborne Concession 2–3, and the dam is ½ km south. It is a small waterbody with woods and reforestation – a pleasant spot with fair landbirding.

(79) Fergus – *Belwood Lake* is another large reservoir lake. It is east on County Road 18 (Belsyde Ave) off Highway 6 at the south end of town. Belwood Conservation Area 5 km on the left provides good views of the dam and west end of the area, and farther east a section of the lake is visible at 1.6 km. Continue east on 18 to County Road 26 (4½ km) and drive north some 3 km to the bridge, which provides views of the east end of the reservoir. There is further viewing possible from the cottage roads south of County Road 19, which runs west back to Fergus. The lake can be good for waterfowl in early spring and late autumn, Red-necked Grebes and herons in migration, and shore-birds in autumn.

(80) **Ferndale** – The country around Ferndale is a flat plain good for Brewer's Blackbirds, possible Western Meadowlark, Upland Sandpipers, and other field species in summer. Loggerhead Shrikes, Eastern Bluebirds, and Grasshopper Sparrows should be looked for in the old fields. The blackbirds tend to be along the sideroads south of the Lion's Head road. The sideroads east of the highway in particular should be covered, and the first north-south gravel road.

(81) **Goderich** – For access to the Maitland River mouth and Goderich harbour drive north through town on Highway 21 to North Harbour Road and turn west. This road is just past the Old Jail and immediately before the railway bridge on the high-way as it curves right down the hill. Drive 1.7 km to the harbour, which is good for gulls and ducks. There is also access to the parkland along the river from this road.

The road to *Falls Reserve Conservation Area* is a little farther north along 21: go to the bottom of the hill and turn right on County Road 31 just the other side of the Maitland River bridge. The area is 8 km east, at Benmiller (0.2 km west of the junction with County Road 1 northbound). This area has good woodland along the river and mixed habitats associated with the flood-plain. There is a falls on the river, which curves round this area.

County Road 1 runs north from Benmiller some 10 km to Nile, where it takes a jog. If you turn right here on West Wawanosh Concession 1 and drive east, at about 2½ km you begin to pass the Conservation Authority lands associated with *Saratoga Swamp*, on the north of the sideroad. These continue for the next 3 km or so, and there are further areas along Concession 2–3, the next side-road to the north. The whole is heavily forested, including stands of white pine, and the mix of swamp, coniferous, and hardwood bush and rough pasture provides an excellent variety of bird habitats.

(82) Guelph – South of Guelph there are a number of locations of interest. For areas southwest, starting from the junction of Highway 6 and Kortright Road just southwest of the city (just past the point the expressway curves to run southeast) turn west on Kortright Road. *Kortright Waterfowl Park* is 2 km along this road, and the heavily wooded banks of the Speed River west can have good landbirding and the Speed itself loitering duck, mostly semi-wild Mallards, although other species can occur. The park itself has a comprehensive collection of captive waterfowl (entry fee). Return east on Kortright Road 1 km to Downey Road, running south. This is Wellington County Road 35. Drive 4.3 km to the third sideroad west and turn on this gravel road; 0.8 km along it passes through Cranberry Bog, a heavily wooded area with good birding, and some 1.5 km farther it passes through another heavily wooded section, the *Little Tract* of Wellington County Forest on the south, and a privately owned bog forest on the north (access by permission). The next sideroad north-south (4.2 km from your turn) is hardtopped County Road 32, on which you will head south; however, first turn right and cover the small lake ½ km north (Neibauer's Marsh), which can yield duck and other waterbirds. Turn and drive south some 4 km, crossing Highway 401. Just over the bridge the *Puslinch Resource Management Area* is on the left, and continues along the north side of the first sideroad east – this will be just ahead, where the road you are on curves right – for 2 km. There are reforestation, hardwoods, and flooded gravel pits, and the whole area is managed mainly with an eye to small game production. Grasshopper Sparrows have bred here and there is a good mix of edge and woodland bird life. The area is also accessible from the service area on the eastbound lanes on Highway 401 between interchanges 282 and 295.

When County Road 32 turns west it runs along the north shore of *Puslinch Lake*. Most of the shoreline is private property but view the lake itself for migrant waterfowl in early spring and late autumn from the end of a small sideroad south 1.5 km from the county road turn. West of here again Pinebush Road runs down the west side of the lake, and at the south end is property owned by the Grand River Conservation Authority giving access to the wooded southwest bay, with further viewing opportunities. Many rarer species of waterbirds have occurred.

Southeast of the city several areas are accessible from County Road 46 (formerly Highway 6 and called the Brock Road). This is accessible at present from Highway 401 by taking Exit 299 northbound. However, at the time of writing there are plans for closing this exit: if this occurs 401 access will be via Highway 6 north (Exit 295). One would then go about 1 km to the light at Wellington County Road 34, turn right, and drive to the Brock Road intersection at Aberfoyle, which is about 4 km north of the present 401 Exit 299.

From Exit 299 drive north 12.8 km to the Stone Road (the second set of lights, just past the College Motor Inn). Turn right (east), go 4 km, crossing Victoria Road after 2 km, to the next crossroad (Watson Road). Turn right and go some 600 metres. A stile and a marked trail lead away to the left (east) at this point, which is about 150 metres north of the Eramosa River.

This is the *Radial Line Trail*. It goes through wet cedar woodland, along the river, open moraine country, pine plantation, mixed deciduous woodland, and open agricultural land. It is marked throughout, and returns to Watson Road about 600 metres south of the original starting point. The complete loop takes 1 to 1½ hours of vigorous walking; bird-watching, it takes considerably longer!

The *Starkey Property* is south of the above. From the stile given as starting point, go south about 1½ km to the village of Arkell, turn left (east) onto Wellington Road 37 (known locally as the Arkell Road), go about 1.2 km to just past the old Starkey Farm (an old stone house with two rows of conifers in front), where a marked trail leads south up the hill. It joins a loop on open upland moraine country and returns to the starting point. The open area has the usual species of such habitat, but also includes Grasshopper Sparrows (some years), Hooded Merganser (breeds some years on small ponds behind the hills), and Henslow's Sparrows (irregular). The southern end of the trail passes through open deciduous woodland.

Guelph Lake is along the north side of Highway 24 some 5½ km east of the Highway 6 Guelph by-pass and immediately east of the intersection of County Road 40. The large lake is visible for some 2 km along 24 east of here. It is good for waterfowl in early spring, and (depending on the state of drawdown) there may be mud flats in autumn, which can be very productive of shore-birds.

A little farther on the road crosses the lake on a causeway which gives good views on either side. About 0.8 km east of the eastern end, turn right (south) in the village of Eramosa onto a dirt road; after 1 km this road crosses a causeway which gives another good overview of the lake, at this point shallower and more overgrown.

(83) Harriston – For the sewage lagoon, drive west on Highway 87 from its intersection with Highway 9 in town. Turn right on John Street, drive two blocks to William, turn left there and cross the tracks; the lagoon road is on the right.

(84) Hensall – The lagoons here are west off Highway 4 south of town. From the junction of Highways 4 and 84 drive south 2 km to Hay Sideroad 15–16, and turn right. The lagoons are 0.7 km along on the right, just over the railway, and easily visible from both the tracks and the road.

About 10 km north of town, in Brucefield, County Road 3 runs west and by following it for two sideroads (4.4 km) and turning north on a gravel road one can drive through good river valley habitats along the Bannockburn River to the *Bannockburn Wildlife Area* at 1.8 km, where one can park and cover the area on foot. It is good for landbirds.

(85) Holland Landing – To reach Holland Landing lagoons, drive north through the village on Regional Road 51, and from its intersection in town with Thompson Road (just south of the post office) continue 1.8 km to Cedar Street on the east. The lagoon gates are 0.6 km along, at the end of this street. To con-fuse you, Regional Road 51 in Holland Landing is called Yonge Street, not to be confused with Highway 11, which by-passes the village to the west; or with old Highway 11, the present access road from the present highway. (Highway 11 is called Yonge Street farther south.)

(86) Kincardine – There are two areas of interest in town and others nearby. The south exit from Highway 21 to Kincardine is Kincardine Street, which runs west 1.5 km to Queen Street, the town's main street.

For the lagoons, go to Queen and turn left (south). Queen ends in ½ km at a cemetery gate. Turn left here on Bruce Avenue and drive 0.8 km to the dump entrance on the right. The lagoons are behind and west of the dump.

Returning to Queen Street, drive north 2 km to Lambton Street, and turn left at the light. The road leads down (½ km) to *MacPherson Park* on the shore, which provides views of the river mouth to the south and of the lake. Scan for ducks and gulls: duck often hang around the river mouth when adjacent areas are frozen.

Some 15 km east of Kincardine in the Township of Greenock is a very large swamp along the Teeswater River. Highway 9 crosses the southern ends of this west of the Highway 4 intersection, but to visit a much richer area go to the junction of these two highways and turn north on Regional Road 20. Drive to the third sideroad (6.2 km) marked to Chepstow, and turn west. The most extensive areas of swamp are about 2 km ahead. There are trails there giving foot access north and south.

South of Kincardine 13 km along Highway 21 is the *Point Clark* road (Huron Concession 2). This leads west some 4 km to the shore and then curves left. At 5 km from Highway 21 is Lighthouse Road, which leads (0.8 km) to the (well-signposted) historic Clark Point lighthouse on the shore. This point is the westernmost promontory along the Lake Huron shore between Cape Hurd and Kettle Point, and hence is an excellent place for viewing southbound waterbird migration in autumn.

(87) Lindsay – The sewage lagoon complex is off Highway 36 north. From the intersection of Highways 36 and 36B (Queen Street) drive north 2.8 km to the point the highway curves right. Turn left at the curve on Ops Concession 6 and immediately (0.2

km) left again on a road that runs down past the landfill site to the lagoons and river.

(88) **Listowel** – The sewage lagoons are 2.1 km south on Highway 23 from its intersection with Highway 86 northwest of town. Drive to Elma Concession 1–2 and turn right; the lagoons are 0.6 km along on the left.

(89) **Mar** – This tiny community is at the corner of Highway 6 and the Sky Lake road and is a convenient departure point for many of the most interesting areas on the Bruce Peninsula.

The *Rankin Resources Management Unit* is a huge and diverse area including Sky and Isaac lakes. Albemarle Sideroad 25, 2 km south of Mar, runs east to Isaac Lake through the waterfowl management unit. Look for marshbirds as the road crosses the marsh at the bottom of the hill and waterfowl and shorebirds both inside and outside the feeding pens. Wilson's Phalaropes occur regularly here. The lake itself (2.8 km) tends to be less productive but has breeding Pied-billed Grebes and Black Terns.

The Sky Lake road runs west from Mar along the south side of the lake, which is too disturbed to yield much except at dawn, when the marshes to the west can yield Pied-billed Grebes, duck, Black Terns, and Marsh Wrens. The bridge at the far west end is the point of entry (southbound) to the Rankin River canoe route, which leads through Isaac and Boat lakes to terminate at Sauble Falls 18 km to the south. The route passes through extensive marshland and the wooded swamps south of Boat Lake.

Two kilometres north of the point at which the Sky Lake road joins the Red Bay road is Red Bay Lodge, set amid fine hardwoods. The wood-lot north of the sideroad to the beach has had breeding Northern Parula Warblers, and 1.1 km farther north is the sideroad west to Petrel Point, where the Federation of Ontario Naturalists has a reserve on the south of the road. Olive-sided Flycatchers have nested here and snipe are common. Listen for Barred Owl at night.

The north-south sideroads both west and east of Highway 6 (readily accessible either way from Mar) are the key roads for covering the marginal farmland and heavy woodlands of the Bruce. Good habitat abounds. Going south on the west side leads to Oliphant while going north on the east leads to Dyer Bay (qv).

(90) Markdale – The sewage lagoons are relatively inaccessible at the back of a farm lane on the west side of Highway 10, 0.8 km north of the main intersection in town with Main Street.

The latter is County Road 12, and 9 km west from here to Glenelg Sideroad 20N one can drive north one sideroad (2.1 km) to Concession 12–13N. Here – particularly east along the concession – is a fine area of cedar–tamarack swamp and wet woodland south of Bell's Lake, itself a conservation area.

(91) Midland – Just south of here is *Wye Marsh*, yet another extensive wetland in the north of Simcoe County. Its main entrance is opposite the Martyr's Shrine on Highway 12, 5.5 km east of the intersection with Highway 27. There are also access points along 27 to the west side of the marsh. The roads and distances going south from the above intersection are Preston Road at 2.1 km, the village of Wyebridge at approximately 2.9 km, and along Sub-way Road at 3.9 km, all running eastbound. Wye Marsh has excellent interpretive facilities (including an underwater observation chamber) and nature trails. In addition to the marsh itself there is a variety of habitats including hardwoods and old farmland in the 1012-hectare preserve, where no hunting is allowed.

(92) Milverton – For the sewage lagoon take Mill Street west in the centre of the village off Highway 19, drive 0.7 km, crossing the tracks; the lagoon drive itself crosses the tracks to the left.

(93) Mitchell – The extensive sewage lagoons at Mitchell are accessible from either Highway 23 or 8. From their intersection north of town take 23 south 1 km to Frank Street. Turn left and drive 0.7 km to the turn on Wellington Street, where the lagoons are clearly visible on the right and the entrance is directly ahead. Wellington Street leads east back to Highway 4 southbound.

(94) Mount Albert – York County Road 13 passes south of Mount Albert. To reach the lagoons turn north on to Centre Street (the main street) and drive 2 km to Doane Road on the right. The lane to the lagoons is 0.7 km along this road on the north.

(95) Neustadt – For Neustadt lagoon turn left as County Road 10 southbound jogs right. The lagoon is over a field on the left beside the railroad tracks at 0.5 km, with the driveway 0.3 km farther on.

(96) New Hamburg – To reach these lagoons, drive west on Highway 7/8 to the Nith River bridge south of town. Turn south immediately over the bridge on Wilmot Township Road 12 and drive 1.4 km; the gate is on the left.

Regional Roads 3 and 5 south of Highway 7/8 provide access to the extensive areas of green space along the Nith River. The best public access is the Montgomery Sanctuary woodlands, via Regional Road 12 across the Nith as one turns east towards New Dundee.

(97) Newcastle – Bond Head, south of Newcastle, has a small harbour and limited marshes along the creek. Take Exit 440 from Highway 401 and take the road south to the lake (about 3 km). The main road leads to the east side; the west is accessible by turning west on a sideroad immediately past the railroad bridge.

The *Ganaraska Forest* is northeast of Newcastle and between Highways 115 and 28. It is a diverse area of over 4200 hectares with mixed hardwoods, red pine reforestation of varied ages, and some open and edge areas. There are many access points, and the Conservation Authority has an excellent map of the area (write the Ganaraska Region Conservation Authority, Box 328, 56 Queen Street, Port Hope, Ontario, L1A 3W4, or the Ganaraska Forest Centre, RR 1, Campbellcroft, Ontario, L0A 1B0), which shows the location of the access points and the very extensive trail network. There are feeders at the centre itself, and the sideroad to the east has shrub plantings and bluebird boxes. The forest has many recreational uses including snowmobiling, horseback riding, and hunting.

No specific rarities have been reported but all the customary woodland species can be expected, with old field species in the open areas and Clay-coloured Sparrows in younger pines. In winter the evergreens attract finches and the berry-bearing trees waxwings.

The main access points from the west are along the sideroad eastbound at the junction of Highways 35 and 115, and the next eastbound sideroad northeast along 115 (some 2.7 km). This has one access point on the south at 1.7 km, and at 7 km is a T-intersection where a right turn leads some 3 km south to the forest centre itself. From the south there are access points off County Road 9 north from Kendall and again along the County Line Road, which is the northbound access to the centre itself.

(98) Oliphant – The waterfront here has been consistently productive of waterbirds. Cover the roads paralleling the shore both north and south of County Road 13 (the main road from Wiarton). The northbound road tends to be best: 2.7 km along this the main road turns east to Red Bay and the shoreroad continues a further 1 km before it dead-ends. The waters off this section often have loitering waterfowl, and Common Snipe are common in the marshes. The beach shelves very slowly at Oliphant, and low Great Lakes water levels expose huge areas of beach. In such periods Piping Plover have bred and large numbers of shorebirds – particularly Red Knot – can occur, with Snow Geese in late autumn. The common warblers of the Bruce can be found along the shore roads behind the cottages.

Returning to the Red Bay road, turn east and continue east on the sideroad past the point where the Red Bay road turns north again. This sideroad crosses the marsh at the north side of *Spry Lake*. Both Marsh and Sedge Wrens occur in summer, with Sora and Virginia Rails, and Common Loons can be seen on the lake itself. This road rejoins County Road 13 1.9 km farther on. There is good birding all along this stretch.

Turn left on the county road (which leads back to Wiarton) and pass the *Rankin River* crossing on the north 1.2 km farther on. Waterfowl, particularly Wood Ducks, occur here.

South from Oliphant on County Road 21, *Sauble Beach* is usually too disturbed for many waterbirds to linger, although the gulls could be checked over. A fine wood-lot behind the beach strip has nesting Pine Warblers. The area behind Sauble Lodge is best.

(99) Omemee – The sewage lagoons are quite small but easy to cover. Turn north on Regional Road 7 (poorly marked but it is opposite the post office in the centre of town and is signposted to

Bobcaygeon), drive 1.5 km and turn left (west). Drive 0.4 km, and the lagoons are on the right.

(100) Oshawa – The well-known Second Marsh here unfortunately is not accessible to birders, and its future continues in grave doubt. *Darlington Provincial Park* (entry fee), accessible from Highway 401 Exit 425, can be of interest outside the hunting season. The beach can have shorebirds and gulls, the marshy edges Sharp-tailed Sparrows in migration, and the ravines other passerine migrants.

(101) Palgrave – The No. 25 Sideroad at the southern edge of the village on Highway 50 runs west to *Palgrave Conservation Area*. Go 1.6 km to the next intersection and turn north. This road ends (2.4 km) in the area, but there is excellent birding along it: in the dry rolling fields to the east Grasshopper Sparrows breed, and in the woods are a good variety of species typical of wet woodlands. The area itself has had Clay-coloured Sparrows regularly in the young pines, but these trees may be growing too tall for this species. Bluebirds and Henslow's Sparrows have also bred, and there are sheltered ponds and much mixed woodland.

(102) Penetanguishene – North of here via Simcoe County Road 35 is *Awenda Provincial Park* (entry fee), which occupies an extensive and heavily wooded section at the north end of the Huronia peninsula. The cover is mainly a fine stand of the typical mixed hardwoods of this region, with all the associated woodland birds. Trails and interpretive facilities are available.

(103) PICKERING – The area east and west of here along the Lake Ontario shoreline provides some of the more consistently productive birding in this part of the region. As an eastward extension from Toronto, urban development is occurring rapidly, but the wood-lots, marshes, and abandoned farmland provide an outstanding mix of habitats, and the lakeshore is a major flyline for migrants. Heavy hawk flights can develop, and waterfowl and shorebird movement can be watched offshore. If water levels are low, extensive areas of mud flat attract shorebirds. The best places are between Port Union on the west and Whitby on the east (Highway 401 interchanges 390 and 412), and can be covered from either direction, although this account goes from west to east.

Coming from the west on Highway 401, exit at Highway 2, Port Union (Exit 390), and turn east on Highway 2. Drive 3 km to White's Road, turn south and drive to *Petticoat Creek Conservation Area*. Park just outside, and walk straight ahead down the track (not the road) into a wooded valley which ends at the lake. Keep to the east side and work up and around, returning to the park entrance (excellent for migrant landbirds).

Return on White's Road to Oklahoma Road. Turn right, proceed 0.8 km to West Shore Boulevard, and turn right again. The foot of this road gives good lake viewing. From this point *Frenchman's Bay* lies to the east; it is good from autumn to spring for waterbirds if it is not frozen over. To cover it, return 0.6 km to Sunrise Avenue and turn east. The end of this road gives views of the south end. Turn north on Breezy Drive and follow this to a small park on the right. From here there are excellent views of the centre and north of the bay. Then continue keeping left to return to West Shore Boulevard and turn right. Follow this road around, covering the marshes at the north end of the bay on foot (good for shorebirds), to the lights at Liverpool Road. The foot of this road gives views of the lake west of the nuclear power plant, and of the small wetland at the east end of Frenchman's Bay.

In winter and early spring large gull flocks, including white gulls, loiter on the ice of Frenchman's Bay. They are visible from here or from the ends of the short westbound streets to the north.

Return now to the lights at West Shore Boulevard and turn right to continue east on Bayly Street. This is the old Baseline Road, which runs due east to Whitby, where it becomes Victoria Street West. The areas of interest are all south of this road. Proceed 0.8 km to Sandy Beach Road, turn south, cross a stream, and over the bridge turn right into the parking lot of *Sandy Beach Waterfront Park*. Cover the woods north of the parking lot, and follow the edge of the water around to the lake.

South of the park the road turns east opposite the nuclear power plant. Continue east, circuiting the boundary of the Pollution Control Plant by turning north on McKay Road and following this road around as it bears east and then south, continuing to the lake as Jodrel Road. This area, together with the river and marshes to the east, is known as the Corner Marsh, or more accurately *Squires Beach*. Turn east (Conmara Avenue) and then north (Frisco Road). In migration periods the trees of this area can produce warblers, the wires swallows and flycatchers, and the gardens and rough land sparrows. Stop before turning onto Frisco Road and scan the lake carefully for loons, grebes, and duck. This area, together with the waters off Cranberry Marsh, can have flocks of Red-necked Grebes in spring and fall (September). One can also cross the field to the east to reach the mouth of *Duffin's Creek*, looking along the shores for shorebirds, checking the riverside trees for landbirds, the marsh for duck and other waterbirds, and in fall the sky for hawks. Continue north on Frisco, stopping just before it turns west again on Montgomery Park Road. This is the 'Corner Marsh' proper, and to the east is Duffin's Creek, with extensive marshes and possible mud flats in the fall; to the north is a good wood-lot and further marshes, and all the large overgrown hedgerows are productive of migrants.

From Squire's Beach return to the first north-south road (Station Road) and proceed north. At present this road passes through a swamp with tamarack and cedar. It is attractive to migrant birds, and the roadside border of winterberry holly is attractive in autumn and winter both in itself and to wintering thrushes, waxwings, and Pine Grosbeaks. However, it is fast vanishing. On reaching Bayly Street again continue east, and on into Ajax, crossing a stream at the bottom of a hill. From here to the main Ajax intersection at Harwood Avenue lie *Ajax Flats*, a patchwork of old fields, industrial development, and new housing on the south. One traditional route into this area has been the Rotary Park (Valley) Road 0.3 km up the hill from the bridge. To the west of this road are the woods and wetlands bordering Duffin's Creek. The surrounding old fields have been good for hawks and owls, especially in winter. At times the south part of this road becomes impassable.

Then cross Harwood and proceed 0.8 km to Pickering Beach Road. Turn south and check the lake at the base of this road, then continue east on Lakeview Boulevard to its end. Before turning north on *Shoalpoint Road* check the lake and shoreline to the east again, then drive north, periodically looking over the marsh on the right and watching the multiflora rose hedge and neighbouring gardens for migrants. This road crosses a small stream as it leaves the housing development, passes through brushy hedgerows, an alder thicket, dense cedars, and an old orchard, and finally rejoins Bayly Street. It can be very productive, and the cedar woods have yielded up to six species of owls in winter.

Farther east 1.6 km a north-south road marks the Whitby boundary and Bayly Street becomes Victoria Street West. Past this ½ km is a poorly marked road at present signposted 'Unaleyi,' running south to Cranberry Marsh. The marsh lies to the east and is visible from the road. There are access points half-way along its length where a grove of trees joins the road, and again just north of the Finnish camp at the end of the road. The lake should be checked for loons (Red-throated are rare here). Cranberry has a rich bird life, with breeding Gadwalls, coots, and (periodically) Little Gulls.

Return to the main road and continue east 0.6 km to Lynde Shores Conservation Area on the south side of the road. Here are a small marsh, an old wood-lot, and heavy thickets worth investigating for landbirds. The woods have trails through them and bird-feeders. There are public toilets and a picnic area here too (the only toilets along this route apart from those at gas stations!). A short distance east the Lynde Creek ('Baseline') Marsh borders both sides of the road. Although disturbed, it usually has some waterbirds present, and Least Bitterns occur here.

Proceed a further 1.6 km; here the grounds and access road to Whitby Hospital run down the west side of Whitby Harbour. Drive to the bottom, watching trees, lawns, and the bayside for birds, and at the end check the lake and shoreline. A dirt road branches off east just before the main road curves right. The former goes to Whitby Yacht Club, passing through cottonwoods and scrub on the way and allowing a closer view of the shoreline to the east. The main road curves around the shore, and just as it turns up the west side of the hospital grounds a short sideroad goes off to the left (west) leading past a small water treatment plant to a rough parking lot near the lake. Park, and walk west along the gravel bar across the mouth of Lynde Creek. Check the marshes, the end of the bar, and the willows. Then retrace your tracks to Victoria Street West.

Brock Road, 0.8 km farther east, gives access to the east side of Whitby Harbour. Turn south on Brock Road at the light and drive 0.6 km to a bridge crossing a stream. The harbour is undergoing constant change (mostly for the worse) but this spot has marsh and mud flats on both sides of the road, and the scrubby trees to the southeast have roosting Black-crowned Night Herons. From here continue south, following the shore to a gravel road running between fuel tanks and the harbour. Check the harbour and the far shore at this point, and proceed along the harbour mouth. Scan the piers, the shoreline to the east, and the lake. Then rejoin the main road, which is now called Water Street and is heading east. Turn north when the road ends in Dunlop Drive and continue until this road ends in Victoria Street East. Turn east here and follow the road around to the Thickson Road and Highway 401 Interchange 412.

At the south end of Thickson Road the lake can be very productive. To the east at this point is the privately owned *Thickson Point*, where the houses bordering the road back onto a wood-lot with old white pines. The road edges and the adjacent gardens should be carefully checked for migrants. A private road to the Corbett Creek water treatment plant goes east from Thickson Road 0.3 km from its end, running down the north side of the woods to *Corbett Creek* and the marsh. Birders are tolerated on this road, and both the marsh and the adjacent woods can be most productive, especially during migration. From here return to Highway 401.

Greenwood and Claremont Conservation Areas are both in the Duffin Creek watershed and are accessible from the Westney Road. This is Regional Road 31, and is 1.6 km east on Highway 2 from the main intersection in Pickering village with Regional Road 24, called Church Street (Highway 401 Exit 400). To reach *Greenwood Conservation Area* go 5 km north and turn left on Greenwood Road. For *Claremont Conservation Area* go a further 5.3 km north crossing Highway 7; the entrance is just around the corner as Regional Road 31 leaves Westney Road and turns onto Concession 7.

Both areas have nature trails through mixed woodlands along the creek and coniferous stands that attract winter birds. Claremont also has extensive multiflora rose hedges along Sideline 12, which is its western boundary. These hedges are often very productive in winter if they have fruited well. This is one of the few places locally where Bohemian Waxwings have appeared with some regularity. To reach it go west from the park entrance about 0.8 km and turn right (north). This road ends at Concession 8. If you then return to Regional Road 31 you can follow it west to Regional Road 1, which will take you back to any of the major highways to the south.

(104) Port Bolster – Although it is so much smaller than the Great Lakes, Lake Simcoe is still a huge body of water and attracts many waterfowl in migration. The most fruitful observation points seem to be primarily in the lake's southeast sector. Along the south shore of the lake proper the shoreline is almost wholly devoted to cottage development, and is paralleled by a road most of the way.

Access is not, however, as easy as this sounds, because the narrow road is well travelled and legal parking areas are scarce or absent. *Sibbald Point Provincial Park* provides one good access area when it is open, as does a small public park on the shore road just west of here. Farther east two fruitful spots are 2.2 km down the *Duclos Point* road, to the left as the main point road turns right, and at the north end of *Port Bolster*, where a small shoreline park is just west off County Road 23, 2.2 km from the intersection with Highway 48.

(105) Port Elgin – The waterfront here can be good for waterbirds, but south of town *MacGregor Point Provincial Park* is far more rewarding. Offshore here large concentrations of loons, Horned Grebes, and other waterbirds occur in autumn migration. The park itself has the usual mixed woodland species (there are woodcock throughout the campgrounds), and small lakes and wetlands, sections of sandy shoreline, and patches of open country provide other habitats. The north-south sideroad which forms the east boundary (the Lake Range Road) also passes through an excellent mix of habitats to the south.

(106) **Port Perry** – To reach the (Nonquon River) sewage lagoons go 4.5 km north on Highway 12 from the junction of 7A in Manchester to the third road to the east. This is Scugog Line 8 (not Durham Road 8, which is the second road), and is an excellent birding road all the way to the lagoons, 3.1 km along on the right. The five lagoons have been most productive, and the adjacent woodland to the north and surrounding fields can be excellent for viewing migrant landbirds.

St Marys – See page 77, Chapter 3.

(107) **Sebright** – Around this small community northeast of Lake Simcoe, and east to Coboconk, lies a flat limestone plain, known as the Carden plain, which has a mix of poor farmland and woodland. Here many of the species typical of marginal farmland occur. Cliff Swallows, Eastern Bluebirds, Loggerhead Shrikes, and Golden-winged Warblers are among the more interesting species that can be found on a tour of the backroads in this area.

(108) **Seaforth** – For the sewage lagoons drive north on Highway 18 from the main intersection in town with County Road 12. Go 2.5 km to Tuckersmith Sideroad 15. Turn left and drive 0.6 km past a cairn on the right and turn right on a gravel road crossing the railroad tracks. The lagoons are just beyond on the left, and visible both from the tracks and (in part) the road.

(109) **Shallow Lake** – *McNab Lake Conservation Area* is some 3 km along the sideroad running northeast from the centre of this village. Its entrance is a poorly marked gravel road on the left, which leads down to the lake past some tall hardwoods where Yellow-throated Vireos and Cerulean Warblers occur (and likely nest). The road from the village crosses a flooded area of old woodland, good for herons.

(110) **Shelburne** – The sewage lagoons are 0.7 km south of the main intersection of Highways 10 and 89. Drive to Greenwood and turn east; the lagoons are on the left at the end of the road. (Going north, Greenwood is the first street on the right after crossing the creek.)

(111) Singhampton – *Devil's Glen Provincial Park*, on Highway 24 east of here, and the *Osprey Wildlife Area*, 11.3 km south of the park and about 2 km west on Osprey Concession IDR, together give an excellent cross-section of the landbirds of this area.

(112) Southampton – The waterfront here can be good for shore-birds and other waterbirds in migration. Turn west off Highway 21 on the main street and drive down to the shoreline.

(113) Stayner – For Stayner sewage lagoon drive east on Highway 26 from the junction of Highway 91 and at 1.3 km turn north on Mowat Street. The lagoon is down a farm lane 1.1 km along on the left.

(114) Sutton – Sutton sewage lagoons are easier to find coming from the east than from Sutton itself. From Highway 48 turn north on County Road 18, leading to Sibbald Point Park. Drive 1.6 km to the first cross-street, Black River Road (Regional Road 80), turn west and drive 2.1 km; the lagoon road is on the south.

Refer to Port Bolster above for details on viewing points along the south shore of Lake Simcoe.

(115) Thornbury – The sewage lagoon is 1 km east of the main intersection of Bruce Street and Highway 26. The short lane to the lagoon goes south off the highway opposite Grey Street.

(116) Tobermory – The small headlands around Tobermory concentrate landbird migrants. There are no specific locations: you should drive to the ends of various roads east and west of the end of Highway 6. There are also several interesting areas nearby. The sewage lagoon may be expanded in the future. It is down a long drive on the west of the highway 0.6 km south of the Cape Hurd Road, but is not worth visiting at present. Cape Hurd itself has some potential as a spot for viewing waterfowl migration, but there is no sure access to the shoreline.

Cyprus Lake Provincial Park (entrance fee) is well east of the highway 11.2 km southeast of town. It is set amid heavy coniferous woodlands, and the birdlife has a more northern character. A little farther north on Highway 6 is the *Dorcas Bay* road, which runs southwest to the bay. The Federation of Ontario Naturalists has a reserve that occupies most of the land to the north of the road (its main interest is the fascinating flora), although there is a little township park at the northeast end of the bay. Again, the bird life is quite northern, and Cape May Warblers have been recorded in summer. Pine Warblers can be found in the pines of the township park and Olive-sided Flycatchers occur over the bogs. There is not usually much in the way of waterbirds, although snipe are very common and terns (Caspian and Common) usually loiter on the beach. Massassauga rattlesnakes are as common here as anywhere on the Bruce – listen for their buzzing, insect-like rattle.

Flowerpot Island is a national park some 4 km offshore from Tobermory. There are a couple of small excursion boats that will take visitors over to the island in good weather, and it is also possible to camp there. The island is uninhabited except for the lighthouse-keepers, and in character it is much like the mainland. However, there is a small bog along the west shoreline that seems to be a good place for lingering migrants. Blackpoll Warblers have summered here on occasion.

Tobermory is the southern terminal for the Tobermory–Manitoulin Island ferry (see Little Current). Also see Wiarton for a discussion on the Bruce Peninsula generally. There is a new proposal for a national park in the Tobermory area at the time of writing.

(117) **TORONTO** – Metropolitan Toronto is a city of over two million population, with all the urban sprawl and heavy traffic that implies. In spite of its size, however, it has a number of excellent birding locales, most of them associated with the Lake Ontario shoreline.

Lake Ontario here and to the west has some of Ontario's largest concentrations of wintering waterfowl – depending on ice conditions elsewhere, between a third and a half of all the birds wintering in the province. Over the years some 35 different species have occurred, with up to 30,000 individuals. The principal species are Canada Goose, Mallard, and Black Duck (all semi-feral), Greater Scaup, Common Goldeneye, Bufflehead, Oldsquaw, and Common Merganser, with smaller numbers of Mute

Swan, Gadwall, American Wigeon, and Redhead. All the water-fowl that occur in the province can turn up, and Snow Goose, Barrow's Goldeneye, and Harlequin Duck have been rare but regular. The common gull at this time is Herring, with smaller numbers of Great Black-backed and Ring-billed. Glaucous and Iceland are regular.

The area can also be of great interest in migration periods with Common Loon, Horned and Red-necked Grebe, White-winged Scoter, and Red-breasted Merganser appearing, as well as the shoreline movements of shorebirds and landbirds characteristic of the north shores of the lower Great Lakes. In late autumn this has been one of the better areas in the province for King Eider, Purple Sandpiper, and Red Phalarope.

The lakeshore is of interest all the way to Hamilton, and because coverage is easier going from west to east the account that follows starts at Highway 2 east of the Queen Elizabeth Way at Burlington.

Pass the hospital, proceed through the traffic lights, and turn right immediately into the parking lot of *Spencer Smith Park*. There are rest-rooms here, and excellent views of the lake. From this point on the highway runs through a virtually continuous belt of housing, and lake viewing is mainly confined to the streets that dead-end at the lake. The following are the main vantage points (the distances are from point to point):

2.3 km *Guelph Line, Burlington*

0.8 km *Sioux Lookout Park, Burlington* A small waterfront park

1.3 km *Walker's Line*

2.1 km *Appleby Line*

1.9 km *Burloak Road and the Pig and Whistle Inn*

0.8 km *BP Centennial Gardens* Scan the Shell pier immediately to the west carefully for gulls, as a number of uncommon species have summered here, and watch for jaegers in autumn. This westernmost section of the lake is the most productive of jaegers (September-October), Red-necked Grebes in spring and fall, and White-winged Scoters in May.

1.8 km *Bronte Road, Bronte* The tame duck flock here usually has some interesting stragglers in winter The road next turns east into Ontario Street, which gives views of the lake to the east. Return to Lakeshore Road via Nelson Street.

1.1 km   *Third Line* (distance from the corner of Nelson Street)

0.9 km   *Coronation Boat Ramp*

2.9 km   *Holyrood Avenue* The tiny Holyrood Park at the foot gives lake access, and good landbird habitat nearby.

0.8 km   *Kerr Street, Oakville* The public is allowed into the grounds of the Water Treatment Plant at the foot of this road, for views of the often unusual diversity of wintering duck which can be expected west of Oakville Harbour.

0.5 km   *Navy Street* Drive south and then take the last street east (Front) and proceed to its end, where *Dingle Park* gives views of the lake. Then return to Lakeshore Road via Dunn Avenue.

0.8 km   *Park Avenue* (distance from Dunn Avenue) This road turns at its base into the *Esplanade*. Return via Howard Avenue.

4.1 km   *Arkendo Drive* View the shoreline east to the St Lawrence Cement Company pier. The area around the creek is good for landbirds.

2.1 km   *Southdown Road* The highway turns north; you turn south and go down the side of the National Sewerpipe plant.

Return to the main road, now going north. At 1.1 km turn onto Orr Road, and proceed 1½ km to Meadowwood Road checking the woods en route. Turn right on Meadowwood and go to its end in Country Club Crescent, then right again, and follow this road until it merges with Watersedge Road, just before both roads end in *Watersedge Park*. The beach in front of the refinery can be very productive. Then proceed north on Meadowwood (passing Orr Road) to rejoin Lakeshore Road. Turn right onto Lakeshore Road and continue east.

East of Meadowwood Road 1.6 km, just west of the Lorne Park Road traffic light, there is an entrance to *Jack Darling Memorial Park*. Drive south to the lake, checking the trees and shrubs en route for migrants, and the beach for shorebirds. Drive west to the parking lot, and from there walk west about ½ km to *Rattray's Marsh*. At the marsh walk along the shingle barrier beach to view the centre of the marsh, or bear right to curve around the top end into the hardwood bush there.

2.9 km *Stavebank Road S, Port Credit* By keeping right it is possible to drive to the Yacht Club parking lot to view the harbour. Then, return, taking the first right turn onto Port Street. At the east end of the large parking lot on the south of this street (the foot of Helene Street) is a very productive bay, off the *St Lawrence Starch Plant.* The long stone pier to the west is worth checking for gulls, shorebirds, and open country species, and adjacent yacht-mooring basins may also have duck and gulls. Return to Lakeshore Road by continuing east on Port Street, which curves around to join the foot of Highway 10.

From Port Credit east to Mimico Creek the waterfowl tend to drop off in numbers and variety, although there can be good birding all along this stretch. Marie Curtis Park along Etobicoke Creek has a small wood-lot and a tame Mallard flock, but *Humber Bay Park*, about 2½ km east of Royal York Road and on either side of Mimico Creek, is better. There is parkland – and parking – both east and west of the stream here. The east side is usually better, with waterfowl congregating in the sheltered waters between the eastern point and the mouth of the Humber River. Continuing east from here the road crosses the Humber and becomes Lakeshore Boulevard.

This area is called *Sunnyside,* and is the most accessible part of the western Toronto waterfront. If you are starting coverage at Sunnyside and wish to cover Humber Bay Park, you can do so by following Lakeshore Boulevard past its junction with the Queen Elizabeth Way at the Humber River mouth (to do so stay in the right-hand lane of traffic), entering Lakeshore Road just east of the Park Lawn Road traffic lights (follow the signs). The east entrance to Humber Bay Park is left at this intersection.

Sunnyside cannot be covered from east to west by automobile but can easily be covered on foot or by bicycle. Persons driving coming from the east (and not visiting Humber Bay Park) should use the left-hand lane of Lakeshore Boulevard approaching the Queen Elizabeth Way intersection. This lane permits a U-turn just east of the Humber mouth. The shoreline can then be covered by a series of right-hand turns into the parking lots, which are accessible only from the eastbound lanes of Lakeshore Boulevard. From each, the neighbouring shoreline and break-wall, and the waters both inside and outside, should be scanned for gulls and duck. Pay special attention to the gaps, and to con-centrations of Mallards which often include individuals of other species. The area is best in late autumn, winter, and early spring, and then is often the most productive easily accessible area for waterfowl in Toronto. One caveat is that after heavy snowfalls the parking lots and drives mentioned may not be ploughed, maintenance of these areas in winter being irregular. Distances are not given here, as most places mentioned follow one another in quick succession.

The first parking lot entry is immediately east of the Humber River junction and U-turn. From this lot you can cover the Humber mouth, and there is usually a large flock of waterfowl panhandlers here in winter. On leaving the parking lot you may wish to check the foot of Grenadier Pond by turning left at the first traffic light onto Ellis Avenue. Otherwise continue east through the light to the next parking lot, and a short way farther on to a small parking lot servicing a food concession just west of Sunnyside Swimming Pool (a large concrete structure). The trees should be checked for migrants.

The next stop is a boat launching ramp west of a footbridge crossing the boulevard. East of the footbridge the divided high-way ends. Continue east past the Boulevard Club to the top of the hill, and enter a parking lot servicing the Toronto Sailing and Canoe Club and *Argonaut Rowing Club*. This is a good spot from which to 'scope the bay.

Continuing east, pass under another footbridge and turn imme-diately onto *Aquatic Drive* (check the grassy areas as well as the water). On re-entering Lakeshore Boulevard one is driving south of the Canadian National Exhibition grounds, with Ontario Place on the right. Continue on to Bathurst Street, which is the major intersection ahead as one passes Tip Top Tailors.

At Bathurst turn right and proceed to the end. Check the Western Gap (the entrance to Toronto harbour) from here, and walk east along the wall by the elevator to view the west end of the harbour.

East of Bathurst Street there is a mix of industry and recreation called Harbourfront. From late October to early April this is worth covering. Turn sharp right at the next light (Spadina Avenue) onto Queen's Quay West and drive a little west and then south to view Toronto Harbour. Then proceed east along Queen's Quay. The parking servicing the Toronto Island ferry docks is about 0.3 km east on the north of the road, and the Toronto Island ferry docks themselves are on the south side opposite the foot of Bay Street. Continue east 1.6 km farther on where Queen's Quay rejoins Lakeshore Boulevard at Parliament Street. The *Victory Mills* loading dock at this point can be very productive.

The next area is devoted to heavy industry. Turn from Queen's Quay onto Lakeshore Boulevard eastbound and bear right around the next bend (0.6 km) to drive south over the lift bridge on Cherry Street. Continue to its foot, where *Cherry Beach*, in spite of its unprepossessing appearance, can be very good. Walk west and check the Eastern Gap and the beach (both gaps seem to attract rarer stragglers: a King Eider spent a winter in this one). In spring and autumn the trees and shrubs concentrate migrant landbirds. This is also a route for migrant hawks and open country birds.

Leaving the Cherry Beach area, take the first right (Unwin Avenue) and drive east 1.6 km curving around the *Hearn Generating Station*. At its east end is a Bailey bridge crossing the outflow of cooling water used by the plant. Park on the east side of the bridge and check the area for gulls and duck. Look for stray small gulls, and check the warm waters of the outer harbour beyond, which concentrate large numbers of duck. The largest flock of Common Mergansers in Toronto winters here, and adjacent shorelines are good places to see Snowy Owls. Opposite is the Eastern Headland. The scrub cottonwood and willow south of the road and west of the bridge can yield Saw-whet Owls in October.

Continuing east to Leslie Street, the entrance to the headland is on the right. Turn north on Leslie Street and drive 0.8 km to Eastern Avenue. From here the Gardiner Expressway gives access to both the west of the city and (via the Don Valley Parkway) the north, and Leslie and Eastern Avenue give access to the east.

The Eastern Headland at the foot of Leslie Street is a spit of land 5 km long extending out into Lake Ontario in a southwest direction. Constructed of landfill by the Toronto Harbour Commission, it is still being developed, but interim use of the area for such activities as walking and cycling has proved very popular. It is wholly undeveloped, except for a paved road along the centre of the spit, a lighthouse and a few temporary buildings at the far end, and some portable toilets near the tip.

The lake side of the headland is armoured and formed into a series of small bays, with shingle beaches falling off rapidly into very deep water. On the north side four bays with sandy beaches have been formed, divided by low fill ridges. These areas are gradually growing over with cottonwoods and willows. They have been colonized by a huge colony of Ring-billed Gulls, with Common Terns and a few Caspian Terns. Wilson's Phalaropes and several species of waterfowl have nested and the entire area is very attractive to shorebirds and waterbirds in both spring and autumn. Not only do open country species such as Horned Larks, Water Pipits, Lapland Longspurs, and Snow Buntings occur in large flocks in migration, but numbers of other passerines occur as well, as do Short-eared and Snowy Owls. Hawks follow the headland west in autumn.

At present the headland is formally open only on weekends between 10:00 AM and 4:00 PM from June to November, and then only to pedestrians or cyclists. A periodic free bus service runs during part of this time from the nearest public transportation access point at Queen Street East and Leslie Street. This bus will stop on request at any point along the headland. There is car parking just inside the first gate at the foot of Leslie. During the nesting period the areas of the gull and tern colonies are off-limits. This kind of arrangement seems likely to continue for the next few years and may be extended, but as the details are likely to change, phone the Toronto Harbour Commission in business hours (to 4:00 PM) for the latest information.

The *Toronto Islands* have been rather eclipsed by the Eastern Headland in recent years, but they offer a wider range of habitats and some of the same quality. Apart from an area at their east end they are entirely parkland, and are accessible only by ferry.

The islands consist of a hook-shaped strip of land enclosing Toronto Harbour, and are islands by virtue of the two shipping channels, one at the east end just west of Cherry Street (Eastern Gap) and the other at the foot of Bathurst Street (Western Gap). The area adjoining the Eastern Gap is called Ward's Island and is largely occupied by housing. The outer shoreline runs roughly southwest for some 3 km, gradually curving to Gibraltar Point at the islands' west end, where it hooks north to terminate after about another 2 km at the Western Gap. The islands just south of this gap are at their widest and this area is occupied by a small airport.

On the Toronto Harbour side of the islands the shoreline is much dissected by channels and lagoons. These create a series of small islands, some of them linked to the main land mass (or one another) by bridges. At the east end these islands are also occupied by housing and yacht clubs, although there are one or two natural areas.

Public ferries run to Ward's Island in the east, to Hanlan's Point in the west – actually the northernmost point of the Islands Park, just outside the airport fence – and to Centre Island. The last is the largest of the chain of inner islands, and is the most heavily developed for recreation. The best birding areas are from Centre Island westwards, and only these are covered here.

Grassy lawns, planted beds of shrubbery, and trees (mostly large old willows and cottonwoods) form the cover over most of the area, but natural vegetation backs the beaches and there are several wholly natural areas, including a fair-sized 'wilderness' area. These natural areas consist mainly of open cottonwoods with an understorey of dense shrubbery, principally dogwoods, and tall grass. A few areas of marsh and wet meadows also occur along the lagoons.

The islands are heavily used, particularly Centre Island, so a trip should start early. There are no cars allowed, but on weekends in summer a small train service runs, and bicycles can be rented (you can sometimes take your own). There are a few food concessions, two small restaurants on Centre Island, and frequent public toilets. In winter, however, an island trip becomes more of an expedition as there are no ferries to Hanlan's Point and few to Centre at that time, everything is closed, and there is negligible shelter. Winter trips are primarily productive of waterfowl, and large flocks of Oldsquaws raft both off the south shore and off the Eastern Headland.

The ferry docks are at the foot of Bay Street. Phone the ferry docks (367-8193 – listed under Metro Parks) for ferry times before setting off, and be sure to pick up a schedule at the dock before embarking; there are none available on the other side.

The trees and shrubbery on the islands are often alive with migrants. Watch for hawks in autumn, especially accipiters, which often congregate in numbers in September, when other features are milling flocks of Blue Jays and hosts of Monarch Butterflies. Scan the beaches and lake, especially the airport beach (closed to access), and wet areas behind the beaches themselves. The wilderness area lies behind the Water Purification Plant, and can be entered through the gate at the north end of the fence along the east side. Only members of the local nature clubs are allowed in from 15 April to 15 July. This area can be good for Saw-whet Owls in October, and migrant passerines in spring and autumn. Mugg's Island, between Centre and Hanlan's, has small Black-crowned Night Heron and gull colonies, and interesting waterfowl often can be seen.

Toronto has many large and productive parks. Two in the west are High Park and Lambton Woods. *High Park* is very heavily used and much abused, but its good areas still attract birds. It is situated south of Bloor Street and east of Keele Street, and the best areas are on the west side. Driving west from Keele go 1 km to Ellis Park Road, which is just past the park, and turn south. At the bottom of the hill (0.3 km) turn left into Wendigo Way, which overlooks a small ravine which can be very productive.

Farther south on Ellis Park Road, check the small marsh at the north end of Grenadier Pond, and then walk south to a footpath located a little way up the hill.

Then drive up the hill and turn left onto Ellis Avenue, which runs down to the Queensway and Sunnyside. Just before the Queensway traffic lights check the lower end of Grenadier on the left. This always has a resident Mallard flock, and the wide water area here often has interesting duck and gulls.

To reach *Lambton Woods* and *James Gardens* go west on Eglinton Avenue to the Humber River, and then south on Scarlett Road (the first intersection west of the Humber River) 0.3 km to Edenbridge Drive. Turn right, drive 1.1 km, and the James Gardens parking lot is on the left. This is a fine mixed woodland with some wet areas and much shrub growth with dogwood, elder and buckthorn. James Gardens has feeders and there are usually open wet areas along the damp banks of the flood plain in winter. Red-headed Woodpeckers breed, Great Horned Owls are regular, and Golden-winged Warblers and Blue-gray Gnatcatchers have been found in summer. Lambton Woods is contiguous with James Gardens, and extends along the west bank of the river as far as the railway bridge, where there is a footbridge to the east bank, along which more marginal areas (Lambton Park) can be covered south of Lambton Golf Course, and extending south to Dundas Street. Lambton Woods is probably the best area of woodland in west Toronto.

In the geographic centre of Metropolitan Toronto is the *Sunnybrook, Serena Gundy, and Wilket Creek Park* complex. There are two main auto entrances: one on the west side of Leslie Street (the second major intersection west of the Don Valley Parkway) just north of Eglinton Avenue and opposite the Inn on the Park. From here the park road curves round, following the river and then curving back over the playing fields of Sunnybrook Park to enter a wood-lot overlooking Wilket Creek.

Wilket Creek is a small tributary of the Don that enters from the north along the line of Leslie Street. It is the narrow valley extending north from the park road at the bottom of the hill as one enters, and it terminates just south of Lawrence Avenue in *Edwards Gardens*, a large formal gardens which can nevertheless yield migrants. The second entry to the park complex is from here, at the corner of Lawrence and Leslie.

These parks have extensive grassed areas with picnic tables and are heavily used – on hot week-ends in summer it has been necessary to close them – but they also have excellent habitat for landbirds and can be quite productive, especially in early morning. Over the years they (and Glendon Hall to the west) have produced Three-Toed Woodpeckers as regularly as anywhere around Toronto, and a pair of Pileated Woodpeckers is resident. They are also good for winter finches, and a large flock of robins and waxwings may winter here.

In the east end, *Morningside Park* is one of the finest natural park areas in the Metro system. From the corner of Morningside Avenue and Ellesmere Road drive south 0.6 km to the park entrance on the right (west). The park road runs for some distance in and there are many walking trails through the deep valley, which has a good diversity of habitats including fine mixed woodlands.

The *Royal Ontario Museum* is at the southwest corner of Bloor Street West and Avenue Road in midtown Toronto. It has a major collection of bird skins, nests, and eggs, and is the official repository for bird records for the province.

On the northwestern fringes of Toronto are two noteworthy conservation areas. *The Boyd Conservation Area* is on Islington Avenue, north of Highway 7 (3.4 km). Boyd has one of the finest easily accessible mature evergreen woodlands in the region. In fact it is rather too accessible, with a hardtopped nature trail through part of it! It is very attractive to winter birds and one of the best places near Toronto to see Pileated Woodpeckers.

Claireville Conservation Area has its main entrance 2.1 km west of the junction of Highway 50 and Highway 7, and a second entrance 1.5 km south of the intersection on Highway 50. It has a mixed woodland, some productive old fields and stream valleys, and a large lake divided almost into two by railroad tracks. Entering the area from Highway 7, drive south and turn left just before the power lines onto a sideroad that runs east towards the woodland. This is a wooded creek valley that is very productive in winter and has become one of the best places in the region to find owls, especially small owls (Saw-whet and rare Boreal), which can be found from late February in the tops of the vine tangles. The sideroad leads to the Highway 50 entrance (usually closed in winter) and it is a relatively short walk from this gate to the woodland. Coming from this direction it is the second creek valley that is the most productive. Returning to the main park road, continue south, crossing the low bridge over the Humber River, and examine the thorn bushes on the south bank of the river along both sides of the road. These may have owls in winter. Cliff Swallows nest under the bridge, and the marsh to the east is interesting in spring.

The water areas can be covered from the road outside the area. From the junction of Highway 50 and Steeles Avenue (2.1 km south of Highway 7) you can turn west and survey the north parts from the Steeles Avenue bridge. Then return to the intersection and turn right on the Indian Line, which runs down the east side of the lake. The part south of the railway bridge can also be covered by continuing south, crossing the bridge below the dam, turning right at the top of the hill into the south entrance to the area marked 'Indian Line Campground,' and driving to the dam gates. Depending on water levels the lake may be productive of shorebirds in fall and of waterfowl in early spring and late autumn.

East of Toronto the areas listed under Pickering are readily accessible and regularly covered by Toronto birders.

(For a more extensive listing of birding areas within 48 km around Toronto, see my *A Bird Finding Guide to the Toronto Region*.)

(118) Tottenham – County Road 10, which runs north through this village to Highway 89 and then, after a jog right, north again to Angus, passes a series of sod farms in the flat country along the Nottawasaga River. These farms are both along the country road itself and along the grid of sideroads to the east and west. They can attract shorebirds in migration, mainly in late spring and early autumn. Specific locations depend on the character of the fields from year to year, the amount of standing water, and the state of migration.

Tottenham sewage lagoon is just past the Conservation Area west of town. On County Road 10 go to the light on Mill Street, turn west, and drive 0.8 km; the lagoon is on the right.

(119) Uxbridge – The area northeast of Toronto includes some extensive stands of pine plantation of varying ages, and oak-pine woodland communities which are of interest botanically and have produced coniferous forestbirds. Many of the woodland roads of this forest are open to the public for hiking and skiing. The lands around Vivian and south of Uxbridge are typical of these woodlands.

Uxbridge is on Highway 47, and the pine zone is on Concession 7 due south of the town, and along Durham Regional Road

21, which runs east from Goodwood. One of the better areas is around the junction of Concession 7 and Regional Road 21, 4 km east of Regional Road 1. These pinewoods are interspersed with open bushy areas (Brown Thrasher, Rufous-sided Towhee, and Field Sparrow) and small pines (possible Clay-coloured Sparrows), and mature trees can yield finches such as crossbills. Recently such birds as Red-breasted Nuthatches and Hermit Thrushes have been recorded here in summer.

(120) **Waterloo** – There are several good areas in Kitchener-Waterloo itself, in addition to the areas covered under Guelph and Cambridge (also see Dorking for the Conestoga Reservoir).

The Columbia and Laurel reservoirs are good for waterfowl and open country species in migration, and Pied-billed Grebe, Canada Goose, Marsh Wren, and Swamp Sparrows nest. They are west from the Conestoga Parkway on University Avenue to Albert Street, then north to Columbia Street West and drive to the University of Waterloo campus. The reservoirs are adjacent to here and to Conservation Drive, reached via Albert Street north to Bearinger Road, and then west again.

Some city parks have natural woodlands. *Waterloo Park* is west of King Street and south of University Avenue; the entrance is off Young Street West, which runs west from King, one block north of Bridgeport. *Lakeside Park* has a small lake that yields waterbirds. It can be reached from the Conestoga Parkway via Homer Watson Boulevard north to Stirling Avenue, then west to Greenbrook Drive. *Hillside and Marsland* parks are in north Waterloo, northeast of Weber and King Streets. Follow Columbia Street East from King Street north to the intersection with Marsland Drive. Access is south of here off Marsland.

Homer Watson Park is south of the twin cities, at the corner of Homer Watson Boulevard and Huron Road. It is the start of a tract of natural land that runs southeast along Wilson Avenue to the Blair bridge over the Grand River. This area includes mixed forests, the Grand River itself, mill ponds and creeks, and extensive trails. The Blair bridge has nesting Cliff Swallows and provides a good look-out for waterbirds. The coniferous stands are good for winter species and owls, and Pine Warblers nest.

Stanley Park Conservation Area is along Ottawa Street East just east of the Conestoga Parkway, and is also accessible from River Road farther east. There are trails here linking with the peat bog in Idlewood Park to the southeast. There are good mixed habitats and it can be especially productive in winter.

The Erb Street Regional landfill site is west on Erb Street just beyond the flashing lights at the Rummelhardt crossroads. It can yield shorebirds and gulls in season.

Schaefer's Woods is an extensive wooded tract of northern character on both sides of Regional Road 14 west of Erbsville. To reach this hamlet drive west on Columbia Street to Regional Road 16 and then north. Barred and Long-eared Owl, Winter Wren, Black-throated Green Warbler, and Northern Waterthrush are among the species that have nested.

North of the twin cities and northeast of Elmira (Highway 85 north) the area bounded by Regional Roads 21, 22, and 86 has mature coniferous plantations and swamp habitats which have yielded such species as Sharp-shinned Hawk, Red-breasted Nuthatch, Golden-crowned Kinglet, Pine Warbler, and Dark-eyed Junco in summer.

Also north of Elmira, on County Road 19 to the west, is the hamlet of Floradale, site of a new reservoir which is proving excellent for wetland species.

(121) **Wiarton** – This town bills itself as the 'gateway to the Bruce Peninsula,' and it is central to many of the most interesting parts of the Bruce. The mix of heavy second growth woodland, cedar bogs, and marginal farmland on the peninsula yields a variety of habitats and an abundance of both forest and open country birds. Most of the species typical of old fields can be found and Turkey Vultures are widespread. There are many small lakes and a long indented shoreline, precipitous on the east (Georgian Bay) side and slowly shelving on the Lake Huron side, where a chain of offshore islands have breeding ducks, gull and tern colonies, and a couple of heronries. The sheltered inner waters are attractive to waterfowl both breeding and in migration, and when the lake levels are low – a cyclic phenomenon occurring over several years – fine shorebird habitat develops. The principal nesting species are Herring and Ring-billed Gulls and Com-

mon and Caspian Terns, along with most of the waterfowl listed
for the breeding season in the south. In migration, open country
species and falcons are noteworthy. See Oliphant for one of the
best areas along Lake Huron. Other areas noted above are Mar,
which provides a jumping-off point form some of the inland
lakes and the backroads; Ferndale, where an area of agricultural
plain has some western species; and Dyer Bay and Tobermory
for areas in the more heavily forested north of the peninsula.

At Wiarton itself the sewage lagoons are usually worth visiting. From the light at William Street in the centre of town drive
south up the hill on the highway 0.9 km to Elm Street. Turn east
and drive 0.3 km; the lagoon road is on the right just before the
cemetery. Wiarton airport is farther east on Elm and might be
worth checking for field species. Dickcissels (on one of their
erratic forays into the province) have occurred here.

Returning, if you cross the highway on Elm Street you can
drive down the hill ½ km and view a marsh on the north which
has been one of the more productive Wilson's Phalarope locations on the Bruce. Other views of this marsh can be obtained
from the roads to the north and east, although at the time of
writing extensive drainage is occurring here.

(122) Wingham – The sewage lagoons are relatively inaccessible – towards the back of a farm ½ km west on Highway 86
from its intersection with Highway 4.

Much easier to get at is the Maitland River both in Wingham
itself, where there is pleasant parkland along it off Highway 4,
and 15 km east of town and just east of Wroxeter. On the south
side of Highway 86 here is Wroxeter Mill Pond, with some
marshy sections and, depending on water levels, mud flats that
can attract migrant shorebirds.

(123) Zurich – The lagoons here are at the back of the playing
fields at the southeast end of town. Turn south on East Street.

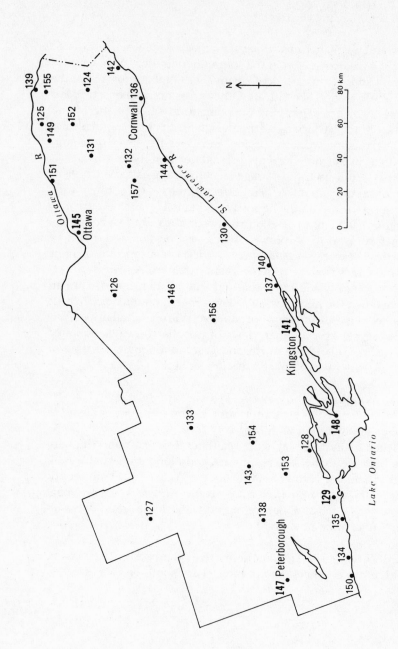

MAP 6 Eastern Ontario

5 / Eastern Ontario

For our purposes eastern Ontario includes all the counties west to, and including, Peterborough and Northumberland, and south of the districts of Haliburton and Nipissing and Renfrew County. It embraces the southern extension of the Pre-Cambrian Shield and the plains to the east.

The Shield areas include most of Hastings, Lennox and Addington and Frontenac, and substantial sections of Peterborough and Lanark counties. They are rugged and heavily forested, mainly with the mixed forest of the Great Lakes–St Lawrence region, but in the Rideau Lakes area just north of Kingston oaks and hickories occur at the northeastern limits of the Deciduous Forest region. This southerly element is reflected in the bird life in that area (see Kingston).

To the south and west of the Shield area is an extensive zone of moraine land and the large drumlin field around Peterborough. The rolling countryside has a mixture of woodlands, reforestation, marginal farmland, and small wetlands that is rich in bird life. Old field habitats also abound in the flat limestone plains farther east, including much of the south of Prince Edward County, and immediately east of the Shield, roughly from the vicinity of Brockville north to Almonte.

The easternmost parts of the region – the United Counties and Prescott and Russell – are heavily agricultural, and the open flat plains south and east of Plantagenet attract hawks and other open country species.

Lake Ontario bounds roughly the western half of the region of the south, and some of the province's most noteworthy areas of migrant concentration occur here (see Brighton and Picton). The St Lawrence River is the region's southern boundary between Kingston and the Quebec border, and it offers the birder a variety of waterfront habitats ranging from marshes between Cornwall and Morrisburg to rocky islands in the Ivy Lea area. In autumn, low waterlevels on the river often produce extensive areas of mud shoreline, attractive to shorebirds.

Extensive field work has been done around the cities of Ottawa, Kingston, and Peterborough. Generally, however, the region has not been extensively worked. Indeed, the easternmost sections are among the least-known parts of the province ornithologically.

There are many areas of poor drainage to the east of the Shield and extensive marshes along the Rideau, all of which look as though they should be most rewarding to visit. They are not included here because, in the absence of more information, it is impossible to identify those of special interest, although brief mention is made of locations that appear to have major potential. Similarly, the Ottawa River is of great interest at Ottawa itself, and could be expected to be productive farther east as well.

In winter the region's rather more severe climate and its proximity to large forest areas seem to result in movements of winter birds such as three-toed woodpeckers and finches appearing here sooner than in areas farther west, and in larger numbers. Owls in particular tend to be a feature of the winter scene. Wolfe and Amherst islands (see Kingston) are noteworthy for winter raptors and the forests around Bancroft and Cloyne for winter finches.

The bird species that occur in this region of the province are generally similar to those that occur over the rest of the south. The existence of the Frontenac Axis of the Shield, however, means that heavy forest cover penetrates farther south here than elsewhere in southern Ontario, and there is a rich assemblage of breeding birds in the more varied habitats that result, with a blending of southern and more northern species. For example, the Breeding Bird Surveys for Mount Julian in Peterborough County and Roblin in Lennox and Addington yield 70 to 80 species, while farther west at Streetsville and Palgrave totals run in the low 60s, with relatively few warblers recorded. Much higher totals are possible farther west with a choice of route that carefully selects habitats; the surveys are essentially standardized samples over randomly selected routes, and as such are a good indication of the overall potential of an area.

Once one leaves the Shield country behind, the variety of species drops again, and the agricultural counties of far eastern Ontario may yield a smaller variety of breeding birds than similar areas farther west. The extensive areas of often poor and ill-drained pasture are reflected in relatively high numbers of American Bitterns, Marsh Hawks, Common Snipe, and Upland Sandpipers, and very high counts of Bobolinks and Red-winged Blackbirds appear. This is one of the strongholds of Gray Partridge in Ontario, but the birds are hard to find.

The areas of limestone plain and moraine share thin soils and a marginal agriculture, and the shrubby, weedy fields provide a stronghold for such species as Eastern Bluebird, Loggerhead Shrike, and Grasshopper Sparrow, although these birds are nowhere common and the shrike is declining seriously even here. Henslow's Sparrows can also occur in suitable areas (heavy forb growth in old fields) but this species is also declining. Known stations near Kingston and Ottawa now appear to be occupied only erratically, and the bird does not seem to occur much farther east.

Other species that occur less frequently in this part of the province are Mourning Dove (although this bird is expanding its range at present), Red-headed Woodpecker, Willow Flycatcher, and Cardinal.

(124) **Alexandria** – For the sewage lagoons, drive into town on Highway 34 and watch for St Paul Street on the east (just next to the Ottawa Hotel). Turn and drive 2.1 km past the cathedral; the lagoon complex is down a long dirt road to the right after the main road has curved northwards.

(125) **Alfred** – The sewage lagoons are at the southeast end of town. Drive to the intersection of Highway 17 and County Road 15 North (15 South is at the other end of town). Turn south opposite the county road and drive 1.6 km, the last section being gravelled. The lagoons are on the left.

The lagoons are in an area of flat, poorly drained farmland, site of the Alfred bog. It is attractive to open country species, Marsh Hawks, and Common Snipe. The bog itself is some 8 km southeast.

(126) Almonte – To reach this community's sewage lagoons, follow Highway 44 southwest through town (past the pleasant Metcalfe Conservation Area) to the highway's end at Highway 29. Cross 29 on to Regional Road 16 and drive 0.7 km, where the lagoons are on the right.

Almonte is on the northwest edge of the Smith's Falls limestone plain. The sideroad running northwest from town just east of the railway passes through some typical habitats.

(127) Bancroft – This town is at the hub of a network of roads that pass through the rugged Shield country south and east of Algonquin Park. The key highways are 62 north to Maynooth (and thence via 127 to the park boundaries) and south to Madoc; 28 southwest to Apsley and Burleigh Falls; and 500 east to Denbigh. There is also a network of reasonably good sideroads, particularly to the north and west. Logging roads and trails are available for hiking. Cardiff, some 15 km west via Highways 28 and 121, has a sewage lagoon, south of the highway, itself south of the townsite.

The bird life is similar to that described under central Ontario, but there is a more southern component with such species as Brown Thrasher being more common, and areas of marginal farmland yield open country birds. Bancroft is one of the few places in southern Ontario where we have seen White-winged Crossbills in summer, and the whole area can be most productive in winter for finches. As in the areas to the north, pinpointing specific locations is impractical, as the interesting species are distributed throughout suitable habitat.

(128) Belleville – Marshes abound along the Bay of Quinte and the west side of Prince Edward County, but accessible marshes are less easy to find. Some good areas are on the roads to Huff's Island, east off Highway 14 some 8 km south of the Belleville bridge. The best areas are along the road 1.7 km from the highway, and ½ km north along the first sideroad from this point (2 km). Extensive cat-tail marshes with open pools and brushy areas are present at these locations.

(129) **BRIGHTON** – This is the nearest community to *Presqu'île Provincial Park*, one of the premier bird-watching locations in the province. The park is 4 km south of town on Northumberland County Road 66, which intersects Highway 2 at the west end of town.

The road runs south to the lake and then curves west to cross the north end of a marsh. From the bridge at this point the sewage lagoons are easy to reach. Immediately east of the bridge a sideroad (Harbour Street) runs diagonally southeastward along the shore. This road winds around for 2.2 km before ending at Prince Edward Street. Turn right there. The lagoons are 0.4 km along on the north.

Returning to the bridge over the marsh, pull off the road and view the wetland on both sides of it. The road then turns south again on the base of the sandpit that forms the point, and the park gate is just ahead (entry fee). It is of interest year-round but much less so in summer. Hunting occurs in autumn from late September, which limits both access to some areas and the numbers of birds that can be seen.

Presqu'île is a hook-shaped peninsula. The base of the point runs south from the park gate and has wide sandy beaches on its west (Popham Bay) side and extensive marshland bordering the sheltered waters of Presqu'île Bay to the east. The road itself crosses an area of open, low-lying sandy pannes between the dunes on each side. Much of this is flooded in spring and some is wet year-round. It is a fascinating area botanically, but not so good for birds. Snipe are common and puddle ducks feed in the wet areas. Migrants fly over and follow the line of cottonwoods along the beach to the west or the heavier woodland that develops to the east. East of the dunes is a series of narrow finger-like spits which are densely forested, mainly with white cedar, but some areas of tall pine occur. These are separated by marshy areas, but marsh viewing is easier elsewhere; however, the woods can be good for migrants, particularly on windy days.

After crossing the pannes the road starts to curve to the east and the park store is on the right. Drive into the parking lot and check the area to the south and west. To the west is the south end of the beach, which has some marsh and shrubby vegetation and a shallow water lead running east at its south end. Between this and the open lake to the south is a narrow sand and gravel point, Owen Point, and farther west there are two offshore islands, Gull Island and High Bluff Island. These support a huge Ring-billed Gull colony and Black-crowned Night heronry. Herring Gulls, Common Terns, and many waterfowl either nest or summer in the offshore waters (Mallard, Black Duck, Gadwall, Pintail, Northern Shoveler, Blue and Green-winged Teal, American Wigeon, Common Goldeneye, and Common and Red-breasted Merganser), and Double-crested Cormorants are regular. Great Black-backed Gulls have also nested.

Owen Point is a major observation point for landbird migration, including hawks, and the loop of shoreline along Popham Bay to the north (the south end of the long sand beach) collects algae and large concentrations of migrant shorebirds. The sand beach itself can also have shorebird and loitering gull flocks along its length. In late May Brant and Whimbrel flocks can be expected, and in October the waters along the lake are one of the best places in southern Ontario for seeing all three species of scoter. The mixture of habitats back from the shore, with juniper, cedar, hardwoods, and open wet and grassy areas, attracts land bird migrants, and woodcock breed.

Past Owen Point the shoreline turns eastward and becomes rocky. Returning to the road, this now also curves east on to the thin limestone plateau which is the 'île' part of Presqu'île. To the north is the main marsh, with excellent marsh viewing along the road. Least Bitterns can be seen here at dawn. To the right the road to the campgrounds and the main part of the park soon branches off. The road one is on follows the north shore to the private cottage area; usually it is better to turn right and go into the park itself, but cover the marsh here carefully first. There is a small launching area here where you can start a canoe exploration of the marshes.

The campground occupies roughly the first half of the south shoreline. There are interior roads to the camping areas: the one running west of the campground entrance crosses a small swamp and marsh along the shoreline and the one running east passes through mixed woodlands and conifer plantations. They are worth covering. The main park road itself continues east and soon divides to form a large loop – a turn right leads to the day-use and picnic area, which is good for viewing migrant waterfowl offshore (loons and diving duck concentrate), field birds and migrant hawks and Red-headed Woodpeckers in the oak trees. A left turn at the intersection leads to extensive mixed woodlands and reforestation, and one emerges to cross an old field (the Calf Pasture) where a sideroad leads north to a boat launch. The small marshy area here can have unexpected waterbirds, and the little point and shoreline willow grove migrant landbirds. This area is especially productive on stormy days when the winds are from some quarter of the south. The open field is good for open country species and watching hawk movement.

The main road continues through scrubby cedar woodlands bordering the cottage area and links up with the other leg of the loop just outside the parking area for Lighthouse Point or Presqu'île Point proper, site of the interpretive centre and heavy shrubby growth that is also good for migrant landbirds.

Presqu'île is not a concentration point approaching the quality of Pelee or even of Prince Edward Point. But it does concentrate migrants (for landbirds, Owen Point, the Calf Pasture, and Lighthouse Point are best) and has an unequalled mix of habitats in a relatively small area. If you own a bicycle, this is the perfect place for it!

Brighton has three motels, and there is a restaurant just outside the park gate. The park campgrounds are, of course, ideally situated, especially High Bluff, which is immediately adjacent to Owen Point.

(130) **Brockville** – North of Brockville there is an excellent wetland and large woods between Highway 29 and Leeds County Road 6 (North Augusta Road) to the east. It lies north of Centennial Drive, which is itself 4 km north of Highway 401. At the east end is an extensive area of woods and wet bush crossed by County Road 6 starting about 1 km north of Centennial Road. On this road the small *Broome-Runciman Dam Conservation Area*, 1.3 km west from North Augusta Road, affords excellent views of the east end of the large lake. To reach the north side go one sideroad north on Highway 29 from Centennial Road (this intersection is marked Airport Road to the west). Turn east and

drive 2.2 km to the entrance of *Buell's Creek Conservation Area* (entry fee) on the south. Linking the two east-west sideroads, and east of Highway 29, is McLarry Road, a rough dirt road which, however, has views of the west end of the lake, and trails leading to it.

To the west of Brockville and well out of town on Highway 2, Brockville Cemetery and the adjacent creek and the St Lawrence River can provide good birding. The portion of the cemetery south of the road is best, but there is no parking there.

(131) Casselman – For the sewage lagoons here, leave Highway 417 and drive north 1.2 km into town. Watch for a sideroad on the right just by the Banque Nationale and before the church (and past the flashing light at the St Isadore sideroad). Turn, drive 2 km to Concession 5, and turn right; the lagoon path is immediately around the corner.

(132) Chesterville – This community also has sewage lagoons. From the south end of town follow County Road 7 (Main Street) north to the river. Cross the bridge and turn immediately on Water Street (right). Drive 0.2 km and turn on a gravelled road that passes the dam and runs along the river. The lagoons are 0.5 km along on the left.

Some 24 km north of Chesterville via County Roads 7 and 6 is the village of *Russell*, which also has a sewage lagoon.

(133) Cloyne – This is the nearest community to *Bon Echo Provincial Park* and is on Highway 41, Lennox and Addington County's answer to Highway 62 at Bancroft. Like the latter, this road traverses wild and rugged country, particularly farther north near Denbigh. It has the same mixture of northern and southern species, and the park is a good base for exploring the area.

Bon Echo is 10 km north of Cloyne and is the largest park in eastern Ontario. In addition to the spectacular Mazinaw Rock, Indian pictographs, and a memorial to Walt Whitman (of all things) it provides 6644 hectares (16,417 acres) of wilderness camping, hiking, and canoeing. This is Shield country and closely resembles the areas described under central Ontario. Prairie Warblers have bred along the shoreline of Mazinaw Lake, outside the park.

(134) Cobourg – The harbour here can yield duck, gulls, and shorebirds. The best access is from Division Street at the junction of Highway 45 in the centre of town. Turn south and drive to the harbour. Check it and drive west to the far side to view the shorelines there and the bay to the east. By taking one of the eastbound cross-streets to D'Arcy Street and driving down to the lake again one can cover the east side of this same bay.

(135) Colborne – The lagoons are rather inaccessible. Coming from the east, go straight ahead on King Street when Highway 2 turns sharp right in town. Drive 0.3 km to Ontario Street and turn left; the sewage lagoons are down a long drive on the right at 0.2 km.

At *Wicklow*, 8 km west of Colborne on Highway 2, Kenwin Park Road goes due south to the lake from the centre of the hamlet. It then curves east along the lakeshore and the pleasant *Haldimand Conservation Area* (with picnic facilities) is on the left, with some ponds to the east and west of it that can yield duck and herons. From Highway 2 to the last pond is 8½ km.

(136) Cornwall – The Saunders Dam and Power Station is at the west end of the city. Coming from Cornwall itself you follow 2nd Street W, which leads to the grounds of the power station. The large parking lot overlooking the water is at present open only during the summer, but at the time of writing there are plans for keeping it open year-round. Below the dam exceptional numbers of Common Merganser and Great Black-backed Gulls congregate in winter, with other waterfowl including Glaucous and Iceland Gulls. There are large gull numbers at other times as well, although the duck disperse once the St Lawrence Seaway opens (usually in March).

From the dam one can get to the headpond by turning left outside the plant gates onto Saunders Drive. Make two more left turns: first on to Power Dam Road and next on to Highway 2 (the banks of the dam are on the left throughout this drive). Continue to the western limit of Cornwall, and immediately before a railroad track crosses the road turn left into *Guindon Park*. The boat launch area here offers excellent views of the headpond. Look over the gulls and waterfowl and then follow

Trillium Drive east, either as far as it will go or out on to Highway 2 again. This gravel park road passes through old field and second-growth woodland habitats, and is good for migrant landbirds, particularly in autumn. Watch for Gray Partridge.

Guindon Park is 5 km from the east end of Long Sault Parkway (see Morrisburg).

(137) Gananoque – The sewage lagoons here are east off Highway 32 immediately north of Highway 401. The lagoon road is on the right 0.2 km north of the 401 exit for Kingston, and there is about 1 km of narrow road to the gate.

The Gananoque waterfront itself is good for migrant waterfowl, which concentrate in the river here in early spring, and the Thousand Islands Parkway between the town and Ivy Lea, some 15 km east, has views of the fine marshes along the St Lawrence. Duck congregate here, too (see Ivy Lea).

(138) Havelock – For the sewage lagoons turn off Highway 7 on to Highway 30, drive 1 km to the Old Norwood Road on the east, and turn. The lagoons are down a narrow lane 0.8 km along on the right (south).

(139) Hawkesbury – Some 18 km east of this town is *Carillon Provincial Park,* located at the first exit from Highway 417 west of the Quebec border. The park is located on the south shore of the Ottawa River just above the Carillon Dam. It provides excellent vistas of the wide river at this point, and has shoreline marshes, second-growth forest, and a beaver pond.

(140) Ivy Lea – This small community is on the Thousand Islands Parkway approximately 15 km east of Gananoque. At Ivy Lea the St Lawrence River is usually open in the winter and both winter and early spring migrant waterfowl can be seen. Canvasback, scaup, Redhead, Common Goldeneye, and Oldsquaw are the usual species, and the occasional Bald Eagle winters.

At the *International Bridge* east of the community an introduced population of Wild Turkeys occurs on Hill Island. I have heard a variety of directions to these birds over the years: what it all boils down to is that they are easiest to find in winter, when they are coming to feeding stations provided by residents on the island. As is the way with feeder owners, their enthusiasm seems to wax and wane and I suppose the birds move around to wherever the pastures are greenest – or corn is thickest, in the present case! They are also more prone to visit feeders when the snow cover is heavier, so snow conditions are also a factor. Probably the best approach is to cross to the island – it is at the end of the first span of bridge, and there is a toll – and inquire. The most recent directions I have seen locate the birds southwest of the highway.

Many of the islands in the river east and west of Ivy Lea form the St Lawrence Islands National Park. The headquarters are at Mallorytown Landing east on the Parkway, and there is primitive camping and good birding on the islands.

Some 5 km north of Ivy Lea on Leeds and Grenville County Road 3 is the village of *Lansdowne*. To find the sewage lagoon here, drive north on County Road 3 into town and up the hill to the point where the road jogs right. At the jog keep right on King Street and drive 0.3 km to the end of the street; the lagoon gate is next to the tracks ahead.

Charleston Lake Provincial Park is about 14 km north of Lansdowne on County Road 3. It is set in Shield country among a network of lakes. There is a diversity of habitats with good birding along the extensive canoe and hiking trails.

(141) KINGSTON – The city of Kingston has the Shield country of the Rideau Lakes to the north and is itself located on the Napanee limestone plain with the offshore islands of Amherst and Wolfe to add to its diversity. There are also several excellent birding spots around the city itself.

The first of these, the *Cataraqui Cemetery*, is on the east side of Sydenham Road 1.4 km south of its interchange (No. 613) with Highway 401, and immediately north of the junction with Highway 2 (Princess Street). There is parking just north of the cemetery itself. The area is small, but the back part especially can be most productive during migration.

Little Cataraqui Creek joins Lake Ontario just west of the city, and the marshes along its lower reaches can yield a rich array of marsh birds in summer, and migrant duck and (depending on water levels) shorebirds in migration. A railroad track along the creek's east bank between the Bath Road and King Street W and about 1 km west of Portsmouth Avenue can be used to gain access to the area, which also contains some hardwood bush that can be productive in migration. Parking is possible both on the south side of Bath Road and the north side of King Street W. The Rideau Trail also follows the creek's east bank.

The *Little Cataraqui Conservation Area* is about 1 km north of Highway 401 on Division Street (Exit 617). It is well marked on the west of the road, and has a large waterbody (good for ducks) and associated mixed woodlands.

Going west from the city on Highway 33 the *Amherstview* sewage lagoons are just beyond the village of Elmwood. Watch for Maple Ridge Drive on your right; 0.3 km ahead are the stoplights at Coronation Boulevard, and the sign for Lennox-Addington County. Turn right here and drive 1 km, crossing the railroad, and turn west on a road marked to the golf course. At 1.9 km this road turns right into the golf course, and a rough track continues on beside the railroad, eventually leading to the lagoons, which have been some of the most productive in the province.

About 10 km farther west on the highway, and 0.3 km west of its junction with Highway 133, is the Amherst Island ferry. The ferries start at 6:20 AM, leaving the mainland hourly on the half hour, and on the hour from Stella (Amherst Island). There is a small fee.

The pattern of birding is similar on *Amherst* and *Wolfe islands*. Both have a network of gravel roads and on both the flat farmland is interspersed with wood-lots and areas of marsh. The land is private, but most birding can be done from the roads. A typical day's trip is devoted to following these roads around and covering adjacent fields, wetlands, and waterfront from them. Where entry on to private property is desired, permission should be sought and the usual courtesies observed. The quality of some of the sideroads varies considerably, and at times they may be in very poor condition, especially in early spring. Refer to Maps 7 and 8 for Amherst and Wolfe, respectively.

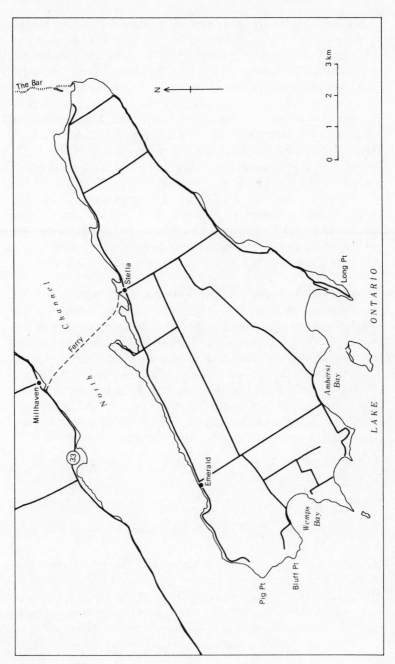

MAP 7 Amherst Island

On Amherst Island the swamps and marshes along the south-west shoreline are rewarding during migration. Waterfowl raft offshore and the gravel beaches at the east end can yield shore-birds. Both islands are excellent for field and open country birds, but their international fame is as a haven for hawks and owls in winter. Ontario's largest numbers of Snowy Owls and Rough-legged Hawks have occurred on Wolfe Island, and Amherst played host in early 1979 to an amazing concentration of ten owl species including an estimated, unprecedented 34 Great Gray Owls. Both islands experience huge build-ups in the numbers of voles and mice and these in turn attract raptors year-round, but particularly in winter. The outbreaks are periodic, so do not expect to drive down to Amherst next January and see ten species of owl! However, the islands usually have fair numbers of the commoner species in any year. Large flocks of Brant occur on both islands in late May.

Wolfe Island is divided into two by Bayfield Bay, with the largest land mass to the west and a long, narrow extension east. It is the west section that is most productive. There are many secluded bays with sand and gravel beaches and bars. Ducks, shorebirds, and gulls congregate here and the waterfowl raft offshore and at the marshy southwest end feed on the adjacent fields.

The ferry for Wolfe Island leaves from Kingston at the foot of Brock Street south of Ontario Street and one block west of Prin-cess Street, which is directly accessible from Highway 401 Inter-changes 613 and 617. A partial ferry schedule at present is:

Leave Kingston		Leave Wolfe Island	
6:15	AM	12:00	noon
7:15	AM	2:40	PM
8:40	AM	4:00	PM
10:00	AM	5:20	PM
11:20	AM	6:00	PM
12:40	PM		

There are several interesting and scenic drives through the *Rideau Lakes* area north of Kingston. One such route is to drive north from the city on Highway 38 to Harrowsmith and turn east, on Frontenac County Road 5. Drive to Sydenham and turn north at the flashing light on to County Road 5A. If one sticks to 5A the route is fairly straightforward. It initially bears generally

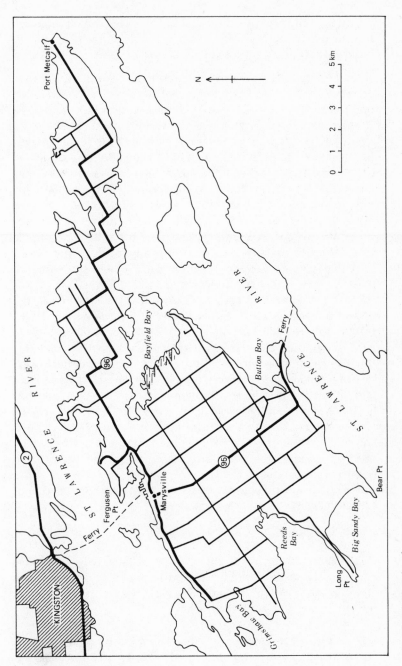

MAP 8 Wolfe Island

northeast, but then winds around back to Highway 38 again. In spite of what the provincial roadmaps imply, at the time of writing it is gravelled for most of its more than 30-km length.

Taking odometer readings from the corner of 5 and 5A, a road to the right at 12.3 km leads to Frontenac Provincial Park, as yet undeveloped. At 14.1 km the road passes through the *Otter Lake Sanctuary* of the Kingston Field Naturalists. At 17.1 km the County Road *bears left* and down the hill into the small community of Desert Lake. If you go straight ahead instead of turning left the road passes through country east of Desert and Canoe lakes. Canoe Lake has Prairie Warblers along the west shoreline (only accessible by canoe). However, it is easy to get lost in the maze of small unmarked sideroads winding through this area (even 5A is unmarked for most of its length) and a topographic map is needed to explore them. Continuing on 5A, after Desert Lake there are more sideroads, but all fairly obviously secondary to the county road. One on the left just after leaving Desert Lake leads to Holleford and back to County Road 5, but the caution above applies here also. County Road 5A eventually joins Highway 38, where a left turn takes you back to Kingston.

These winding roads are warbler country, and the woodlands of this southerly extension of the Shield attract southern warblers as well as more northern ones. Nashville and Canada Warbler are recorded in boggy coniferous areas, but Otter Lake has Cerulean and Golden-winged Warblers. In 1981 the Rideau Lakes area had breeding records of both Louisiana Waterthrush and Northern Three-toed Woodpecker, southern and northern species in remarkable proximity. Recently Golden Eagles have been reported here in summer.

It is also beautiful country, particularly in autumn. Just do not expect to be able to cover it in a hurry!

Lakefield – See the Peterborough account.

(142) **Lancaster** – To reach the sewage lagoons, drive north on Highway 34, cross the railroad, and turn east at once on John Street. Drive 0.2 km to the point the street turns; the lagoon road continues east alongside the tracks.

(143) **Madoc** – The sewage lagoons for Madoc are on the west of Highway 62 beyond the south end of town (0.6 km past the

playing field at Seymour Street). They are visible from the highway.

(144) **Morrisburg** – Some of the most interesting parts of the St Lawrence River are between Morrisburg and Cornwall on Highway 2. The *Upper Canada Migratory Bird Sanctuary* includes Upper Canada Village, but its main entrance is well marked approximately 14 km east of Morrisburg. The feeding ponds and viewing tower are 2.6 km south, and there are some 6 km of well-laid-out nature trails passing through old pasture, swamp, maple wood-lot, and cedar woods, with several viewing blinds. In migration the whole place can be alive with birds, especially Canada Geese. Drive 0.5 km farther to the causeway and view the water areas on each side for ducks and shorebirds, and the trees on Nairn Island (the campground to the south) for migrant landbirds.

Some 6½ km east of here is the start of *Long Sault Parkway*, a scenic toll road linking a number of islands which are entirely devoted to parkland. The area acts as a migrant trap to some extent, and offers excellent views of the St Lawrence. Watch for Bald Eagles in summer. There is hunting here, so the area is less productive in autumn for waterbirds than the sanctuary. The parkway rejoins the main highway 7 km farther east. Even if you do not cover the Long Sault Parkway, Highway 2 itself can be most interesting because of the many areas of marsh, open water, and mud flats between Morrisburg and Cornwall (qv).

(145) **OTTAWA** – Ottawa, with its green belt and its abundance of parks, has many areas of interest to the birder in the city itself. Parkways follow the river between Britannia on the west and Rockcliffe Park on the east, and the wooded areas and ravines of Rockcliffe Park itself can be rewarding. *Britannia*, however, is probably the most productive area. It lies northwest of the intersection of Highway 7 (Richmond Road) and Highway 17 (Carling Avenue). Britannia Road (off Carling just west of the above intersection) leads north to Cassels Street, where a right turn leads to the Britannia Filtration Plant.

It is possible to park both outside and inside the plant grounds, and cover the river and rapids, the beaver pond to the south, and the wooded areas. Access to the pinewoods east of Britannia

Road can be gained from the cross-streets. The whole area is a migrant trap, and hawks move across the river at this point. Gulls and ducks can be seen on both the river and the pond.

A good location farther downtown is the area of the *Arboretum*. Take the Rochester Street exit from Highway 417 (the Queensway). Drive south to Carling Avenue, then west one block to Preston, then south again to join Highway 16 (the Driveway), and turn right on 16 and continue to the traffic circle, where 16 continues south, the Driveway turns west into the experimental farm, and a road to the east enters the Arboretum. This again is a migrant trap, and the pines attract finches and Bohemian Waxwings in winter.

The *National Museum of Natural Sciences*, at Metcalfe and McLeod Streets, has a permanent exhibit hall on the birds of Canada, and is the centre for bird information and records for Canada as a whole.

Interesting areas to the west of Ottawa include Shirleys Bay and Richmond. At *Shirleys Bay* there is a long dyke leading out into the Ottawa River, and this is the site of some of the most outstanding waterbird finds, especially shorebirds, in the region. To reach it follow Carling Avenue west from Britannia and through Crystal Beach (the road is the old Highway 17, and watch the river for waterfowl en route). Watch for the well-marked Moodie Drive stoplight, just before the Bell Northern Research Laboratories, on the left. Continue 2.4 km farther along Carling and watch for a sideroad on the right marked to the Connaught Rifle Ranges. Turn there, and follow the road to the river. This is Shirleys Bay. Follow the road around to the left and drive 0.4 km from the turn and park near a rough track on the right. Then walk down the track and out on to the dyke. Most of the birds are on the west side of the dyke.

Moodie Drive, noted above, is Ottawa-Carleton Regional Road 10, and if you return to it drive some 20 km south to the village of *Richmond*, which has two areas of note. Approaching Richmond from the Ottawa side, watch for the intersection of Regional Road 8, signposted to Manotick, on the left. Turn on to this road and drive 0.8 km to the sewage lagoon on the right, which can be rewarding. Then return to Regional Road 10 and continue 1.8

km into Richmond, where Regional Road 5 enters, signposted to North Gower and also on the left. Turn here and drive 1.8 km to the railroad crossing. Park and walk about 3 km down the railroad tracks on the southwest side (on the right leaving Richmond) until a swamp opens out on the left. From 1976 to 1978 Yellow Rails were recorded here, and the area is also good for Sedge Wrens, Least Bittern, and other species. The open country around Richmond is productive of open country birds, and Gray Partridge occur.

Southeast of the city is *Mer Bleue*, a large peat-tamarack bog that occupies a large area between Blackburn and Carlsbad Springs. The area has yielded some remarkable breeding records, including Hawk Owl and Palm Warbler. The area lies east of Highway 417 and south of Innes Road. Drive some 3 km east on Innes and turn right on Anderson, bearing south to cross the west end of the bog.

To the west of Ottawa along the river (near Arnprior) is *Fitzroy Harbour Provincial Park* with vistas of the widening river above one of the dams. Then downriver Regional Road 9 passes Constance Creek to its east. There is an interesting variety of habitats on the sandy soils in this area.

Ottawa seems to experience a rather different mix of migrant waterbirds from that in areas farther west. Most noteworthy is the regular occurrence of small numbers of Arctic Tern on the river in late May or early June. Conceivably the river offers a flyway to James Bay from the St Lawrence, by-passing the land masses farther east. It also seems to do particularly well with winter birds. Good numbers of finches and three-toed woodpeckers occur periodically, and the city has played host to numbers of Gyrfalcons, Great Gray Owls, and Bohemian Waxwings more frequently than have other places. Perhaps these birds also use the river valley to move southeast. Winter is also a good time for Gray Partridge, which are particularly common around Ottawa.

(146) **Perth** – *Stewart Park*, behind the town hall, can be good for landbird migrants. Entering Perth on Highway 43 from the north, the highway turns left in town and then right again onto the main street (Gore Street W); the Town Hall is 0.3 km south

on the right. If you continue south on Gore Street 2 km (it becomes Lanark County Road 1) you can visit *Perth Wildlife Reserve*, 2.2 km down a sideroad to the east. Half-way down you pass the Perth sewage lagoons. The reserve itself has a baited pond and a 3-km nature trail with views of the Tay Canal and adjacent marshland.

Highway 43 between Perth and Smith's Falls, and again east of the latter, provides views of marshy areas along the Rideau.

East of town 2 km on County Road 4 is the southern part of the extensive *Long Swamp*, north of the road. It is good in summer for warblers and in winter for finches and waxwings. The same area is on the south along Highway 7 east of Perth, while on the north is the even larger area of Blueberry Marsh.

The highway continues eastwards to Carleton Place, with Mississippi Lake to the south. The lake is heavily devoted to recreational uses, but may be worth investigation in migration periods. There are marshy areas west along County Road 10 (about 25 km east of Perth, signposted to Lanark).

Some 4 km south of *Carleton Place*, Highway 29 passes Goodwood Marsh on the east and Mississippi Lake, now on the west. The sideroads along this stretch should repay exploration.

(147) PETERBOROUGH – There are two fine parks in Peterborough itself, and many interesting areas in the vicinity, particularly to the north along Highway 28. Entering Peterborough along 7B from the west, follow the road round south to its intersection at Parkhill Road (7B is Otonabee Road, but just prior to this intersection it bears sharply right on Reid Street).

To visit *Jackson Park*, turn right on Parkhill Road and drive 1.1 km, crossing the bridge and turning into the park opposite the intersection with Monaghan Street. This is a large, well-wooded park, excellent for viewing landbirds. It is possible to walk along the almost disused railroad track for several kilometres.

Mark S. Burnham Provincial Park is southeast of town on Highway 7, 0.6 km past the lights at the intersection of Peterborough County Road 30. It is also a fine area of woodland with some marshy areas. Both these parks have the customary breeding birds and are rewarding during migration.

To visit the areas north of town turn left on Parkhill Road from 7B, following the signs to Highway 28 north, drive 0.8 km and turn left on Water Street, which becomes the highway. Just before the Trent University Campus the road forks, one branch crossing the Otonabee River, but bear left to follow the main highway.

The first location is *Miller Creek*. Watch for the intersection of Highway 507 and bear diagonally left on to this. Drive 1 km north to the 7th Line of Smith Township, turn left (west) and drive 5.2 km to Miller Creek Conservation Area. The area is an old railroad track which passes through a swamp. Walk south along a path to find an area that is good for marshbirds.

Returning to Highway 28, continue north to *Lakefield* and cross the Otonabee River bridge. Turn right immediately on Water Street and drive 0.8 km to Peterborough County Road 33. Turn left on it and drive 0.5 km to the sewage lagoons on the east, where many rarities have occurred over the years, including the province's second Spotted Redshank in 1980.

From the lagoons continue on County Road 33 to Highway 134 and turn north towards Young's Point. This highway shortly joins 28 and you continue north on it. Turn east on County Road 6 (Stoney Point Road) and follow the signs in order to visit both *Warsaw Caves Conservation Area* near the village of Warsaw and *Petroglyphs Provincial Park* near Nephton.

Both areas have had Olive-sided Flycatcher breeding. The provincial park has Gray Jay throughout the year and the pines along the road have proved a good place for Red Crossbills. Three-toed woodpeckers also occur.

Highway 28 continues to *Young's Point*, where a fine stand of White Pine on South Beach Road (on the right just before the highway crosses the bridge) can yield northern species, including Parula and Yellow-rumped Warbler.

North of Young's Point Highway 28 is also the access highway to some outstanding wilderness canoe trips in the Shield country between Burleigh Falls and Apsley. Anyone planning such trips needs detailed topographic maps so more detailed information is not necessary, but one route starts from the access road at Long Lake, west through Loucks, Cox, Cold, Gold, Cloudy, Bottle, and

Beaver lakes and into Cachacoma and Mississauga. Cachacoma and Mississauga are on Highway 507, from which one can cover the same route travelling eastwards. Farther north a second access road off 28 leads to Anstruther Lake and a trip through Rathburn, Copper, and Serpentine lakes.

These trips will yield the typical Shield thrushes and warblers, and nesting Turkey Vultures. Along Long Lake there is a population of Prairie Warblers.

Returning to Lakefield again, the Otonabee River affords fine birding both north and south of town. To the north the river widens to form *Lake Katchawanooka*, visible from County Road 25, which runs along the west bank, and with a marsh at the south end accessible from Lakefield Municipal Park.

South of Lakefield the return trip along River Road – which you turned off to go to the lagoons – provides a beautiful and rewarding drive back to Peterborough along the east bank of the *Otonabee River* and the Trent Canal.

There can be good birding all along this route, as the river is a flyway. Watch under bridges for Cliff Swallows, and the river for waterbirds. The road follows the river closely until just past the Trent University campus, when it crosses to join Highway 28 at the Y-intersection noted in the directions for the route north. From here return to Parkhill Road, and – if proceeding east – turn left and drive to Television Road, which is County Road 30 and which leads south to Highway 7 just west of Mark S. Burnham Park. Westbound travellers can reach these same areas via this route by reversing the directions.

(148) PICTON – The southern part of Prince Edward County has several outstanding birding areas. Picton, the largest town in the county, forms a convenient departure point for these locations because the main roads radiate from the town. Approach Picton from the north via Highways 14 and 33 from Belleville, and from the west and east via Highway 33. Old field habitats abound on the thin limestone soils to the south.

Prince Edward Point, one of the premier migrant concentration points in the province, is located at the southeastern tip of the county. The route to the point differs depending on whether one

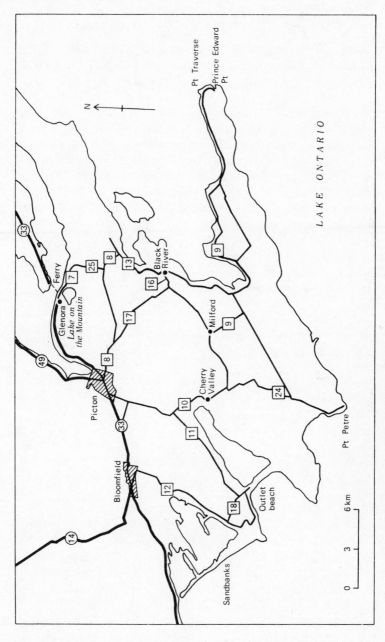

MAP 9 Picton and Southern Prince Edward County

is coming from east or west. From the east, take the Adolphus-town-Glenora Ferry (free, every 15 minutes). This is about 35 km from Kingston, and the point is some 40 km by road from the ferry. Leaving the dock at Glenora, first check your gasoline. There are no gas stations on the roads you are about to follow. If you need gas, go straight to Picton and get some. Otherwise turn left at the top of the hill on to Country Road 7, which then passes Lake-on-the-Mountain Provincial Park. The Lake-on-the-Mountain motel here is the nearest to the point, and one of few in this part of the county. Continue to County Road 25 (2.4 km from the park, marked to Waupoos); turn right, then to County Road 8 (2.4 km also to Waupoos); turn left and then at 1.8 km bear right on County Road 13 (to Milford), and follow this road around to Black River. Drive through the hamlet and then follow the directions in the paragraph after next.

Coming from the west, turn south in Picton on to County Road 8 to Waupoos. (Note the caution above about gasoline.) One can now drive around to the right-hand turn on to County Road 13 described above, or bear right off 8 on to County Road 17 at about 2½ km, and drive to the point 17 turns right. Turn left here and drive east on County Road 16, which joins Road 13 just outside the hamlet of Black River. Turn right and follow 13 south.

At Black River east and west routes join. Continue straight on at the junction with County Road 9 on the right, which goes to Milford, and which is also the road to Point Petre. Milford has the nearest gas station to the point, so note the intersection: it is not signposted at present, but is opposite the Mariner's Memorial Park and Lighthouse. County Road 13 ends at this intersection, by the way; at the next road sign you will find you are on County Road 9! Rose's Lane, 3.6 km farther on, is the next important intersection.

At Rose's Lane one can take an alternative route to the point by turning right on a gravel road. Dealing with this route first, drive 1.7 km and turn left, checking the creek en route for bitterns and duck. The low cedars to the northeast of the creek have had Clay-coloured Sparrows in summer. Around the corner, the old fields to the right are good for hawks. Yellow Rails have occurred in migration in some of the weedy wet areas (about ½ km along) and Sharp-tailed Grouse are present but rarely seen. If the fields are being grazed over the grass may be short enough for plover and other open country species on migration. A side-road to the south at 3.2 km, which leads to the shore, is sometimes passable. Otherwise continue east to rejoin the main road at 7.1 km from your turn-off.

Proceeding on the main road past the Rose's turn-off, a further 2 km will lead to Smuggler's Cove, the nearest campground to the point. *Little Bluff Conservation Area* is next (2.2 km) and has a small marsh to the left on the way in. A stop street 4 km from here marks the entry from the right of the alternative route from Rose's Lane. Follow the main road left.

From this point on the bushes and weeds along the road can be alive with migrants. Hawks are often moving down the point, and the open water to the left, although usually not very productive, can yield loons and grebes. Just as the paved road ends (1.1 km) a track to the right which passes a marsh on the south shore, may be passable. Next, a pond by the road (2.6 km, at present just past a mailbox marked 'Wannamaker') can be surprisingly productive of shorebirds and other species. Ontario's first Chestnut-collared Longspur was observed here and Cliff Swallows have nested on the adjacent barn.

At 2.3 km you enter *Prince Edward Point National Wildlife Area*, and the most productive parts of the point. Drive through Traverse Woods, excellent for landbird migrants. Past here the road curves at Point Traverse. Watch for hawks, duck on the pond to the right and on the lake, and landbird migrants everywhere. About 1 km farther on turn right through the fishing village (no facilities) of Long Point Harbour and enter another wood-lot as the road deteriorates rapidly. It curves around the harbour and about 1 km from the harbour dock arrives at the Lighthouse Bird Observatory entrance. This is on Prince Edward Point itself. The observatory is run by Kingston Field Naturalists, and has an active banding program.

The best areas here are off the point and along the south shoreline to the west for gulls and diving duck. Huge rafts of scaup and merganser occur in autumn and gull movements occur in migration times. The water between Point Traverse and Prince Edward Point often have scoter and Oldsquaw and the shoreline rocks have shorebirds. The swampy woodland at the harbour, although small, can be most productive, and all the old fields can be alive with sparrows and other migrants. Hawks and other diurnal migrants tend to drift down to the point from Point Traverse and then mill around over the fields to the west. Saw-whet Owls are regular in October, but hard to find during the day.

Point Petre is at the other end of the county, and it also concentrates migrants. To reach it from Prince Edward return to the County Road 9 junction noted above, turn left, and drive 1.5 km to the curve in the road where Royal Street goes off to the left. Turn on to this gravel road, which runs virtually due west for 7½ km before curving to join County Road 24. Turn left on to this road and drive 3 km to *Point Petre Recreational Area*. Watch for Eastern Bluebirds on the wires along this stretch of road. The main road continues 1.7 km to the lighthouse station. Any of the small roads down to the shore on the west can be interesting, and on the west just at the start of the recreational area is a picnic area in a wood-lot. This overlooks Soup Harbour and gives excellent lake viewing for waterfowl. A gravel road 0.3 km on the east past here leads back towards Prince Edward. Its condition, and more particularly that of sideroads running south from it, can be uncertain, and you should have a topographic map if you plan to explore.

Petre badly needs more coverage. Although it is nowhere near as productive as Prince Edward, the mix of birds tends to be different and the opportunities for lake viewing are better. Whenever we have visited Petre we have always seen something we had missed earlier at Prince Edward.

To get to Petre without visiting Prince Edward drive southwest on the Cherry Valley Road (County Road 10) from the west end of Picton and turn left in Cherry Valley continuing on 10 to the junction, at about 2 km, of County Road 24 on the right. Turn here; this road leads directly to the point.

There are some other good locations on this side of the county. Some 14 km from Point Petre via County Roads 24 and 10 (along the route just described) is the junction on the west of County Road 11, which runs along the north side of East Lake. *Beaver Meadow Conservation Area* is on the right 0.8 km along 11. This has trails in a swampy woodland, and a lake which can yield herons and such species as Wood Duck, which may be hard to find elsewhere.

Continuing west, County Road 11 leads to *Sandbanks Provincial Park*. At 7.6 km you come to a T-intersection; turn left here on County Road 18. The *Outlet Beach* section of the park is 0.7 km ahead, and incorporates the heavy cedar cover along the barrier beach fronting East Lake. This can be good for finches, but Sandbanks proper is more interesting. To reach it turn off County Road 18 on to County Road 12 just before the Outlet Beach Park area. This road leads along the shore (lake viewing) 3 km to a stop street, with the park gate immediately opposite. Sandbanks has coniferous plantations, magnificent sand dunes, a long sandy beach, and many small sedge-margined pools backing the first line of dunes and along the entry road. These can be excellent for shorebirds.

From the park gate you can turn left to continue on County Road 12, which leads back to Highway 33.

(149) **Plantagenet** – There are sewage lagoons here. The town is south of Highway 17. Turn right on County Road 9, drive south 0.7 km to Pitch Off Road, on the left just before the bridge over the river. Turn and drive 0.4 km. The lagoons are on the left.

The South Nation River here has a reputation for flooding the countryside in spring – conditions that elsewhere concentrate waterfowl and shorebirds. The situation at Plantagenet still needs investigation.

(150) **Port Hope** – The east side of the harbour is accessible by driving south on Mill Street as Highway 2 turns east from the river at the east end of town. Turn west at this intersection instead, cross the river, and drive ahead to John Street, and then turn south there to drive down to the west side of the harbour. There are parking areas at the very end of King Street (past the nuclear plant) and a beach to the west.

Willow Beach is accessible from Highway 401 Exit 456 (the Wesleyville Road). Drive some 3 km south to the T-intersection, turn left, and drive another 1 km to a small gravel road running to the lake. Turn south; ½ km down is an abandoned railroad track which can be followed east to a rich area of woods and marsh. The area is private property but naturalists are welcomed, and it is also possible to go to the end of the road to view the lake.

(151) Rockland – Rockland lies off Highway 17 south of the highway. The sewage lagoon is on the north side of the highway roughly half-way between the main business exit to town and the Laurier Street exit to the east.

(152) St Isidore de Prescott – The sewage lagoons here are down a farm lane off County Road 3 at the north end of town. Take County Road 3 west (marked to Embrun), and drive 1.3 km to a paved road on the right, which becomes a farm lane after ½ km. The lagoons are to the northwest.

(153) Stirling – Stirling is at the junction of Highways 14 and 33. For the sewage lagoons, drive to the end of 33 in town, and just before the junction of Highway 14 turn right (south) by the bank on to Henry Street. Drive 1.2 km and turn right into the lagoon drive.

South of Stirling off Highway 33 – itself with scenic views of the Trent River and Canal – Northumberland County Roads 5 and 28 run west from Frankford to Highway 30. To their north is the extensive area of swamp and marsh south of the Percy Reach section of the Trent. A network of backroads leading to this area and crossing it invite exploration by a birder with the appropriate topographic maps.

(154) Tweed – To reach the sewage lagoons go 0.3 km north of the river bridge at the north end of town. Turn right on Hastings County Road 9 (or 39 – both signs appear!). Drive 1.6 km and turn south on a narrow dirt road. The lagoons are beside and visible from this road, 0.8 km along on the right.

(155) Vankleek Hill – To reach the sewage lagoon here, turn east from Highway 34 on to Main Street (County Road 10), drive 1.1 km, crossing the railroad, and turn right on a gravel road. The lagoon is 1.3 km along on the left.

(156) Westport – A couple of areas are of interest in Westport, quite apart from the village itself (which must rate as one of Ontario's most beautiful) and the marshy areas surrounding it. The sewage lagoons are on the west of Highway 42 down a farm lane 0.2 km south of the intersection of the highway and County Road 10.

By turning on to this county road one can drive up the hill at the northeast side of town and turn into the *Foley Mountain Conservation Area* on the right at the top. There are excellent mixed woodlands here including tall red cedars, and the ridge forms a flyline for migrant landbirds. Continuing on towards Perth, County Road 10 runs through some farming country. Watch the wires for Eastern Bluebirds.

South of town County Road 10 runs through typical Rideau Lakes countryside en route to Kingston (qv).

(157) Winchester – For Winchester sewage lagoons, follow County Road 3 (Main Street) as it runs east through town, and continue on it as it turns north (now Ottawa Street). The lagoons are down a long dirt road 2.2 km farther on from this point.

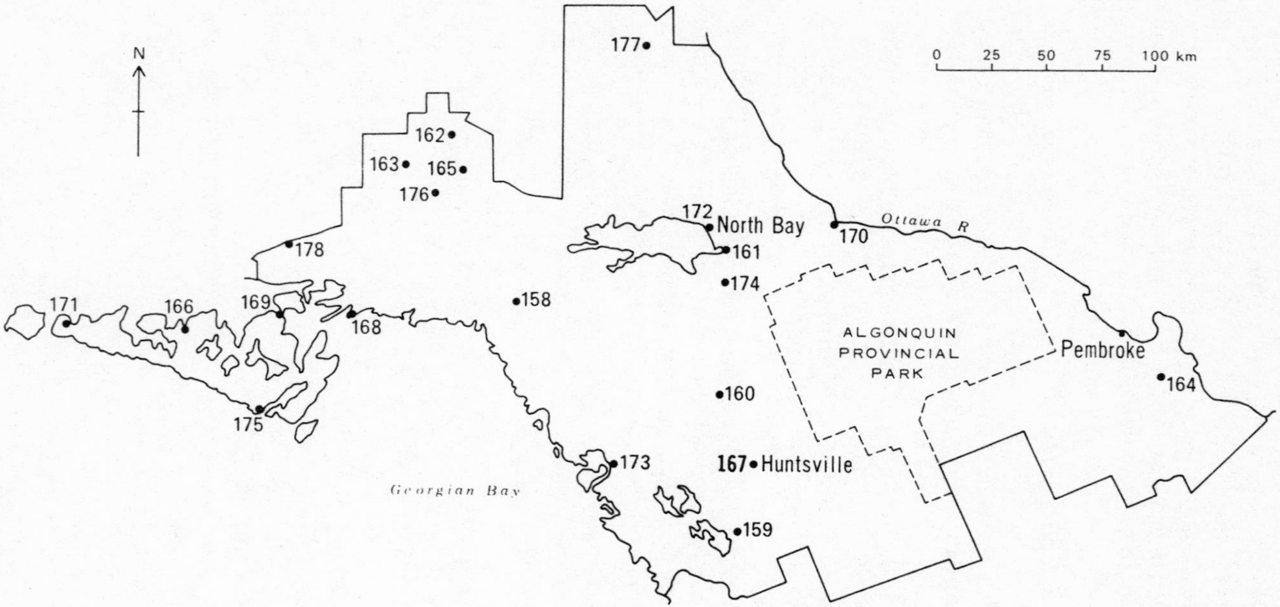

MAP 10 Central Ontario

Pembroke

•164

Ottawa R.

ALGONQUIN
PROVINCIAL
PARK

170

North Bay

172
161•
•174

160•

167•Huntsville

•159

177•

173•

158•

Georgian Bay

162•
165•
163•
176•

168•

178•

169•

175•

166•

171•

N

0 25 50 75 100 km

6 / Central Ontario

We are arbitrarily defining central Ontario as Renfrew County and the districts of Haliburton, Muskoka, Parry Sound, Nipissing, and Manitoulin, together with the regional municipality of Sudbury and those parts of Sudbury District that lie south of Highway 17.

This part of the province is within relatively easy reach of the large population centres of the south, and much of it is 'cottage country,' providing summer week-end retreats for these centres. In many ways it is transitional between north and south. Many birds of the northern forest reach their southern limits in this region, and southern species become rare north of here.

Most of the region is forested Pre-Cambrian Shield country, but there are areas of farmland along the Ottawa River, north of Sudbury, and on the limestones of Manitoulin Island as well as in isolated pockets elsewhere, particularly along Highway 11 south of North Bay.

The abundance of water in the region is not paralleled by an abundance of waterbirds, as the Shield lakes are relatively infertile and in many places around Sudbury dead. There is little to attract either shorebirds or open country species. By contrast, the forests, particularly of the Algonquin Highlands between Highways 11 and 17, are diverse, with some southern hardwoods mixing with spruces and other boreal species. White Pine, Eastern Hemlock, and Balsam Fir are major constituents of the forest, and north of North Bay the Temagami forests become heavily dominated by White Pine. Bird life is equally varied and rich. It is probably one of the best areas in Canada for breeding thrushes and warblers, and there is a strong northern component to the bird life as well. Many southern species reach their northern limits through the region, and are much scarcer – or become scarcer – than in areas farther south.

The forests in the immediate area of Sudbury and Falconbridge are impoverished as a result of pollution from heavy metal deposits. Scrub birch and aspen, with large expanses of bare rock, make the area unappealing to the eye and as a birding locale. There are, however, some noteworthy locations (see Sudbury, Garson).

Manitoulin Island is in marked contrast to the Shield areas. It resembles the northern parts of the Bruce Peninsula, and like it is a tilted limestone plateau with shelving beaches on the south, much marginal farmland, poor drainage, and thin soils.

In this region the birder encounters a problem which intensifies farther north. Good habitat abounds, and the selection of good birding locations is more a matter of watching for changes in the forest composition than of following directions in a book. At the same time, areas that are relatively commonplace in southern Ontario – marshes and open country – are often scarce and attract rarities.

The following species breed in this region but are not found farther south, except occasionally or in limited areas:

Merlin	Philadelphia Vireo
Spruce Grouse*	Tennessee Warbler
Black-backed Three-toed	Cape May Warbler
Woodpecker*	Bay-breasted Warbler
Yellow-bellied Flycatcher	Wilson's Warbler
Olive-sided Flycatcher	Rusty Blackbird
Gray Jay*	Evening Grosbeak
Common Raven*	White-winged Crossbill
Boreal Chickadee*	(erratic)
Solitary Vireo	Lincoln's Sparrow

Some of these birds are relatively rare even in this region itself, particularly in the south. Four – the grosbeak and the first three warblers listed – tend to increase in numbers during periods when the larvae of the Spruce Budworm moth become exceptionally abundant. In recent years budworm infestations have occurred widely and these birds have become quite common. In less favourable times – for the species, not the forests – their ranges appear to contract northwards.

Species at or close to the northern limits of their normal breeding ranges in this region are:

Turkey Vulture	Pine Warbler
Northern Parula Warbler	Red Crossbill (erratic)

The area is not noted for migrant concentrations, although Mississaugi Light at the west end of Manitoulin Island is important. Movements of loons and raptors are noteworthy here as well as landbirds, and in spring large flights of White-winged Scoters, Oldsquaws, and Whimbrel pass along the south shore. The province's largest recent concentrations of Red-necked Grebes have also been recorded off the island, but the locality is not readily accessible.

Algonquin Provincial Park is noted as one of the best places for persons living farther south to see winter finches in season. The region as a whole, however, is above all noteworthy for the wealth of woodland breeding birds. This is the place to go not only to hear most of the thrushes and wood warblers on their nesting grounds, but also to become familiar with such species as Barred Owls, which are rare and local farther south.

(158) Bigwood – Some 15 km south of this small community on Highway 69 is *Gundy Lake Provincial Park*, an excellent Shield park which contains a Great Blue heronry. Saw-whet Owl, Whip-poor-will, Boreal Chickadee, Warbling Vireo, and Golden-winged Warblers have been recorded.

The forests both north and south of Bigwood are excellent for characteristic coniferous forest species such as three-toed woodpeckers and warblers.

(159) Bracebridge – The extensive and productive sewage lagoon complex here can be reached from Highway 11 by exiting on the interchange south of town (marked Highway 118). This is Muskoka District Road 4: turn towards Bracebridge and drive 4.7 km to Beaumont Drive (Muskoka Road 16) on the left, which follows the river. Turn and drive 0.8 km to James W. Kerr Park also on the left. Drive in and walk up the hill at the back to reach the lagoons. From Bracebridge itself drive south through town to the river bridge and then turn right on to Beaumont Drive as above. The lagoon area is excellent for landbirds in migration as well as duck and shorebirds.

(160) Burk's Falls – The lagoons here are situated east of town. Exit east from Highway 11 at the Highway 520 junction, and drive through town down towards the bridge over the river. Yonge Street is the first street running east, south (0.2 km) of the bridge. Turn east and drive 1.1 km to a point where the road turns south at the railroad tracks. Turn north on an old dirt road beside the tracks, and go 0.4 km. The lagoons are across the tracks from this point.

South of town 13 km Highway 518 runs northeast to Kearney and Sand Lake. This road passes through marsh and spruce swamp habitats, as well as cleared land. It has yielded an excellent mix of old field and forestbirds.

Sundridge, some 18 km north of Burk's Falls on Highway 11, also has a sewage lagoon. Farther north again, 11 km at South River, is the road to Mikisew Provincial Park. Breeding birds seen here include Philadelphia Vireo and Yellow-rumped Warbler.

(161) Callander – This town is on a bay at the eastern end of Lake Nipissing. A road along the shore allows easy views of the lake. There are three exits to Callander from Highway 11, and southern one providing best access to this road. Opposite the 'Nipissing District' sign 0.3 km past the northernmost exit to town is a rough dirt road running west. This crosses some old fields to the sewage lagoons, 1 km from the highway. The whole area can be quite rewarding.

(162) Capreol – To reach the sewage lagoon in this, the northernmost community in the Sudbury Regional Municipality, continue on from the end of Regional Road 84 (Dennie Street) to the flashing light at Hanna Avenue. Turn left and go 0.3 km, following the street as it curves right (now as Young Street) and crosses the tracks. Turn left and bear immediately left again on a gravel road. Drive 0.7 km and cross a bridge to the right; the lagoon is straight ahead.

(163) **Chelmsford** – The sewage lagoons here have been consistently productive. To reach them from Highway 144 northbound, turn right at the stoplight on to Regional Road 14 (Errington Street). Continue 1.6 km to a four-way stop at Main Street. Turn left, cross the bridge, and turn right (0.3 km) on Montpellier Street. This road turns (0.4 km) to cross the railway, and the lagoons are on the left 0.6 km farther on.

(164) **Cobden** – At Cobden Highway 17 parallels the west shoreline of Muskrat Lake, and some 7½ km north of town the road crosses the Snake River and the wetlands associated with it. The latter also parallel the road to the west. A westbound sideroad about ½ km south of the river bridge leads to this area: turn left at the T-intersection.

Some 25 km northwest of Cobden is Pembroke. There is access to the *Sand Lake Gate* of *Algonquin Provincial Park* from a point 3.2 km farther northwest of this town on Highway 17. Follow a road (paved for a few kilometres and then gravelled) west for 32 km to the Sand Lake Gate (permits available there) on the eastern boundary of Algonquin Park. Proceed into the park on Sand Lake Road through young forests of birch and poplar, and extensive pine stands (both red and white) – which are dramatically different from Algonquin's west-side hardwoods. Common birds of the pine forest include Olive-sided Flycatcher, Pine Warbler, and Dark-eyed Junco.

About 10.5 km in from the Sand Lake Gate is the Barron Canyon Trail. This trail (about 1½ km long) leads to and along the edge of the spectacular Barron River Canyon (with 100-metre vertical granite walls), before looping back to the parking lot. Common birds in the gorge include Yellow-bellied Flycatcher, Hermit Thrush, Northern Waterthrush, and Dark-eyed Junco (all of which should be heard from the top). Close to the water's edge (far below), Barn Swallows and Eastern Phoebes build their nests on the vertical rock walls – a contrast to their usual sites on man-made structures.

Another 8.5 km along Sand Lake Road brings you to the turnoff (left) to Achray on Grand Lake. Here there is a campground on the lake, with a good beach.

Upon returning to Sand Lake Road, there is a choice of returning to Pembroke (turn right), or taking a left turn and driving some 35 km farther on to Lake Traverse. An extensive area near Lake Traverse was clear-cut to salvage the jack pine forest killed by budworm in the past, a section which may produce American Kestrels, Eastern Bluebirds, Rufous-sided Towhees, and Field Sparrows. Watch along the road and in adjacent ponds for Wood Turtles and Blanding's Turtles, both of which are 'specialties' of Algonquin Park's 'east side.' Typical birds along the road in summer (varying with the particular year) include Evening Grosbeak, Purple Finch, Pine Siskin, and Red Crossbill. Stops along the way may yield Solitary and Warbling Vireos and the usual variety of Algonquin warbler species.

(165) **Garson** – The sewage lagoons here have yielded some of the most interesting waterfowl records in the Sudbury region. They are 1.5 km west of Regional Road 86 on O'Neil Street West, which is ½ km south of the light at Margaret Street. Cross the tracks and turn right immediately on Heino Street. The lagoon gate is 0.2 km along on the right. If coming from Sudbury, a faster route is to drive 5 km from the intersection of Highways 17 and 84 in town to Donnelly Street (signposted as the Kirkwood Mine Road). Turn left and proceed to O'Neil, turning *right* there and left on Heino, just before crossing the tracks.

(166) **Gore Bay** – This town is the administrative centre for Manitoulin Island, and to reach it you will pass through some typical Manitoulin countryside. The entire island is a well-known place for birds, but like the Bruce Peninsula – which it resembles – it is difficult to pinpoint specific localities. The poor pastures are excellent for Upland Sandpipers – possibly one of the largest populations of this species in Ontario occurs on the island – and like the Bruce used to be good for Eastern Bluebirds and Loggerhead Shrikes. Common Ravens are significantly more common than on the Bruce, and Turkey Vultures less so.

Highway 540, running across the north of the island and now paved for all but its last 9 km or so, links some of the best birding areas: Mississagi Light near Meldrum Bay to the west, the Gore Bay area, and Little Current on the east.

At Gore Bay, the sewage lagoons are on the west side of the western leg of Highway 540B, which loops into town and out again, and 1.4 km from the main highway.

Continuing west on 540 from this intersection, at 5.4 km the main highway turns left and the road to the airport continues straight ahead. After some 4 km this road crosses a causeway to Barrie Island, where there is wetland associated with the waterfront. American Bittern, duck, snipe, and other waterfowl occur. Both the airport and the fields of Barrie Island have at different time been dancing grounds for a flock of Sharp-tailed Grouse. They have not been reported recently, but my guess is that they are still in the general area and a systematic search might find them. This flock was once a mixed population of Sharp-taileds and Greater Prairie Chicken. This was the only occurrence of the latter in Ontario in recent years, but none has been seen since 1969 and the birds are apparently now Sharp-taileds only.

Return from here to the main highway and turn right to drive south 8.3 km, crossing the causeway between Wolsey Lake and Bayfield Sound. At the south end of this is Indian Point, site of a highway picnic area. It does not look like a migration concentration point, but it can be a good one. When you have birded this area and the adjoining waters, continue on 540 to Mississagi Light or return to Little Current.

(167) **HUNTSVILLE** – On Highway 11 driving north from town and shortly after the Highway 60 junction is *Arrowhead Provincial Park*, with an interesting nature trail along the river.

Huntsville is best known, however, as the nearest large community to the *Algonquin Provincial Park* Highway 60 corridor.

Algonquin (entry fee) is both the oldest provincial park and, with an area of over 7600 square kilometres, one of the biggest. Highway 60 between Dwight and Whitney crosses the southwest corner of the park, and is the main public road through it. The interior is accessible by canoe, and there are over 1600 km of canoe routes. Specific routes will not be identified here because to my knowledge none offers significantly different birding to that available elsewhere in the region; however, the canoe routes and hiking trails are undoubtedly the best way to see the park.

Algonquin occupies an area of rolling highlands, and the forest – and other flora and fauna – presents a mix of southern and northern species. Although this kind of mix is typical of the region generally, Algonquin has a particularly rich mixture, and much of the variety is accessible in the relatively short distance along Highway 60. There is a good museum with a skilled and knowledgeable interpretive staff which can be of great help to the visitor in giving directions regarding specific species. There are several fine nature trails as well as a couple of major hiking trails, all accessible along the highway.

Algonquin Park is noted for its wildlife-viewing opportunities, for both mammals and birds. In spring and early summer, Black Bears, Moose, Beaver, and White-tailed Deer are frequently seen at close range. The park has become famous as a place to hear Timber Wolves in late summer and early autumn.

Birders are primarily drawn to Algonquin for its northern specialties, and warblers on their breeding grounds. Boreal forest species such as Olive-sided Flycatcher, Gray Jay, Common Raven, and Boreal Chickadee occur commonly along Highway 60 in the park. In addition, careful searching in favoured locations can yield Spruce Grouse, Black-backed Three-toed Woodpecker, Yellow-bellied Flycatcher, Rusty Blackbird, and Lincoln's Sparrow. Remember, however, that Algonquin's continuous forest cover can make these birds very difficult to find.

Common Loons nest on most of the larger lakes, but ducks are scarce. The commonly observed raptor along Highway 60 is the Broad-winged Hawk (frequently perched along the utility lines). Ospreys are occasionally noted over lakes near the road, and one should listen at night for Barred and Saw-whet Owls, both of which are common.

Outside the breeding season, the park is worth a visit in late autumn through early spring to see winter finches and resident species. Both eagles occur rarely during this period as well, feeding on wolf-killed deer.

There is good birding along the 43 km of Highway 60 between the Huntsville turn-off (Muskoka Road 3) and the park gate. The fields in this stretch represent a habitat not available to any extent in the park itself, and can yield field species including (occasionally) Grasshopper Sparrow. Some sideroads can be most interesting, particularly the network accessible along Canal Road (Muskoka Road 23) on the south, 4 km from Muskoka Road 3; and Limberlost Road on the north 5.9 km farther on (Muskoka Road 8, to Sinclair Township). These are narrow, winding roads, often gravelled, going through good warbler country. Drive slowly, parking and walking along the roads from time to time.

In Algonquin itself much birding can also be done from the highway, but it is busy and if you plan to do this get out at dawn ahead of the traffic. Stop regularly, selecting variations in the habitat along the road, and drive with the windows open. Most of your 'watching' will be done by ear! In addition to the marked nature trails, there are many sideroads, some disused, and old trails along the road that can be explored on foot. It is emphasized again that naturalists at the museum can provide detailed information on particular species at the time of your visit. Be sure to stop in.

Some specific locations of interest follow, but no attempt has been made to be exhaustive. The distances given are from the West Gate: the distances along the highway within the park are marked in this manner also.

0 km	The West Gate
3 km	The Oxtongue River Picnic Grounds and start of the Western Uplands Hiking Trail. The heavy spruce to the east used to be good for Spruce Grouse; it is years since I have found the birds there, but it may be worth checking. Gray Jay and Boreal Chickadee are frequent.
7.2 km	The Whiskey Rapids Nature Trail. This is an excellent nature trail, and in my experience one of the more productive spots for Boreal Chickadees.
16.7 km	The Hardwood Hill Picnic Grounds. Black-throated Blue Warbler and other deciduous woodland species occur here.
20.1 km	The Park Museum and Interpretive Centre
22.3 km	An abandoned railroad bed here offers a good walk in either direction.
30.6 km	The road to the airfield. A very productive spot for fieldbirds and rarities (an island of open country); also waterbirds on Lake of Two Rivers.
35.6 km	The Trailer Dump Station. Golden-winged Warblers have occurred in the shrubbery here.
42.5 km	The Spruce Boardwalk Trail. Olive-sided Flycatchers are regular, and there is a good chance of spotting Spruce Grouse in the bog.

45.2 km   The Beaver Pond Trail. A varied and productive nature trail through wetlands and coniferous habitats.

46.3 km   The Opeongo Lake Road. At the south end of Opeongo Lake are some of the best marshy areas accessible from the highway.

53.0 km   There is a gravel pit here on the north side, and a small bog adjacent to it. Spruce Grouse are possible.

55.8 km   The East Gate

The Algonquin Park Museum has produced a series of priced publications on the park's flora and fauna. Birders would be particularly interested in the booklet on birds (price: $1.00), which includes an annotated list with arrival and departure dates. In addition, illustrated trail guide booklets (each with a different natural or human history theme) are available for each of nine trails along Highway 60.

General information and a publication price list are available from: Ministry of Natural Resources, Box 219, Whitney, Ontario, K0J 2M0. Current bird-finding information can always be obtained at the Park Museum (km 20), or by phone ([705] 633-5592).

For the eastern side of Algonquin see the section under Cobden.

There are several campgrounds in Algonquin and three commercial lodges that take guests. Outside the park there are motels at Oxtongue Lake, Huntsville, and Whitney.

(168) Killarney – This community is 67 km from Highway 17, and *Killarney Provincial Park* is situated astride Highway 67 just northeast of it. This is a large wilderness park, but unlike for Quetico and Algonquin, its birding potential is little known. It has yielded records of species as diverse as Connecticut Warbler and Warbling Vireo in summer. Once again it is a canoeist's park, and offers some of Ontario's most beautiful scenery.

(169) Little Current – This is the first town encountered driving on to Manitoulin Island from the north, on Highway 6. Low Island can be interesting at times during migration, particularly in regard to open country species. Southbound, turn right (north) at the intersection of Highways 6 and 540. This road leads down to the business section. Bear left at the bottom of the hill, and follow the main street on west up the hill (Robinson Street) 0.8 km to Hayward Street on the left. On the right is a gravel road which leads down to the town park on Low Island.

The sewage lagoons are off 540 west of town. Go west 0.5 km past the highway maintenance yard, which is just before the corner at the end of town. The lagoons are 0.6 km down a track on the left. Highway 540 westbound leads to other good birding locations (see Gore Bay and Meldrum Bay).

(170) Mattawa – For the sewage lagoons here, turn off Highway 17 westbound just the other side of the river bridge on to the road that follows the west bank of the river. The lagoons are between it and the sideroad. *Samuel de Champlain Provincial Park* west of here has good forest land typical of the area.

(171) Meldrum Bay – At the end of Highway 540 on Manitoulin Island just outside this community is a small paved road (at least it starts out paved) running some 10 km westwards to *Mississagi Light*. The lighthouse here has a campground and picnic area on the limestone pavement, all set in open cedar woodlands. This is a migrant trap of note, as birds following the south shore of the island westwards end up here, and it is also a good spot for watching waterbird movements. Loons both fly south down the straits and concentrate here, and Red-necked Grebes gather nearby. Significant hawk flights can develop.

(172) North Bay – The shoreline road here provides views of the east end of Lake Nipissing. Frank's Bay, at the north end of town, also has good landbird habitat adjacent to it.

(173) Parry Sound – This town has a number of interesting areas nearby. Mill Lake, on both sides of Highway 69 as it by-passes town, can be productive of waterfowl in winter, but Powerhouse Falls on the Seguin River, accessible via River Street northbound off the south exit of 69B, is even better. The 69B south entry to town also passes the extensive coniferous plantations on Tower Hill, which are good for winter landbirds. The feeders and mountain ash trees on Belvedere Hill (off Waubeek Street) attract Bohemian Waxwings and landbird stragglers at this time, and the dump off McDougall Road gulls and ravens.

At *Otter Lake* off Highway 69 some 10–12 km south of town there is a bog where Olive-sided Flycatcher and Blackburnian and Palm Warblers have occurred in summer. Follow the Bradshaw Marina sign. Nearby, at *Oastler Lake Provincial Park*, Prairie Warblers have been recorded.

Both Highways 518 and 124, running northeast from Parry Sound, are good birding roads, and the sideroads off both highways can be very productive. I have no specific locations to suggest, but the areas around Waubamik, Dunchurch, and Ahmic Lake on Highway 124, and around Orrville on 518, have been reported as excellent.

The wild coastline south of Parry Sound is the site of probably the largest remaining concentration of Prairie Warblers in Canada. The birds frequent open rocky areas with white pine, oak, and juniper cover, where they are locally abundant. At present there is no ready road access to this area, but by boat or canoe the birds occur around Spider Bay, Spider and Cowper lakes, and the west end of Conger Lake, along the east shore of Blackstone Harbour, and along the shorelines of Moon Island. Farther south again they occur on some of the islands of Georgian Bay Islands National Park, along the Gibson River near its outlet to Go Home Lake, and along Twelve Mile Bay, which is accessible via District Road 12 off Highway 69. My guess is that they occur elsewhere all along this coastline as well.

Killbear Provincial Park, northwest of Parry Sound, is on a peninsula which looks as though it should be good for migrants. The forest is hemlock and maple, and Barred Owl, Whip-poor-will, and Red Crossbill have occurred. Prairie Warblers should be looked for in season.

(174) Powassan – There is a sewage lagoon here that can be viewed from a distance by turning west from Highway 11 on Highway 534, and driving 0.4 km. Park just past a barn. The lagoon is across the fields to the north and can be covered with a 'scope.

(175) South Baymouth – If you take the ferry from Tobermory to Manitoulin Island and points north you will arrive here. It is a good place for migrant concentrations at times, when the trees and shrubs around the cottages and motels near the ferry docks can be alive with birds. A short distance up Highway 6 (about 1 km) is a park area on the west which can be productive.

Manitoulin's south shore is a good place to see large flights of Oldsquaws, White-winged Scoter, and Whimbrel in May, and waterbirds generally; there are few easily accessible locations, but South Baymouth itself gives some views, and *Providence Bay* farther west also has a good sand beach. (see Gore Bay, Little Current, and Meldrum Bay for other locales on this island.)

The Tobermory–Little Current ferry (the *Chi-Cheemaun*) is a large car ferry that crosses four times daily from mid-June to the beginning of September; and outside those times twice daily (except Fridays) from late April to mid-October. The crossing takes 1¾ hours, and reservations and fee schedules are available from Owen Sound Transportation Company, Box 336, Owen Sound, Ontario, N4K 5P5. I have never heard of anyone seeing anything very noteworthy from the *Chi-Cheemaun*; all we have seen are gulls and hummingbirds!

(176) Sudbury – This city is unlikely to make anyone's list of the bird spots one most wants to visit, but *Kelley Lake*, just south of Highway 17, can be most productive. An excellent assortment of shorebirds and duck occur on migration, and Wilson's Phalaropes are among the species recorded in summer.

The east end is the most productive, and it is easiest to approach the lake from the south, along Southview Drive. From the city drive west on Highway 17 to Kelley Lake Road and turn south, or south on Regent Street to Bouchard Street and turn west. Both these streets lead to Southview, and you then drive west, with lake viewing all along the road on your right. This road finally enters the South-west By-pass, linking Highways 69 northbound and 17 westbound, and the by-pass itself runs along the shoreline of the west end of the Lake.

The traveller using the by-pass should watch for Southview Drive on the east – it is some 4 km northwest of the lights at Long Lake Road.

There are small sewage lagoons at three communities east of Sudbury: *Verner* and *Warren* on Highway 17, and *St Charles* on Highway 535.

(177) Temagami – The small sewage lagoon can be reached by turning east at the Water Tower on to O'Connor Drive. Follow this road 0.7 km to the end of the pavement, turn right, and drive a further 0.2 km, where the lagoons are straight ahead at a bend in the road.

(178) Webbwood – The sewage lagoon here is along a gravel road at the west end of town. Turn north, drive some 1½ km, and turn left to the lagoon.

7 / Northern Ontario

Northern Ontario as treated here is all of Ontario north and west of the districts of Nipissing and Manitoulin, and the south end of the District of Sudbury. It includes the area of Sudbury north of the Regional Municipality and Highway 17. However, the extreme western part of the area – the District of Rainy River west of Highway 812 – is dealt with in the next chapter.

This enormous region represents unusual difficulties to the compiler of a finding guide. Roads are few and population centres are scattered. Forests are less diverse than those farther south and some habitats, mainly open country and marsh communities, are scarce or absent over huge areas. Bird life is less varied but can be rich in numbers, and the typical forest habitats and associated birds are widespread even along major highways. Hence many species that might be novel to a travelling birder in summer are easy to find, and other species are either absent or elusive everywhere.

There is no information on the bird life of much of northern Ontario, and relatively little detailed information even on the more settled regions. It is customary to hypothesize that it is pretty much the same as that in similar areas which have been covered.

The Trans-Canada Highway routes are those used most commonly by people travelling across the north, and for many miles they are the only through roads. If one considers Highway 71 running along the east of Lake of the Woods as a linking road between Highways 11 and 17, these highways form two huge

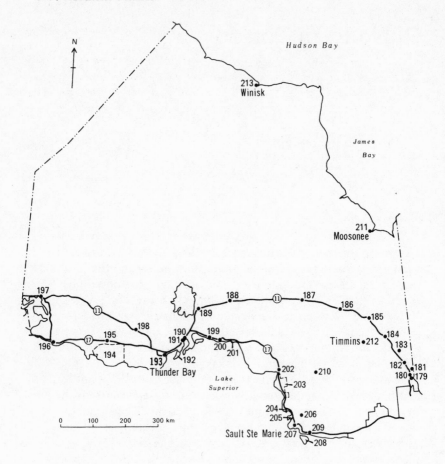

MAP 11 Northern Ontario

loops, one west of Thunder Bay and the second between Nipigon and North Bay. Because so many birders in the north are en route to a specific destination and will be travelling these roads, the sequence of the first part of this account will follow Highway 11 westwards and Highway 17 back, although we hope the directions to specific locations are adequate for an approach from either direction.

The forests associated with the more southern parts of the settled north are still the mixed hardwoods described in earlier chapters. The change to boreal forest is most easily seen when driving through Lake Superior Provincial Park, where the maples in the south are gradually replaced by birch and spruce to the north end. The boreal forest varies in its composition, and hence in its bird life. Along the north shore of Lake Superior it is still quite varied, but in the Clay Belt itself south and west of Cochrane stands of black spruce can dominate the scene for miles. Farther west, jack pine becomes important both in the mixed forests between Thunder Bay and Fort Frances and through much of the boreal forests between Hearst and Dryden.

Significant areas of agriculture displace the unrelieved forest cover in the two Clay Belts, north and east of Sault Ste Marie, and again around Thunder Bay and Dryden.

Several species of birds have ranges that include the settled areas of northern Ontario but rarely occur farther south in the breeding season. These are:

Horned Grebe
Sharp-tailed Grouse*
Sandhill Crane
Solitary Sandpiper
Bonaparte's Gull
Hawk Owl*
Great Gray Owl*

Boreal Owl*
Northern Three-toed
  Woodpecker*
Orange-crowned Warbler
Palm Warbler
Pine Grosbeak

Most of the above are difficult to find even in the north. Golden Eagles are very rare breeders and breed well north of any roads.

As in the Shield areas of central Ontario, beaver dams can create open wetland conditions that are otherwise absent, and towns and communities – though at times not very pretty – often provide the only open country for miles, and so are worth checking for field and edge species. In southern Ontario one finds more birds along the network of gravel roads than along the highways, and similarly here the secondary roads – if any exist – can fill a similar role. The canoeing birder can find much excellent country, particularly in Quetico and Lake Superior provincial parks, or (for real challenge) the wild rivers to the north.

The bulk of northern Ontario is inaccessible even by road. Only a couple of roads and one railway go north of 51°N, and none reaches the north coast. Hence the Hudson Bay lowlands and the sea coast require special arrangements for visits. The second part of this account will deal with both these areas (see Moosonee and Winisk) and with some of the communities and roads not associated with the Highway 11–17 loops.

In *A Naturalist's Guide to Ontario*, W.K.W. Baldwin characterizes the Hudson Bay lowlands as 'a vast peatland wilderness,' and points out that this huge area south of the coast comprises one-quarter of the land surface of the province. Canoe trips into this region are becoming more common but are really outside the scope of this book since their prime objectives are unlikely to be birding. The Moose via the Missinaibi, Mattagami, or Abitibi rivers, and the Albany and the Winisk, are the rivers that seem to be most popular with canoeists at present. To get a taste of this flat, desolate country by rail, see Moosonee.

North again, mainly around Cape Henrietta Maria, is a belt of tundra along the Hudson Bay coast itself. A large number of species is present in summer along the coast or on the adjacent lowlands that occur nowhere else in Ontario at that time except as non-breeding stragglers from migration. These are:

Arctic Loon	Rough-legged Hawk
Red-throated Loon	Willow Ptarmigan
Snow Goose	Semipalmated Plover
Greater Scaup	American Golden Plover
Bufflehead	Whimbrel
Oldsquaw	Greater Yellowlegs
Common Eider	Lesser Yellowlegs
King Eider	Pectoral Sandpiper
White-winged Scoter	Least Sandpiper
Surf Scoter	Dunlin
Black Scoter	Semipalmated Sandpiper

Stilt Sandpiper

Northern Phalarope

Parasitic Jaeger

Black Guillemot

Gray-cheeked Thrush

Water Pipit

Blackpoll Warbler

Common Redpoll

Tree Sparrow

White-crowned Sparrow

Fox Sparrow

Lapland Longspur

Smith's Longspur

A number of other tundra and arctic species, such as Sabine's Gull, Snowy Owl, and Snow Bunting, have been seen here in summer as well, but probably as non-breeders. Note that, of the above list, the Common Eider, Willow Ptarmigan, Black Guillemot, and Smith's Longspur can be seen in Ontario only in this area.

Northern Ontario's potential for migration watching has never been fully explored, but opportunities abound. The southern tip of the Sibley Peninsula has produced, among other rarities, Scott's Oriole and Fork-tailed Flycatcher. Heavy passage occurs along the northern Lake Superior shoreline, where enormous counts of Rough-legged Hawks and winter finches have been reported, and areas north and east of Sault Ste Marie have been identified as good for migrants at various times. There seems to be little indication that Lake Superior plays a major role in waterbird movements.

The north coast, particularly the south end of James Bay, presents a wholly different dimension. It is already recognized as one of North America's major fall staging grounds for shorebirds and waterfowl, and as a southern pocket of sea it should concentrate seabird migrants as well. The jaegers, Sabine's Gulls, and kittiwakes that appear at the south end of Lake Huron in late autumn come from somewhere and it is likely that they come from here. Similarly the movement of Arctic Terns and some other species up the Ottawa River in spring may end at James Bay. But how these species get from south to north or vice versa – if in fact that is what occurs – remains to be established.

Northern winters are long – a month or more longer than in the south, with freeze-up in November and little amelioration until April – so most birds retreat from the region in that season. Grouse, ravens, Gray Jays, woodpeckers, and finches remain with the odd goldeneye and merganser on open water. Noteworthy birds at this time include the owls, which start nesting activities early and whose calls build to a peak in March and April. Merlins and Sharp-tailed Grouse can be more conspicuous than usual at this time.

THE HIGHWAY 11–17 LOOPS

Highway 11 north of North Bay runs through white pine forests in the Marten River area, which are noteworthy for Hermit Thrushes in June. Marten River and Finlayson Point are pleasant provincial parks in the area. Refer to Chapter 6 for directions to the lagoon at Temagami.

North of Latchford the highway enters the mixed landscape of the Little Clay Belt, with farmland interspersed by mixed woodland. In the southern part of this area there are sewage lagoons at North Cobalt, New Liskeard, and Earlton.

(179) **North Cobalt** is east of the main highway. The small lagoon is not worth a special detour unless you are travelling on Highway 11B anyway. Follow it around to the junction of Highway 567 in town. Turn southeast onto 567 and proceed 1.6 km to Groom Drive on the right. Turn and drive 0.3 km; the lagoon is on the left.

For the (180) **New Liskeard** lagoon, continue north on Highway 11 to the junction of Highway 65. Just past this intersection (0.1 km) on the west is a gravel road, Dymond Road 3, which runs 0.6 km to dead-end at the lagoon.

Highway 65 itself runs northeast to the Quebec border. Some 23 km from its junction with Highway 11 is (181) **Judge**, at the Blanche River crossing. In mid-April Canada Geese congregate in the wet fields south of here on both sides of the river, followed later in April by ducks.

The north end of Lake Temagami is noted for Brant in early June: I have no specific viewing areas to suggest, but the waterfront at Haileybury and New Liskeard gives excellent views of Wabi Bay, and farther north there are sideroads east off Highway 65 on the way to Judge.

Continuing north on Highway 11, the town of *Earlton* is just west of the highway, but the sewage lagoon is rather hard to get at. Follow the main street (10 Avenue N) to 10 Street West. Turn west and drive about 1 km to a small cemetery on the north. The lagoon is at the back of this and to the west.

South of Englehart, a drive in to *Skeleton and Clear Lakes* off Highway 569 can be productive in summer. From Highway 11 drive 10 km east on Highway 569 to the point where it turns south. Turn north on a good gravel road, following it around (it bears generally north and east) to a T-intersection at the top of a rise (5 km) where the road turns right. Turn left and drive 2.2 km to Clear Lake, then continue 2.1 km to Clear and Skeleton Lake access points.

On this route the highway crosses typical clay belt farmland, and the gravel roads run through excellent mixed woodland habitats. Ospreys and Common Loons occur on the lakes and Common Ravens nest on the cliffs at Skeleton Lake. Watch for red foxes in the farm areas: they are common on the Little Clay Belt.

Back on the main highway again, the (182) **Englehart** lagoons are probably the most productive ones in this region. They can be reached by turning east on First Street at the south end of town. Drive 1.1 km, crossing the tracks, to Lagoon Road. Turn left and drive 0.8 km to park at a point alongside the railroad and by two storage tanks. A track leading away from the railroad leads to the lagoons. The woodlands surrounding them yield sparrows and warblers – the shrubby areas have Lincoln's Sparrow – and the lagoons themselves waterbirds.

Also at Englehart is the excellent *Kap-Kig-Iwan Provincial Park*. It follows the deep river valley and has a variety of habitats, some quite southern in character. Some southern birds, such as White-breasted Nuthatch and Northern Oriole, have been found here.

The localities around (183) **Kirkland Lake** are not worth a detour, but this rather populous area at the north end of the Little Clay Belt is a destination for many travellers. Highway 66 runs through Kirkland Lake to the Quebec border, and traverses some varied habitats – the roadside rest areas are delightful. Travelling east from Kirkland Lake, the town dump (sanitary landfill) is on the south side of the highway 11.1 km from the railroad crossing at the east end of town. This attracts scavenging birds and can be particularly interesting in winter. East of *Larder Lake* (from the Highway 624 junction) Station Road at 1.5 km passes through some good wetlands ½–1 km from the highway. Proceeding east a further 8 km and the highway itself passes some areas of slime deposit to the south that can yield shorebirds in season.

Going west from Kirkland Lake the Culver Lake park at the west limits of *Swastika* (1 km from the railroad crossing at the east end of the village) is down a gravel lane on the south of the highway. There are mixed habitats here, including a spruce swamp which is good for birds year-round.

Continuing along Highway 11, (184) **Matheson** is the next area covered here, although both *Ramore* to the south and *Val Gagné* to the north of this community have small sewage lagoons. At Matheson turn east off Highway 11 on to Highway 101 east, and drive 0.7 km to the Black River bridge. Where there are flats to the south, gulls and duck loiter, and the marshy edges of the river should be scanned as well. Return to Highway 11 and cross it, driving 0.7 km west to an old gravel pit on the right. Just east of this is a small pond, which also often has gulls and ducks.

Highway 101 westbound to Timmins intersects with Highway 11 north of Matheson. However, those using Highway 144 from Sudbury as an alternative route to Highway 11 north will cut the corner by using Highway 67, which joins 11 farther north (see Timmins below).

North of here Highway 11 leaves the Little Clay Belt, the 40 km between the intersection of Highway 578 and the town of Cochrane passing through areas of boreal forest with black spruce and tamarack bogs. The heavier evergreens along here have yielded finches including White-winged Crossbills, the more open areas Connecticut and Palm Warblers, and bushy sections Lincoln's Sparrow.

(185) **Cochrane** itself is in the Clay Belt proper. To the north of town is *Lillabelle Lake*, noted for its prairie-like quality and bird

life. In fact, around this lake it is sometimes difficult to believe one is in northern Ontario!

To reach the lake take Highway 579, which is the road running north into town from Highway 11 as the latter turns west. Follow 579, which itself turns west and then, outside town, north again. Continue north on Lillabelle Lake Road when Highway 579 again turns west. This road continues north 5.0 km to the north end of the lake, and then curves around the end. There is excellent lake viewing from here, and an area of marsh and scrub across the road to the north.

From here continue east 2.8 km to the next sideroad south. Turn south, drive 2.5 km, and turn right on a sideroad just past Cochrane airport. This road leads to a seaplane base on the lake, and affords further views of its southeast end. Return to the main road and continue south to Cochrane. Lake specialties include Red-necked Grebes, Ruddy and other ducks, and Black Terns.

Cochrane is a jumping-off point for flights into the James Bay goose camps and for the Ontario Northland Railway's Polar Bear Express to Moosonee (qv).

Some 15 km east of town is *Greenwater Provincial Park* off Highway 11 14 km north of the highway. The park is situated on an esker overlooking a series of lakes. We have noted Spruce Grouse and Solitary Sandpiper, and Lincoln's Sparrows are present in summer and probably breed here.

Between Cochrane and Smooth Rock Falls the character of the forest is similar to that south of Cochrane. This is one of the best stretches of black spruce forest along either highway, and such species as Cape May, Bay-breasted, Palm, and Connecticut Warblers should be listened for.

From Smooth Rock Falls and Hearst much of the country along the road is devoted to marginal agriculture, and there are old fields and scrub. A few small lakes along this stretch can be productive of both duck and Black Terns.

At (186) **Moonbeam** Highway 581 runs north 13 km to *Remi Lake Provincial Park*, which is one of the few accessible localities for breeding Bonaparte's Gulls, and in which Orange-crowned Warblers have been reported in summer. The town itself has a sewage lagoon. To reach it, take the first street north at the east end of town (Leonard Avenue), then right at once on to Cimon Drive. Continue 0.3 km to René Brunelle Avenue; the lagoon is to the east.

Other communities with small lagoons in this area are *Fauquier,* east of Moonbeam, and *Val Rita,* west of Kapuskasing.

The spruce forests around Kapuskasing are known to have populations of both Boreal and Great Gray Owls. Hope of finding them is slim, however, unless one comes in very early spring prepared to spend time tracing their calls.

Around **(187) Hearst,** gravel roads go north on either side of the Mattawishkwia River crossing at the east end of town. The road on the northeast side turns away from the river at 0.7 km, where a small flooded gravel pit and some scrubby areas on the north side of the road can be productive. The road on the northwest side follows the river for some distance through pleasant mixed habitats.

The Hearst lagoon is southeast of town. Turn south at the light on Highway 583. Drive 1.4 km to the point the highway turns right. Turn left here on the gravel road past Ecole Louisbourg and drive 1.5 km to the next T-intersection. Turn right (south) and drive 1 km to the extensive lagoons on the west of the road.

Fushimi Lake Provincial Park, west of Hearst and north of the highway, has Bonaparte's Gulls, and probably other northern species.

Highway 11 west of Hearst, and especially west of the Highway 631 junction, enters a long stretch where the forest is unbroken by settlements. Initially the land continues very flat and the forest composition is spruce, tamarack, and aspen, but west of the Thunder Bay District line the country becomes more rolling and jack pine, white birch, and balsam fir become more common. This is geographically the northernmost part of the 11–17 loops, and the fine forest should be checked for the more northern species noted above. This is the only area south of Moosonee where I have found Orange-crowned Warbler in summer.

Roadside lakes become more frequent from Klotz Lake on. This lake has a small provincial park, and another west of Longlac

(*MacLeod*) is set among mixed forest on another lake. The shore of Long Lake just west of (**188**) **Longlac** is good for migrant shorebirds, and the marshes there are quite extensive.

The lagoon at (**189**) **Beardmore** is accessible by a bush road. Approaching town from the east, take the dirt road on the right immediately before the bridge crossing the river. Bear left, and left again on small dirt roads; the second bush road in leads to the lagoon.

At Beardmore the highway curves more sharply southwards towards Nipigon and Lake Superior. *Blacksand Provincial Park* provides views of Lake Nipigon to the west; there is no good viewing of this large lake from the highway itself, but the road does pass through the rugged country along its southeast shoreline prior to dropping down along the valley of the Nipigon River. At Nipigon, Highways 17 and 11 westbound join.

(**190**) **Hurkett** is located off the main highway on a loop road, Highway 582. Between here and the Wolfe River crossing is the entrance to *Hurkett Cove Conservation Area*, an area of beach, marsh, alder swamp, and forest that provides a view over the waters of Black Bay. It is about 3 km off the highway.

The country around Highway 11 between Hurkett and Thunder Bay is very rugged but patches of farmland begin to appear in the immediate vicinity of the road itself. At (**191**) **Dorion** the fish hatchery has always been noted as a good birding spot: the area is sheltered and the water open even in winter. It is rather a long way off the highway, however, although the access roads traverse some good mixed habitats as well. Eastbound the hatchery road is at the east end of town, and westbound it is 1.4 km past the Wolf River Road. The sideroad's only sign is 'Fish Hatchery,' and it is west of the highway.

To reach the hatchery, after turning on to the road, bear right at two T-intersections at 1.9 and 2.2 km, and then drive another 2.7 km. It is straight ahead at a bend of the road. The sheltered valley here is particularly good for migrants in poor weather. We have always found this and the entire Thunder Bay area good for Pileated Woodpeckers.

Some 8 km past the fish hatchery turn-off is the road to Ouimet Canyon Nature Reserve Park. The reserve protects the very unusual flora of this spectacular, deep canyon.

(192) Sibley Provincial Park turn-off is about 33 km from the hatchery, 34 km from the north end of Thunder Bay, and the park itself is 38 km from the main highway, on a slow, winding secondary road (Highway 587) which is gravelled at its lower end. If you plan to visit Sibley, it will take time!

However, Sibley is worth a visit. It is a fascinating area for both plants and animals; be sure to get maps and bird and plant lists at the park gate (entry fee). Moose are particularly common. There are miles of hiking trails along the shoreline and up to the top of the bluffs but there is no automobile access to views of Lake Superior in the park itself.

The park occupies most of the southern part of the peninsula, whose rugged cliffs (Thunder Cape) form the famous 'Sleeping Giant' that dominates the view from the Thunder Bay water-front. The park is heavily forested, mainly with balsam fir, but with major stands of white pine and swamps of black spruce and white cedar as well. Hence it is excellent for the warblers of the coniferous forest: in all, 22 species of warbler have been recorded, Connecticuts regularly and Northern Parula on occasion. As the peninsula is also at the northern edge of the mixed forest zone some more southern species can be found; over 206 species are listed on the park check list. The best birding areas within the park are Pickerel Lake, east of the highway, and the outlet of Lake Marie Louise, which is along the scenic drive to the west of the campground gatehouse.

At the southern end of the highway is the cottage community of Silver Islet, with open grassy areas and vistas of the lake. It is here that many rarities have been noted during migration, the peninsula representing the most accessible migrant trap along Lake Superior. Mckenzie Point and Silver Harbour Conservation areas, south of the road between Sibley and Thunder Bay, both provide views of the east end of Thunder Bay.

(193) THUNDER BAY has several interesting areas in and around the city itself. The first, Boulevard Lake Park, is the most accessible to the traveller and the only one that does not entail a major detour from the by-pass route west via Highway 102. Take the easternmost exit (ie, the first travelling west) from Highway 11–17 to Thunder Bay (11B–17B, Hopper Street). Drive 3.2 km south to the point the road curves right to become Cumberland Avenue. Go across the light, cross the bridge, and turn (0.4 km) into a parking area in the park on the right. This is the south end of *Boulevard Lake Park*. Walk up the hill to the north and check the woods and shrubbery for migrant landbirds and the lake itself for waterbirds.

The Thunder Bay waterfront was under extensive development at the time this guide was being prepared, so it is not possible to identify specific waterfront locations. The area around the mouths of the Neebing and MacIntyre rivers has extensive marshes; the visitor might check the roads leading to the harbour and waterfront for suitable access points.

Chippewa Park is a productive area to the south of the city. Follow Highway 61B south (via the Kingsway, Ford and Frederica streets, and Woodward Avenue) to the Kaministiquia River swing bridge. Continue 0.7 km to a T-intersection where 61B turns right. Turn left and follow the Chippewa Park signs 6.5 km to the park on the shore of Lake Superior.

Cover the woods and underbrush for migrants and the shoreline for waterbirds. Both Cape May and Black-throated Green Warblers have nested. The area is also productive in winter.

If you have more time and wish to visit some of the more productive farming areas near Thunder Bay a drive through Paipoonge Township can be worth while, and a pleasant change from forestbirds. From Chippewa Park return to Highway 61B and continue on until it links up with Highway 61. The following drive is only one possible route to follow. The distances given are from point to point.

From 61B–61 intersection, continue south past Loch Lomond Road and watch for some sewage lagoons on the left of the road (1.5 km) belonging to the Thunder Bay Correctional Centre, whose entrance is a short distance farther on. These lagoons can yield shorebirds and duck. (From here south to the intersection with Highway 130, the area west of Highway 61 is the Slate River valley. Any of the sideroads can yield interesting birds.) At 3.4 km turn west on Paipoonge 5 Sideroad. Continue to the next crossroad, which is Concession 2 (2.1 km). Turn right and check the river crossing and the wet area just beyond it (1.4 km). Then return, continuing south past 5 Sideroad, and watch for a wet area on the right (3.8 km) just before Highway 130 intersection (0.4 km). Turn right on Highway 130 and drive to the Kaministiquia River bridge (6.9 km). Park and check the river, particularly the path running down from the southeast side of the bridge, and also check the gravel pits nearby (Rough-winged Swallows have occurred). Highway 130 returns you to Highway 11, but an alternative – slow and rather rough – road west follows the north bank of the Kaministiquia from the village of Rosslyn to Stanley. From Highway 130 at the Kaministiquia bridge continue to the railroad crossing and turn left immediately on the far (north) side (1.6 km). This is the Harstone Road, which leads to the village of Stanley on Highway 588 (11.9 km) through excellent habitat, which also continues west of Highway 588. At Stanley you can turn right to return to Highway 11, but first turn left and drive down the hill to check the river again for waterfowl. You return to Highway 11 just east of Kakabeka Falls.

In the opposite direction Highway 588 runs some 45 km west from Stanley to *Whitefish Lake*, which is noteworthy as the only reliable nesting place for Red-necked Grebes in the area. The route is through farms and mixed woodlands which have yielded many of Thunder Bay's records of more southern birds.

A couple of areas are not covered on the above route. *Thunder Bay airport* is at the junction of Highways 11–17 and 61. The short grass around the airport perimeter can yield Western Meadowlark, Upland Sandpiper, and Bobolink. LeConte's Sparrows have occurred here.

Highways 11–17 at this point are westbound on Arthur Street. If you drive east on Arthur (it is a typical urban strip of motels, gas stations, and fast food stands) you will come to the urbanized *Vicker's Park* on the right. Believe it or not, this can be very good for migrants. Get there early, before the dogs and children!
Highway 11–17 continues west through the mixed forests along the Kaministiquia River valley to Shabaqua, where 17 goes north and 11 turns left. The stretch of Highway 11 between

here and Fort Frances is beautiful but relatively uniform in character. It runs through superb forests in rugged Shield country. At one time none of this countryside seemed to roll quite as much as the road itself, but the road has been rebuilt. This is a more diverse forest than any the traveller will have encountered since leaving the area of Sault Ste Marie. Sugar maple and basswood reappear in forests dominated by white, red, and jack pines, together with white birches, balsam fir, and white spruce. Communities are few, and ones along the road even fewer.

There are two areas of note. **(194) Quetico Provincial Park** is a vast roadless wilderness area accessible only by canoe. There are two highway access points, the main one at the park's only highway campground at Dawson Trail. There is an excellent interpretive program here, and even if you do not propose to travel in the park it is a good idea to contact the naturalists, who can often direct you to interesting locations.

In Quetico the birds of the forests breed undisturbed. Some 26 pairs of Bald Eagles nest every year and other raptors include Merlin and Osprey. Six species of owls occur in summer, and nests of five (Barred, Great Horned, Hawk, Great Gray, and Saw-whet) have been located. Both three-toed woodpeckers are resident, and crossbills and Pine Siskin are usually present. Connecticut Warblers are regular summer residents along with 21 other warbler species. The owls are most vocal in early spring, and are not usually readily found at other times.

One thing the park lacks is areas of marsh, but that deficit was relieved by a marsh that developed in association with Steep Rock mine at nearby **(195) Atikokan**.

The Steep Rock marsh is on the mine property, but visitors are allowed with permission. Turn off on Highway 11B to Atikokan and drive 4 km to Mercury Avenue on the right. Turn there and follow the signs to the airport, following Mercury around 1.7 km to Larson Avenue. Turn right again and follow the signs around (bearing left off Larson) to the start of the private mine road 4 km farther on. Ask permission at the gate and proceed to the marsh. This is along the road to the look-out, which gives a view of the gigantic open pit mine in operation. The marsh's most noteworthy breeding birds are Red-necked Grebes and Yellow-

headed Blackbirds, but it is a good place for waterfowl generally.

As you approach Fort Frances you cross stretches of Rainy
Lake and see more superb Shield scenery. West of the town,
however, you enter the agricultural areas described in Chapter 8,
and these continue along the first section of Highway 71 north.

At (196) **Emo**, 6 km east of the junction of Highways 11 and 71,
the sewage lagoon is at the north edge of town, east of the Emo
Township Line and along the road past the racetrack.

Highway 71 is less interesting for the Lake of the Woods specialties than the areas farther west, described below. By Caliper
Lake one is once again in rugged Shield country and mixed
forest, which continues along Highway 17 east and west of
Kenora.

The highway west through (197) **Kenora** passes some marshy
areas and the open waters of the north end of Lake of the Woods.
I have never seen White Pelicans here, but recent reports suggest
they are beginning to appear more in this part of the lake, so they
are worth watching for. After Kenora the road continues through
fine mixed forest similar to that described under the Highway 11
section past Quetico. There is a good mix of warblers including
Northern Parula, Bald Eagles should be watched for along the
lakes, and Black-billed Magpies are possible at dumps.

Going east from the Highway 71 intersection you will soon
enter the large area of burn resulting from a major forest fire that
crossed Highway 17 in 1980. This should be good for woodpeckers, including three-toeds, for some time. Farther east again
there is heavy forest, with much pine. Around Dryden, however,
there is a zone of farmland, and when the forest resumes it is
dominated by tall conifers through to English River. This heavy
boreal forest yields all the usual warblers and northern birds.

The section from English River to (198) **Upsala** has more areas of
black spruce bog and small lakes. One such near English River
has a pleasant roadside rest area where there should be Rusty
Blackbirds and Lincoln's Sparrows. The largest single area of bog
along the road is some 20 km west of Upsala; in fact this is the
only extensive area of muskeg along the entire Highway 17

route. It is also the only place on this route that we have seen Palm Warbler, and Connecticut Warbler can be heard in the general area.

There is nothing else of particular note until Thunder Bay, and the section thence to Nipigon is discussed above.

Shortly east of Nipigon the highway begins to play hide-and-seek with Nipigon Bay, and there is easy and frequent waterfront access east of **(199) Rossport.** We have never observed much of note on the waters here – loons and mergansers – but the scenery is superb and (if you are driving through from the west) it is a pleasant change from the forest. Close by is *Rainbow Falls Provincial Park,* with the birch-spruce habitats typical of this area.

At **(200) Terrace Bay** is one of the few beaches along this section of the lake: it is at the mouth of the Aquasabon River, and the road to it (southbound just east of the hospital, south of the highway) passes the small sewage lagoon.

Some 2 km east of Terrace Bay (or 1 km west of Airport Road if you are headed west) is one of the more extensive areas of dwarf spruce along Highway 17 across Lake Superior. This looks like Palm Warbler habitat, although we have never seen one here.

The highway then continues east to Marathon through rugged country along the lake. The cooling influence of Lake Superior affects the forest composition, even to the extent of creating an alpine barren zone along the immediate shoreline, as in **(201) Neys Provincial Park.** This is a fine park at the mouth of Little Pic River. There is good birding here, and farther east along the *Heron Bay* road (Highway 627). Pukaskwa National Park on the shoreline south of here is still being developed.

Past Heron Bay the highway turns inland and winds through heavy forest en route to Wawa. Some 20 km west of White River is a smallish area of new burn along the highway, which is worth watching for woodpeckers. *Obatanga Provincial Park* is set in tall spruce forests (Solitary Vireos nest in the campground) and has a network of canoe routes. Solitary Sandpipers have occurred in summer.

There are three locations of interest in the **(202) Wawa** area. Going west, the lagoons are situated 1.2 km past the Highway 101 turn-off to town, and eastbound they are just past the Magpie River bridge. Turn north on a gravel road (not the road to the highway works yard, which is farther east) and the lagoon gate is about ½ km along where the road turns right. The lagoons are exceptionally productive, with breeding Gadwall and summering records of Ruddy Duck and Canvasback. The shrubby sections nearby along the river have American Bitterns and Lincoln's Sparrow, and Merlins hunt over the entire area.

At Highway 101 the main highway turns southwards. The road to *Magpie High Falls* is 1.7 km south on Highway 17 past 101 turn-off on the west (the lake side) of the road. It runs through heavy coniferous forest, which is good for Hermit Thrushes, to the falls, which are well worth seeing in themselves. A much longer side trip is to *Michipicoten Harbour* 11 km along Mission Road, 5.1 km south of the Highway 101 turn-off and 0.8 km north of the Highway 17 Michipicoten River crossing. The harbour itself is ugly, but the road en route passes through excellent habitat and passerine movement along the shoreline occurs in migration times.

Highway 101 to Chapleau and Timmins offers an alternative route to 17 southbound, via Highway 129 (see Chapleau).

(203) Lake Superior Provincial Park is an exceptional area from every point of view. It offers the most dramatic scenery to be seen on either of the northern Ontario Trans-Canada routes; it is fascinating botanically, the transition between boreal and mixed forest gradually occurring as one drives south; and it has a mixture of southern and northern bird species. There are canoe routes, nature and hiking trails, and an interpretive program in summer which can give assistance in locating birds.

In general, the northern species, such as Boreal Chickadee, are commoner in the north of the park (down to Old Woman Bay) and some southerners such as Wood Thrush seem to reach their northern limits in the area. By the time you have reached Agawa Bay it is very obvious that you are back in the Mixed Forest zone!

Continuing south, the **(204) Batchawana Bay Road** (Highway 563, on the west) is short – 5½ km – and has some potential as a migrant trap. At the end take the left branch of the road, to the docks, and cover the surrounding alders, as well as the road in.

Another interesting sideroad is the (205) **Goulais River Road** (Highway 552 west) which enters some of the farming country north of Sault Ste Marie. Drive some 3 km, turn left and cross the river, and 1 km farther on bear right. This gravel road heads through some cottage country along the river (heavy cedar) before turning south to cross a swampy area. (There are two spur roads off to the right; keep left.) It is all good birding. On returning to Highway 17, note that the area of black spruce referred to below is about 4 km south of Goulais River Road.

The Sandhill Crane is one of the much sought-after species in Ontario, and the tracts of wild country between (206) **Searchmont and Wabos** are reputed to have a fair population of the birds. They are shy and not easily seen. Highway 558 to these areas is a good birding road through most of its length if there is ever a chance to take your eyes off the road. It is narrow, winding, quite busy, and there is no place to stop, but you can hear things, including such deciduous woodland species as Black-throated Blue Warblers and Scarlet Tanager.

Another area of black spruce bog where Sandhill Cranes have been seen is on Highway 17 itself, in a valley 8 km north of the 558 intersection. (I should warn you that we have never seen one there.)

You are now approaching (207) **Sault Ste Marie**. If you wish a side trip but do not want to wrestle with city traffic, *Hiawatha Park* offers an alternative. Some 9 km south of the Highway 558 junction watch carefully for the 5th Line left of the highway. (This sideroad is signposted to both the Kinsmen's Hiawatha Park and the fish hatchery.) Turn and drive 3.8 km east to the point where the road bears sharply right. The park (well marked) is on the corner; turn left to the entrance. There are the usual amusements, but there is also an extensive area of mixed woodlands with deep ravines and a network of trails. Leaving the park one can continue straight ahead, instead of bearing right to go back out via the 5th Line. This is Landslide Road, which at some point turns into Old Garden River Road, and after 7.4 km joins Highway 17 just after it has turned east to by-pass the city. The fish hatchery, 0.7 km off Landslide Road, is a sheltered spot which might attract birds.

Westbound, to reach this park follow the by-pass round to the Old Garden River Road, which is at the light immediately east of the far end of the by-pass (about ½ km from the latter intersection). Turn right and follow the above directions in reverse. (Note that going this way you by-pass the last Sault gas stations.)

Sault Ste Marie has some reputation as a migrant concentration area, and the St Mary's River downtown can also provide good birding. As noted above, Highway 17 by-passes the city around its northeast perimeter. If you are heading south (ie, eastbound) continue straight ahead instead of turning left on the by-pass. You will then be on Pim Street, which finally angles southwest and crosses Wellington Street to Queen Street East. Travellers heading west approach the city on Wellington Street; continue past the by-pass and drive to Pim (about 3½ km), which runs one-way southwest.

Turn right (west) on Queen, and go 11 blocks to Huron Street. This is the access street for the International Bridge, but turn south to the *Sault Locks*. The Canadian lock is at the foot of Huron. Cross to the lock and then drive west along it, checking the river for waterfowl and the trees for landbirds. Unfortunately the wild centre section bordering the rapids is inaccessible – the only clear vista of the rapids I know of is from the middle of the International Bridge – which would require a manouvre that is not recommended!

From the locks return to Queen Street and turn east. At the next block (Andrew) traffic is channelled south to Bay Street, and by keeping to the right-hand lane and bearing right one can continue east on Riverview Drive, which also affords excellent views of the river below the locks. Return to Bay and continue east. This street finally curves to rejoin Queen Street, which leads back to Highway 17 again via Pim or Wellington – just follow the road signs which bear left (north) on to Church Street to the intersection of the two roads.

To visit *Bellevue Park* continue east on Queen Street East (stay in the right lane when the 17B traffic swings left). The park is at the corner of Lake Street about 3 km farther on. It too affords river views and is good for landbirds in migration. Lake Street runs north to 17B just west of the by-pass intersection.

West of the city two highways end at points near the mouth of the river, and should be good for viewing of migrants and waterfowl. Highway 550 goes to *Gros Cap*, and Highway 565 leads around the airport to *Pointe des Chênes Park*, also overlooking the river.

East of Sault Ste Marie, Highway 17 runs through farm country whose chief claim to birding fame is nesting Brewer's Blackbirds. These birds have been long established here, with other farmland species, including some more southern species at their northern limits (see Chapter 6, on central Ontario).

(208) **St Joseph Island** is south of Highway 17 on Highway 548. This highway, a gravel road for about half its length, circles the island, on which farmland (mainly pasture) alternates with deciduous woodland. Sharp-tailed Grouse have occurred here.

The southwest end is accessible by road and is a federal bird sanctuary and historic site (old Fort St Joseph). It should also be a migrant concentration point. Although there was not much evidence of this the one time we were there, we would recommend a visit if you are birding around the Sault area, perhaps as part of a day on the island as a whole, since these places vary in quality with the status of migration. There are mixed woodlands and marshes at the point as well as open areas around the old fort itself. The fastest way of getting there (it still takes 30-40 minutes) is to cross the bridge and take the right branch of Highway 548 towards Richard's Landing. A little over 7 km from the bridge the highway turns right and No. 10 Sideroad enters from the south. Turn on this sideroad and follow the paved road 12.5 km – the last section going west on P line to rejoin Highway 548 again, now a gravel road. Continue south on this road, and drive straight ahead following the signs to the fort when the highway turns left. The road turns right at 4.2 km, then left, and right again. In all, the distance is about 38 km from the bridge.

The road east to Sudbury continues through mixed farming and wooded country along the North Channel of Lake Huron. It is tame country after the forests farther north and there are many small communities, but the sideroads to the north quickly become forest roads, and the marshes and open water along the lake can produce waterbirds. Sandhill Cranes are frequently reported from the forest areas to the north, but precise directions are not available.

At *Desbarats* there are marshes along the road, and at **(209) Bruce Mines** there is a small sewage lagoon. Turn north on Highway 561 and drive 1.2 km to the Trunk Road on the right. Turn, and then bear immediately left on a gravel road. The lagoon is on the right at 0.2 km and can be viewed from the road.

East again, at *Thessalon*, the alternative highway route from the north – Highway 129 – intersects. There is a sewage lagoon here as well. At Sowerby there are more marshes, and then between *Iron Bridge* and *Blind River* the river parallels the road and there are swampy sections and areas of marsh along the highway. The rest of the route continues through the typical Shield country described under central Ontario.

OTHER AREAS IN THE NORTH

The highways to such locations as Red Lake, Pickle Lake, Manitouwadge, and Hornepayne all traverse forested lands and offer opportunities to observe the birds of the northern forests. Those to Red and Pickle lakes represent the farthest north it is possible to travel by road in Ontario. They are not discussed here because as far as I know they do not offer birds or birding opportunities different from those in the areas discussed above.

(210) Chapleau – This community is at the junction of highways 101 and 129, which form an alternative route to Highway 17 east and west through Sault Ste Marie. Highway 129 has had a good reputation as a birding road in the past, for the characteristic forestbirds. There are several provincial parks near Chapleau, perhaps the most noteworthy being *The Shoals*, outstanding for its northern wetland communities and associated bird life.

(211) Moosonee – A trip to Moosonee is the easiest way to reach arctic tidewater, although the community itself is located some 20 km upriver from James Bay. From late June to the beginning of September the Ontario Northland Railway operates a daily excursion train, the *Polar Bear Express*, to Moosonee from Cochrane. At other times of year the train runs less regularly. There is free parking at Cochrane station and the train leaves in early morning, the trip taking about 4½ hours. The return train leaves shortly after 5:00 PM.

For about half the journey the train crosses the huge muskeg of the Hudson Bay Lowlands, the only easy access to this area. It is desolate country, with miles of stunted black spruce bog; it is also fascinating, and you will be busy looking for Sandhill Cranes, Hawk Owls, and the more common species (such as bitterns and Red-tailed Hawks) that you can hope to see from the train.

At Moosonee there are several areas of note. The town itself, and the townsite of Moose Factory across the Moose River, yield open and edge habitats; west of the railroad and airfield is boggy spruce woodland; *Tidewater Provincial Park* has trails in spruce forest; and the river itself has tide flats. Downriver at the mouth there is Shipsands Island to the north and North Point to the south (sic!). Shipsands is noted as one of *the* places to see LeConte's and Sharp-tailed Sparrows and Yellow Rails, and the river mouth generally (including the mainland just north of Shipsands) is a fine place for observing migration in progress. Species that have been reported from the Moosonee area in summer and not already mentioned above include Sharp-tailed Grouse, Arctic Tern, Marbled Godwit, Black-backed and Northern Three-toed Woodpeckers, (Gray-cheeked Thrush), Northern Shrike, Orange-crowned Warbler, Palm Warbler, (Blackpoll Warbler), Pine Grosbeak, (Common Redpoll), Fox and White-crowned Sparrows. This does not mean you will see even half of these because most of them are quite thinly distributed, and those in parentheses are likely not even regular in occurrence. Noteworthy among the commoner breeding birds are American Bittern, several species of ducks, Marsh Hawk, Common Snipe, Herring Gull, Alder Flycatcher, Tree Swallow, Gray Jay, Common Raven, Swainson's Thrush, Ruby-crowned Kinglet, Philadelphia Vireo, Tennessee Warbler, Yellow Warbler, Wilson's Warbler, and Lincoln's Sparrow.

During migration it seems almost anything can turn up, as the coast not only is a major flyway in autumn for waterfowl, shorebirds, and such northern specialties as Gyrfalcons, but also seems to be the place that many misplaced southern, western, or even Asiatic species end up (Canada's first-ever Little Stint was noted in this area). Recent work has shown a small but significant late autumn movement of true pelagic species along the shoreline as well.

More than casual observation of such movements entails something of an expedition, and locations on Hannah Bay east of the Moose estuary may be more suitable than the Moosonee area itself. The Cree Indians operate goose hunting camps along the bay and can provide the expertise and facilities needed for a trip to such places as Netitishi Point, some 20 km east of the Moose. Knowledgeable guides are essential, as the waters of James Bay are hazardous and the coast is dangerous. Enormous numbers of shorebirds – principally Semipalmated Sandpipers and Red Knot – gather on the vast tide flats, and most of the North American population of Hudsonian Godwits is believed to assemble here. Other common shorebirds include American Golden Plover, Whimbrel, Pectoral Sandpiper, yellowlegs, and Sanderling. Major flights of Snow Geese and Brant occur.

For less ambitious undertakings, travel across and down river is by hiring a Rupert's House canoe and Indian guide at the waterfront, and camping is possible on the mainland north of Shipsands, at Tidewater, and indeed on any suitable area of crown land. If you plan to camp at all remember you will have to be wholly self-sufficient, and it is prudent to keep the Ministry of Natural Resources advised of your plans. There are also two lodges in town, operated by Ontario Northland. Trips at the height of the tourist season may present problems in lining up transportation, since all the Indians tend to be tied up running groups back and forth to Moose Factory, a more remunerative activity than taking one down the estuary!

Further details on fares, schedules, and planning can be obtained from:

Ontario Northland Transportation Commission
805 Bay Street, Toronto, Ontario, M5S 1Y9 (416) 965-4268
(for train schedules, lodge reservations)

Ministry of Natural Resources, Moosonee District
Box 190, Moosonee, Ontario, P0L 1Y0 (705) 336-2987
(for Tidewater Provincial Park, wilderness travel information)

(212) Timmins – Timmins is located on Highway 101 and is the base for commercial air flights into the far north. It also has some good birding in the immediate vicinity. To the west in Mountjoy Township is a farm area that can be good for open country birds.

Access to the city from Sudbury is via Highway 144, which is one of our own favourite highways for northern birding. Once you are past Cartier (and also past all the gas stations) the country is wild and there is excellent birding. We have noted Connecticut Warblers along here in heavy woodland beside the lakes – which is quite different habitat than is associated with this species elsewhere in the province. The best birding is south of Gogama.

Highway 101 east from Timmins has a few lakes along the road, the best for birding being Porcupine Lake about 9 km east of town and between South Porcupine and Porcupine. At the east end the river crosses the road, to enter the lake to the south, and there are extensive marshes on the north side. This is 0.3 km past the Cochrane-Temiskaming Resources Centre on the north of the road.

Bob's Lake is just east of here again on the south of the road. There is a small sewage lagoon near its outlet into Bob's Creek, at the southwest end of the lake.

Between the junctions of Highways 610 and 67 along Highway 101 is a high bridge over the Rupertshouse River. A picnic area at the northeast end offers good views of the river, which may have waterbirds.

Kettle Lakes Provincial Park is 3 km north on Highway 67 from its intersection with 101. The woodland and many small lakes here are good for birds, and Solitary Sandpipers occur in summer.

(213) Winisk – Ontario's northern coast offers birders the enticing array of nesting species listed at the beginning of this chapter, and its potential for migration watching is virtually unknown. Just looking at the map suggests that points such as Cape Henrietta Maria could make some southern Ontario hot-spots look bland by comparison.

Winisk is an Indian village, and has limited accommodation at the Ministry of Transportation and Communications building. One can take a commercial flight in via Austin Airways from

Timmins. Once there one is confined to the area one can walk around the airport, but this gives a sampling of the tundra habitat in the area and at the coast.

Both food and accommodation are provided at the MTC building, and air service is weekly, with flights at present in on Mondays and out on Tuesdays. They leave Timmins at 8:45 AM and arrive (after a stop at Moosonee) at 12:30 PM. The return plane leaves at 11:30 AM for arrival at Timmins 4 PM. Rates, reservations, and further details can be obtained from: Austin Airways, Box 1160, Timmins, Ontario, P4N 7H9 (705) 264-9521. To reserve accommodation at Winisk, call Winisk 33.

There is commercial air service into some of the other communities along the coast, but to visit *Polar Bear Provincial Park*, for example (itself larger than the province's five southernmost counties put together), then you will have to charter your own aircraft. You can camp on the tundra, but most recent birding trips have made use of abandoned radar sites 415 and 416 for this purpose. These are about 30 km south of the cape, but still on the tundra. Again, it is prudent to make arrangements with the Ministry of Natural Resources prior to undertaking such an expedition (see the address under Moosonee above), and if you plan to do much actual travelling on the ground you may be required to use the services of a guide. Although such trips are undertaken more and more frequently, it should be emphasized that they are not to be undertaken lightly. The coast is dangerous, and there are no readily accessible sources of assistance in an emergency.

8 / Rainy River and Lake of the Woods

West of Fort Frances the character of the landscape changes sharply from a rugged country of mixed forests and lakes to flat farmland interspersed with mixed bush. This southern corner of extreme western Ontario is not only remote from the rest of the province geographically: its bird life is very different as well. With average summer temperatures similar to those at Toronto many southern birds which do not appear in most of the north do appear here. Poor drainage and severe winters produce 'boreal' islands of black spruce bog, with associated northern birds. Most striking to the visitor from southern Ontario, however, is the presence of some prairie birds and other animals that are rare or absent elsewhere in the province. The marshes of Lake of the Woods are host to Yellow-headed Blackbird colonies, and Ontario's only colony of White Pelicans breeds on the lake's islands. Black-billed Magpies occur regularly, American Avocets have nested, and Sprague's Pipits have been recorded.

The area's remoteness from the population centres of the south has meant it has been poorly covered by birders, even though its unusual character and rich diversity were recognized as long ago as 1929. Not only do the breeding birds differ from those elsewhere in the province but the mix of migrants appears to be quite different too. Much remains to be found out about the seasonal bird changes here: doubtless many surprises still can be expected.

The northern character of the area is strong, and the wooded areas have a similar, but richer, mix of species to those described

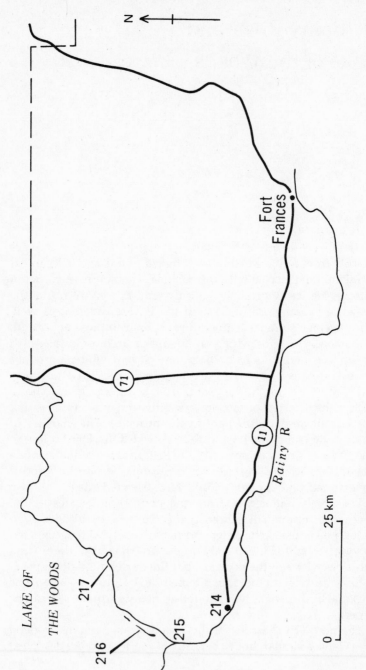

MAP 12 Rainy River and Lake of the Woods

for the rest of northern Ontario. Ravens are widespread, both species of three-toed woodpecker apparently are rare residents, and both Gray Jays and Boreal Chickadees occur. A number of species that are regular in summer in southern Ontario reappear in the extreme west of the province, or (asterisked below) north of the Minnesota border between Rainy River and Thunder Bay:

Wood Duck
Turkey Vulture
Mourning Dove*
Whip-poor-will* (rare)
Red-headed Woodpecker
Great Crested Flycatcher*
Eastern Wood Pewee*
Rough-winged Swallow*
  (rare)
Purple Martin*
White-breasted Nuthatch

House Wren*
Marsh Wren*
Gray Catbird*
Brown Thrasher*
Loggerhead Shrike (rare)
Warbling Vireo
Pine Warbler
Northern Oriole*
Scarlet Tanager*
Indigo Bunting*

Of these species, Whip-poor-will and Loggerhead Shrike do not appear to have been seen on visits in recent years. At least four additional species (Screech Owl, Wood Thrush, Yellow-throated Vireo, and Golden-winged Warbler) have also been recorded and possibly now breed in the area.

The following species, mainly with western ranges, have been reported in larger numbers from this area in summer than from elsewhere in Ontario:

White Pelican
Bald Eagle
Sharp-tailed Grouse
Sandhill Crane
Yellow Rail
Franklin's Gull
  (non-breeding)
Wilson's Phalarope
Short-eared Owl

Black-billed Magpie
Sedge Wren
Connecticut Warbler
Western Meadowlark
Yellow-headed Blackbird
Brewer's Blackbird
LeConte's Sparrow
Sharp-tailed Sparrow
Clay-coloured Sparrow

The flora also has some western components, and Franklin's Ground Squirrel and White-tailed Jackrabbit occur, their only Ontario stations.

Most naturalists' visits have been between mid-April and mid-October. The time of ice going out on Lake of the Woods appears to vary widely in May, but open water may occur along the channel between the mainland and the Sable Islands even when the rest of the lake is frozen. Information on the ice conditions at a specific time can be obtained from the Fort Frances District Office of the Ministry of Natural Resources.

Good waterfowl concentrations occur in April and early May, and there is hawk movement including good numbers of Rough-legged Hawks. Sandhill Cranes can also be expected. Shorebirds in late May include both Marbled and Hudsonian Godwits, rare elsewhere in spring, and Harris's Sparrows can be looked for in sparrow flocks. June is the best period for breeding birds.

By mid-July shorebirds are moving again, and very large numbers are possible along the lakeshore in early August, when huge concentrations of Franklin's Gulls can occur in the Sable Islands channel. September brings hawk movement. By late September and early October flocks of Sandhill Cranes can be seen, and Harris's Sparrows can be relatively common in flocks of White-crowneds. Peak passerine movement is in May, and again in August and September.

Western species, and northern birds that migrate principally through the prairies, have turned up much more frequently in this region than farther east, and with additional coverage many new records can be expected.

CAUTIONS AND HAZARDS

Most of the areas described here are private property; naturalists should use consideration and respect signs. Boating or canoeing on the Lake of the Woods can be hazardous, as it is a shallow, rough lake, full of dead-heads from logging days. There are the familiar northern Ontario clouds of mosquitoes and black flies, especially in June, when ticks can also abound in the wild rice and other vegetation.

WHERE TO GO

There are two main highways to the Rainy River area. From the east Highway 11 from Thunder Bay crosses the southern portion of the region as far as the town of Rainy River. From the north the link with the Kenora area and the main Highway 17 Trans-Canada route is Highway 71, which ends at Highway 11 about half-way between Fort Frances and Rainy River.

The main areas of interest are west of Highway 71 and north of 11, and all the areas described here lie south and west of Lake of the Woods Provincial Park and the main road to it (Highway 621). However, it must be re-emphasized that the region is poorly known, and other locations could be fruitful as well.

To reach the sewage lagoon at (214) **Rainy River**, take an odometer reading at the MTC Patrol Yard and Ontario Provincial Police Station on the south of the road as you enter town. Drive 0.7 km and turn north, then a further 0.3 km and turn west on a gravel road which leads (½ km) to the lagoons. Shorebirds and duck can be expected, and large numbers of Wilson's Phalaropes have been seen here in late May.

On returning to the road from the lagoons, a left-hand turn leads north on one of the more interesting sideroads which joins Highway 600 after about 7 km. Other sideroads should be carefully covered as well. The first to the west of this road (1.4 km north of the lagoon road) also leads to Highway 600. The fields to its north were the site of Sprague's Pipits summering in 1979.

Highway 600 is the main road through the areas of greatest interest, although it too is gravelled for most of its length. To reach it drive directly through Rainy River and turn north on 600 as Highway 11 ends. After 5 km a turn west on to River Road will lead you approximately 6 km farther on to Rainy River itself. The oaks and hardwood bush here can be good for migrant landbirds, and the river for gulls and other waterfowl. From the river the road bears north, and 11.3 km from the turn on to River Road it crosses a creek and bears left. Cover the creek at this point, and west of here to its mouth at the river. Then continue north 1.8 km to the sideroad to (215) **Budreau's Oak Grove Camp**, which is 2.1 km west on the river. The oak woods at the camp are noteworthy for their dominant tree – Hall's Oak, at one of its few Ontario stations – as well as the western character of other elements in the flora. The camp is also an excellent spot for landbird migrants, and is one of the few places offering accommodation in this area (May–November). Continue north on River Road, which turns east, then north, and finally runs east again to rejoin Highway 600, some 30 km from the initial turn-off. Watch along the last eastbound section particularly for Sharp-tailed Grouse, and listen along this route in summer for Connecticut Warblers in poplar woods, and in the farming and edge habitats watch and listen for Cliff Swallows, Eastern Bluebirds, Loggerhead Shrikes, Brewer's Blackbirds, and Clay-coloured Sparrows. Most meadowlarks are Western, but the occasional Eastern is reported.

Some of the most productive areas of Highway 600 are now to the south. The country between 5 and 6 km south is having new drainage ditching installed at the time of writing, which may influence water levels in what have been wide expanses of grassy marsh. Yellow Rails, Sedge Wrens, and LeConte's Sparrows now breed in this habitat, but they are fussy about water levels. Ideally the rails need about 15 cm of water although the acceptable range of water depth seems to be between 3 and 30 cm. If the area is dry the birds should be sought in suitable habitat elsewhere in the area. These open marshy areas are also habitat for Short-eared Owls and occasional Sandhill Cranes, and hosts of waterfowl and shorebirds in spring.

Highway 600 runs east from its intersection with River Road and then turns north. The abandoned school buildings of the almost invisible community of *Harris Hill* are 10 km from the intersection. A small dirt road here, which finally degenerates to little more than a cart track, runs west 5.2 km to the shore.

The shoreline at this point opens on the channel between a long line of sandy islands, the **(216) Sable Islands**. These are excellent for shorebirds – Piping Plover, Marbled Godwit, and American Avocet all occur – and the channel between the islands can yield pelicans, cormorants, ducks, shorebirds, and gulls – including thousands of Franklin's Gulls in August. There are colonies of both Double-crested Cormorants and Common Terns on the lake, so these birds can occur in large numbers, as can Black Terns. Forster's Terns also should be looked for. The shoreline itself is a flyway for hawks and passerines (watch for Bald Eagle and Osprey), and the marshes to the south have Yellow-headed Blackbirds, Sora and Yellow Rails, as well as Marsh Hawks and

Sandhill Crane. Sharp-tailed Sparrows can be found in the shorter vegetation. In spite of its seeming remoteness, the land here is still private property and the visitor should use discretion.

Return to Highway 600 and continue north 1.7 km to the next intersection, where the highway turns east. Continue north to the *Government Dock* (1.9 km), and once again cover the lake, the marshes to the west off Windy Point, and the woods for landbirds. At the point where the road curves right to the dock is Windy Bay Lodge, which is a second place offering accommodation, boats, and guide services (mid-May to October).

From the above intersection Highway 600 runs east 11.6 km to cross Highway 621. Turn north on 621 and drive 4.6 km to (217) **Lake of the Woods Provincial Park**. This park is to the west, on the lakeshore. There are Connecticut Warblers along the entrance road, and the 'Aspen' campgrounds provide fine views of the shoreline north, and west to Windy Point. Look for pelicans, huge flocks of cormorants, as well as Bald Eagle and Osprey. Flocks of gulls gather at the mouth of the Little Grassy River immediately to the south, and the marshes associated with this probably will yield the wetland species that occur elsewhere in the region. There is a small colony of Yellow-headed Blackbirds here. The bog in the park has yielded both Palm Warbler and Gray-cheeked Thrush (probably a non-breeder) in summer. There are also Franklin's Ground Squirrels and Gray Squirrels in the picnic area.

When driving on the roads of the area generally, a careful watch should be kept for Sandhill Cranes in open areas, including hayfields, and for both Short and Long-eared Owls in the evenings. Black-billed Magpies can occur anywhere, but are most likely to be found at dumps.

Highway 621 south is the fastest way to return to Highway 11 and, if desired, Highway 71.

9 / For the Visitor

Public transportation outside cities in Ontario is rather limited, but there are bus, rail, and air links between major centres. Most international or transcontinental flights arrive at Toronto, the hub of the provincial transportation network. Cities with major airports are marked on the provincial roadmap.

Ontario's principal road network is the system of numbered queen's highways. Most of these roads (those numbered to 99) are surfaced and of good all-weather quality, and the Queen Elizabeth Way and the 400 series are all major, divided, controlled-access highways. Other highways, numbered 100 and up, are secondary roads, and, in some cases, may be gravelled. In southern Ontario the county and regional road systems (in black on the provincial roadmaps) are generally equal in quality to most of the main highways. The gravelled township roads are usually laid out in a grid pattern. They can be in poor condition in winter and early spring, but are good for birding.

For further travel information write: Ontario Travel, Queen's Park, Toronto, Ontario, Canada M7A 2E5 or call (416) 965-4008 (weekdays). Free material includes a Traveller's Encyclopaedia, listings of accommodation and campgrounds, and a provincial roadmap. Be sure to get the roadmap, as most commercial maps do not give the county road numbers. The encyclopaedia is useful as it tells you all the interesting things a tourist likes to know, and which I have almost ignored. In Toronto, the Toronto Transit Commission, (416) 484-4544, has route information and a ride guide showing its subway and surface routes.

If you intend to do much birding in the province more detailed maps will be of value. The Ministry of Transportation and Communications publishes a series of 1:250,000 maps that show the township road grids as well as the more major roads (available from MGS Services, 5th Floor, 880 Bay Street, Toronto, Ontario, Canada, M7A 1N8; toll free call 1-800-268-7540). For even more detailed work the national topographic series, with maps on 1:50,000 and 1:25,000 scales, are invaluable. These are available from the Map Distribution Office, Department of Energy, Mines, and Resources, 615 Bruce Street, Ottawa, K1A 0E9. There is a charge for all the more detailed maps.

ACCOMMODATION

There are hotels in all the larger centres, and good to adequate motel accommodation over most of the province. Information on these is provided in the travel information referred to above. The accommodation booklet is arranged alphabetically by community; you sometimes have to dig a little to find the appropriate community listing. Where accommodation is scarce I have noted the relevant facilities in the text for the more important areas.

The camping information is arranged similarly, but note that very few campgrounds are open year round. Planning a camping trip after the Canadian Thanksgiving week-end (the second in October) or before the 24 May holiday week-end can be difficult for this reason. We have found the information in the campground directory unreliable in this regard, so write or phone to confirm.

The provincial park campgrounds are infinitely superior to most private campgrounds from a naturalist's point of view, although they usually provide a more limited range of facilities. I have not attempted to mention all the provincial parks, but the Ministry of Natural Resources puts out a booklet listing them, and another giving information on rates, seasons, and the (limited) reserve camping arrangements. You can get these booklets from Ontario Travel as well on request, but you must write the ministry directly for another useful map, a Guide to Conservation Areas (Ministry of Natural Resources, Whitney Block, Queen's Park, Toronto, Ontario M7A 1W3).

If you are going to do much travelling in the province some understanding of the parks systems will be useful. National and provincial parks range from huge, roadless wilderness areas to quite small campground parks, but most offer camping in good natural settings. Conservation areas are run by one or other of the 39 conservation authorities across the province, each organized on a watershed basis. Their areas fill a regional park role, but include some extensive natural tracts of land with no public facilities, other developed areas with camping facilities similar to those in the provincial parks, and many smaller picnic and day use areas. Some town and city parks (especially in Hamilton and Toronto) have good natural areas, but few have camping facilities.

FINDING LIKE MINDS

The Federation of Ontario Naturalists (355 Lesmill Road, Don Mills, Ontario, Canada, M3B 2W8, phone [416] 444-8419) is the provincial naturalists' organization. It has member clubs in the following communities:

Barrie, Belleville, Brantford, Brockville, Chalk River, Chatham, Georgetown, Guelph, Hamilton, Huntsville, Ingersoll, Kingston, Kirkland Lake, Kitchener/Waterloo, Leamington, London, Midland, Niagara Falls, North Bay, Oakville, Orillia, Oshawa, Ottawa, Owen Sound, Peterborough, Pickering, Port Hope, Richmond Hill, St Catharines, St Thomas, Sarnia, Sault Ste Marie, Simcoe, Stratford, Thunder Bay, Toronto, Walkerton, West Lorne, Woodstock.

These groups vary considerably in their degree of activity. Most meet monthly from fall through spring, and often have field trips to good local areas. To contact them, check with the local library or write the Federation of Ontario Naturalists' head office. The FON offers a range of trips in the province, as do some freelance nature operators.

Other nature organizations in the province that are of interest to birders include The Canadian Nature Federation, 75 Albert Street, Suite 203, Ottawa, K1P 6G1, and Long Point Bird

Observatory, Box 160, Port Rowan, N0E 1M0. Directions to the National Museum of Sciences and the Royal Ontario Museum appear under the Ottawa and Toronto accounts respectively. There are many environmental and trail groups, but they are only peripherally interested in our subject.

Perhaps the best references for persons to contact (because they are updated fairly often) are the periodic supplements to *Birding* (the American Birding Association, Austin, Texas). Local nature clubs and the Federation of Ontario Naturalists can also, of course, often put people into contact with knowledgeable local birdwatchers.

It might be worth while repeating the ABA's rules of etiquette with regard to telephone calls. Try to call between 8:00 AM and 9:30 PM local time, and preferably between 7:00 and 9:30 PM. Local callers might well follow the same advice: many of the people you will contact receive many requests for assistance and are glad to be of help, but to be awakened from a deep sleep at 11:15 PM by a call from a complete stranger who is planning a trip to Africa next year and would like some pointers strains hospitality to the breaking point! Many birders go to bed early, which is something to remember if you are a nighthawk yourself.

HAZARDS LARGE AND SMALL

Outside the major centres traffic can be agreeably light, but Highways 400 and 401 always seem to be busy, and the Queen Elizabeth Way is usually hectic. The northern Trans-Canada routes are very busy in summer, as are highways to the various cottage areas on weekends. From Hamilton east to Oshawa the lakeshore is heavily urbanized. Toronto itself is a typical big city and Hamilton, London, and Ottawa are large urban areas as well.

Driving can be really hazardous in winter, and also in early spring and late fall, when the full gamut of icing conditions can be encountered. If you are coming in winter be prepared to deal with severe cold, and with all the problems – including exposure – this can create.

Ontario's large mammals are not dangerous provided you use common sense, which includes not feeding deer at the roadsides.

One is unlikely even to see timber wolves or brown bears, and unprovoked attacks on humans are almost unknown. (Polar bears occur only along the north coast and I am told they can be dangerous.)

There is only one poisonous snake in Ontario – the Massassauga Rattlesnake – which occurs along the southern Lake Huron-Georgian Bay shorelines and in places along Lake Erie. It is commonest in the Bruce Peninsula, where you can often find one in summer if you try. It is a small snake and not very aggressive, so not very dangerous, but be aware of it and listen for the buzzy, insect-like rattle. These snakes like dry mounds in boggy areas.

Ontario has its fair share of bugs. In the extreme west, wood ticks occur (see Chapter 8); mosquitoes are very common everywhere from late May through August or even later; and there are stable, deer, and moose flies and no-see-ums (midges). Black flies are small black Simuliid flies that will accompany you in clouds in sunny areas, mainly in June. They occur all across the north and are expanding southwards; they are common in the Shield areas and in parts of the Bruce Peninsula. They like to get in around hat and wrist bands and the like, where they gouge out little pits which can itch unbearably for the following week. Liberal and frequent applications of fly dope are needed to discourage these and other biting flies, which are all at their most abundant in June.

Poison ivy in Ontario is a sprawling groundcover, but climbing in the southwest. It is common in many of the best migration hot-spots, so if you are unfamiliar with its distinctive three leaflets and white berries learn to identify it. Any part of the plant can produce an irritating rash on contact.

BOOKS THAT WILL HELP

The appropriate floras and the like are those covering northeastern North America. I assume the reader will be familiar with these, and the relevant popular field guides.

Basic National and Provincial References

Godfrey, W. Earl. *The Birds of Canada*. 1966. National Museums of Canada

James, R.D., P.L. McLaren, and J.C. Barlow. *Annotated Checklist of the Birds of Ontario*. 1976. Royal Ontario Museum

Finding Guides

Goodwin, Clive E. *A Bird Finding Guide to the Toronto Region*. 1979. The Toronto Field Naturalists
Judd, W.W. and J. Murray Speirs. *A Naturalist's Guide to Ontario*. 1964. University of Toronto Press

Regional Distributional Lists

Beardslee, Clark S. and Harold D. Mitchell. *Birds of the Niagara Frontier Region*. 1965. Buffalo Museum of Natural Sciences
Brewer, A.D. *The Birds of Wellington County*. 1977. Guelph Field Naturalists Club
Devitt, O.E. *The Birds of Simcoe County, Ontario*. 1967. The Brereton Field Naturalists' Club
Erskine, Anthony J. *Birds in Boreal Canada: Communities, Densities and Adaptations*. 1977. Canadian Wildlife Service
Kelley, Alice H. *Birds of Southeastern Michigan and Southwestern Ontario*. 1978. Cranbrook Institute of Science
Mills, Alex. *A Cottager's Guide to the Birds of Muskoka and Parry Sound*. 1981. Published by the author
Nicholson, John C. *Birds of the Sudbury District*. 1974. Published by the author
– *The Birds of Manitoulin Island*. 1981. Published by the author
Ontario Ministry of Natural Resources. *Birds of Algonquin Provincial Park*. 1977. OMNR
Quilliam, Helen R. *History of the Birds of Kingston*. 1973. Kingston Field Naturalists
– and Ron D. Weir. Supplement to above. 1980
Sadler, Doug. *Birds of the Peterborough Area*. 1973. Peterborough Field Naturalists
Speirs, J. Murray. *Birds of Ontario County*. 1973–9 (6 sections). Federation of Ontario Naturalists
Stirrett, George M. *The Birds of Point Pelee National Park*. 1973. Parks Canada (four sections covering spring, summer, autumn, and winter)
Todd, W.E. Clyde. *Birds of the Labrador Peninsula*. 1963. University of Toronto Press (includes parts of northeastern Ontario)

Tozer, G. Ronald and James M. Richards. *Birds of the Oshawa-Lake Scugog Region, Ontario.* 1974. Published by the authors

Books on Related Subjects

Banfield, A.W.F. *The Mammals of Canada.* 1974. University of Toronto Press
Case, Frederick W., *Orchids of the Western Great Lakes Region.* 1964. Cranbrook Institute of Science
Chapman, L.J. and D.F. Putnam. *The Physiography of Southern Ontario.* 1969. University of Toronto Press
Dore, William G. and J. McNeill. *Grasses of Ontario.* 1980. Agriculture Canada
Froom, Barbara. *Ontario Snakes.* 1967. Ontario Ministry of Natural Resources
– *Ontario Turtles.* 1971. Ontario Ministry of Natural Resources
Groves, J. Walton. *Edible and Poisonous Mushrooms of Canada.* 1962. Agriculture Canada
Hewitt, D.F. *Geological Guide Books: Geology and Scenery.* 1969. Ontario Ministry of Natural Resources. *No. 1 Rainy Lake and East to Lake Superior; No. 2 North Shore of Lake Superior; No. 3 Peterborough, Bancroft and Madoc*
Hosie, R.C. *Native Trees of Canada.* 8th Edition. 1979. Fitzhenry & Whiteside
McKay, Sheila and Paul Catling. *Trees, Shrubs and Flowers to Know in Ontario.* 1979. J.M. Dent & Sons
Rowe, J.S. *Forest Regions of Canada.* 1972. Canadian Forestry Service
Scoggan, H.J. *The Flora of Canada.* (4 volumes) 1978. National Museum of Natural Sciences
Walshe, Shan. *Plants of Quetico and the Ontario Shield.* 1980. University of Toronto Press

10 / Systematic Lists

The lists that follow summarize the seasonal status of Ontario birds. They are divided by order. The first four columns represent roughly the following seasons:

S = Spring: 15 March to 15 June (relates generally to migration)
Su = Summer: 15 May to 15 July (relates generally to breeding)
F = Fall: 1 July to 15 December (relates generally to migration)
W = Winter: 1 December to 30 March (relates to wintering species)

The abundance symbols used in the seasonal columns are as follows:

a = abundant   Easy to find in all suitable habitat throughout much of the period
c = common   Easy to find during part of the period, and then seen on most field trips to appropriate habitat, and occurring through much of the season
f = fairly common   Seen regularly in good areas during the period; but usually only in small numbers, or present during a relatively short part of the season
u = uncommon   To be expected, and likely to be recorded on at least one or two trips to good habitat over the period, but scarce (or hard to find)
r = rare   Occurs annually (sometimes in small numbers) but can often be missed in the season even with regular field trips
o = occasional   Less than annual in occurrence
e = exceptional   Has occurred, but not to be expected

Species that have occurred fewer than 15 times in the last 20 years are listed separately at the end.

The seasonal status has two columns, one for southern Ontario and the other for the north. The status of birds in the small central Ontario section tends to be closer to that of birds in the south, but in many respects is intermediate in character between the two. These assessments are for the regions as a whole: many species are locally common in one part of a region, but otherwise scarce. This is particularly true of extreme northern and western Ontario, and the northern section probably errs heavily on the side of conservatism because of the lack of comprehensive seasonal data from there.

The lists are intended to guide the user, not to provide a definitive statement on the birds of Ontario. They are based primarily on the seasonal data provided by observers over the last 35 years. I believe they are accurate, but I have not, for example, searched the literature exhaustively for isolated occurrences of out-of-season birds.

	SOUTH				NORTH			
	S	Su	F	W	S	Su	F	W
ORDER GAVIIFORMES								
Common Loon	c	u	c	r	c	c	c	e
Arctic Loon	e	–	o	–	–	r	–	–
Red-throated Loon	r	o	r	o	o	r	o	–
ORDER PODICIPEDIFORMES								
Red-necked Grebe	u	r	u	o	u	r	u	e
Horned Grebe	c	o	c	r	r	r	u	e
Eared Grebe	r	e	r	o	o	o	–	–
Pied-billed Grebe	f	f	f	o	u	u	u	e
ORDER PELICANIFORMES								
White Pelican	e	e	e	–	r	r	r	–
Double-crested Cormorant	u	u	u	o	r	r	r	e
ORDER CICONIIFORMES								
Great Blue Heron	c	c	c	r	c	c	c	–
Green Heron	f	f	f	e	–	e	e	–

	SOUTH				NORTH			
	S	Su	F	W	S	Su	F	W
Little Blue Heron	o	e	o	e	–	–	e	–
Cattle Egret	r	o	r	–	e	–	e	–
Great Egret	r	r	u	e	–	–	e	–
Snowy Egret	o	e	e	–	–	–	–	–
Louisiana Heron	e	e	e	–	–	–	–	–
Black-crowned Night Heron	f	f	f	o	e	e	e	–
Yellow-crowned Night Heron	e	e	e	–	–	–	–	–
Least Bittern	r	r	r	–	–	o	–	–
American Bittern	f	f	f	o	f	f	f	–
Glossy Ibis	o	e	o	–	–	–	–	–
ORDER ANSERIFORMES								
Mute Swan	r	r	r	r	–	e	e	–
Whistling Swan	u	o	u	r	r	e	r	–
Canada Goose	a	f	a	u	a	f	a	o
Brant	u	e	r	e	u	e	r	–
White-fronted Goose	o	e	o	e	e	–	e	–
Snow Goose	u	o	u	o	r	r	r	–
Ross's Goose	–	–	–	–	–	o	o	–
Fulvous Whistling Duck	e	–	e	–	–	–	–	–
Mallard	a	a	a	f	c	c	c	r
Black Duck	c	c	c	u	c	c	c	r
Gadwall	c	c	c	u	r	r	r	–
Pintail	c	u	f	r	u	u	u	–
Green-winged Teal	c	u	c	r	c	u	c	–
Blue-winged Teal	c	c	c	r	f	u	f	e
European Wigeon	o	–	e	–	e	–	–	–
American Wigeon	c	r	c	r	c	r	c	–
Northern Shoveler	f	r	f	o	r	r	r	–
Wood Duck	f	f	f	o	r	r	r	–
Redhead	c	u	c	u	r	o	r	–
Ring-necked Duck	c	r	f	o	f	u	f	e
Canvasback	f	r	f	r	o	–	–	–
Greater Scaup	c	o	c	c	u	r	u	r
Lesser Scaup	c	u	c	r	u	u	u	–
Common Goldeneye	c	r	c	c	c	c	c	r
Barrow's Goldeneye	o	–	o	o	e	–	–	–

	SOUTH				NORTH			
	S	Su	F	W	S	Su	F	W
Bufflehead	c	u	c	c	c	r	c	o
Oldsquaw	c	r	c	c	f	r	f	o
Harlequin Duck	r	e	r	r	–	–	e	e
Common Eider	e	e	e	e	r	r	r	r
King Eider	o	e	o	o	r	r	r	r
White-winged Scoter	f	o	f	o	r	r	r	–
Surf Scoter	u	e	u	o	u	r	u	–
Black Scoter	u	–	u	o	u	r	u	–
Ruddy Duck	u	r	u	o	–	e	–	–
Hooded Merganser	c	u	c	o	u	u	u	e
Common Merganser	c	u	c	f	c	c	c	o
Red-breasted Merganser	a	u	a	r	c	u	c	e
ORDER FALCONIFORMES								
Turkey Vulture	f	u	f	e	r	r	r	–
Goshawk	u	r	u	r	r	r	r	r
Sharp-shinned Hawk	f	r	c	r	u	r	u	–
Cooper's Hawk	u	r	u	r	r	r	r	–
Red-tailed Hawk	c	c	c	a	c	f	c	o
Red-shouldered Hawk	u	u	u	o	r	r	r	–
Broad-winged Hawk	f	u	c	e	u	u	u	–
Rough-legged Hawk	f	o	f	u	f	r	f	u
Golden Eagle	r	o	r	o	r	r	r	–
Bald Eagle	r	r	r	r	r	r	r	o
Marsh Hawk	c	u	c	r	c	u	c	–
Osprey	u	r	u	e	u	u	u	–
Gyrfalcon	r	–	r	r	r	–	r	r
Peregrine Falcon	r	r	r	o	r	o	r	–
Merlin	r	r	r	r	r	r	r	r
American Kestrel	c	c	c	f	f	f	f	–
ORDER GALLIFORMES								
Spruce Grouse	r	r	r	r	r	r	r	r
Ruffed Grouse	c	c	c	c	c	c	c	c
Willow Ptarmigan	e	–	–	–	r	r	r	r
Sharp-tailed Grouse	r	r	r	r	r	r	r	r
Bobwhite	r	r	r	r	–	–	–	–
Ring-necked Pheasant	f	f	f	f	e	e	e	e

| | SOUTH | | | | NORTH | | | |
	S	Su	F	W	S	Su	F	W
Gray Partridge	u	u	u	u	r	r	r	r
Turkey	r	r	r	r	–	–	–	–
ORDER GRUIFORMES								
Sandhill Crane	r	o	r	e	r	r	r	–
King Rail	o	o	o	e	–	–	–	–
Virginia Rail	f	f	f	o	r	r	r	–
Sora	c	c	c	o	u	u	u	–
Yellow Rail	r	r	r	–	r	r	r	–
Common Gallinule	c	c	c	e	–	r	–	–
American Coot	c	u	c	r	c	u	c	e
ORDER CHARADRIIFORMES								
Semipalmated Plover	c	o	c	–	u	r	u	–
Piping Plover	r	r	r	–	r	r	r	–
Killdeer	a	a	a	o	c	c	c	–
American Golden Plover	u	o	u	o	r	r	r	–
Black-bellied Plover	c	r	c	e	u	o	u	–
Ruddy Turnstone	c	o	c	e	u	o	u	–
American Woodcock	c	c	c	o	u	u	u	–
Common Snipe	c	c	c	o	f	f	f	–
Whimbrel	f	o	u	–	r	r	r	–
Upland Sandpiper	u	f	u	–	r	r	r	–
Spotted Sandpiper	a	a	a	e	c	c	c	–
Solitary Sandpiper	c	r	c	–	c	u	c	–
Greater Yellowlegs	c	r	c	e	c	r	c	–
Lesser Yellowlegs	c	u	a	e	c	r	c	–
Willet	r	o	r	–	–	r	–	–
Red Knot	f	o	u	e	r	r	r	–
Purple Sandpiper	o	e	r	r	–	–	–	–
Pectoral Sandpiper	c	o	a	o	u	r	u	–
White-rumped Sandpiper	u	o	u	–	r	–	r	–
Baird's Sandpiper	r	e	u	–	r	–	r	–
Least Sandpiper	u	r	a	–	u	r	u	–
Dunlin	a	o	a	o	u	r	u	–
Semipalmated Sandpiper	c	r	a	e	u	r	u	–
Western Sandpiper	r	r	r	–	–	–	–	–
Sanderling	u	r	c	e	r	–	r	–

	SOUTH				NORTH			
	S	Su	F	W	S	Su	F	W
Short-billed Dowitcher	f	o	c	e	r	r	r	–
Long-billed Dowitcher	o	o	r	–	–	–	–	–
Stilt Sandpiper	r	o	u	–	r	r	r	–
Buff-breasted Sandpiper	e	–	r	–	–	e	o	–
Marbled Godwit	r	e	r	–	r	r	r	–
Hudsonian Godwit	o	o	r	–	r	r	r	–
Ruff	o	e	o	–	–	e	e	–
American Avocet	o	–	e	–	e	e	e	–
Red Phalarope	o	–	r	r	–	–	r	–
Wilson's Phalarope	u	u	u	e	r	r	r	–
Northern Phalarope	r	–	u	–	o	r	r	–
Pomarine Jaeger	e	–	r	–	r	e	r	–
Parasitic Jaeger	–	e	r	o	r	r	r	–
Glaucous Gull	u	o	u	f	r	r	r	o
Iceland Gull	r	e	r	u	r	e	r	o
Great Black-backed Gull	f	r	f	f	–	e	e	–
Lesser Black-backed Gull	e	e	o	e	–	–	e	–
Herring Gull	c	u	c	c	c	c	c	r
Thayer's Gull	r	–	r	r	r	–	r	–
Ring-billed Gull	a	a	a	u	u	u	u	o
Black-headed Gull	r	o	r	o	–	–	–	–
Laughing Gull	r	o	r	e	–	–	–	–
Franklin's Gull	r	r	r	o	r	r	r	–
Bonaparte's Gull	c	u	a	r	r	r	u	–
Little Gull	r	r	r	r	–	–	–	–
Black-legged Kittiwake	r	e	r	r	–	–	–	–
Sabine's Gull	e	–	r	–	–	o	o	–
Forster's Tern	r	r	r	–	–	–	–	–
Common Tern	f	f	f	e	u	u	u	–
Arctic Tern	r	r	–	–	r	r	–	–
Caspian Tern	u	u	u	e	r	r	r	–
Black Tern	c	c	c	–	u	u	u	–
Black Guillemot	–	–	–	e	r	r	r	r

ORDER COLUMBIFORMES

Rock Dove	a	a	a	a	u	u	u	u
Mourning Dove	a	a	a	f	r	r	r	e

	SOUTH				NORTH			
	S	Su	F	W	S	Su	F	W
ORDER CUCULIFORMES								
Yellow-billed Cuckoo	u	u	u	–	r	r	r	–
Black-billed Cuckoo	f	f	f	–	r	r	r	–
ORDER STRIGIFORMES								
Barn Owl	r	r	r	r	e	e	e	–
Screech Owl	u	u	u	u	e	e	e	–
Great Horned Owl	f	f	f	f	f	f	f	f
Snowy Owl	r	o	u	u	r	o	r	u
Hawk Owl	o	e	o	r	r	r	r	r
Barred Owl	r	r	r	r	r	r	r	r
Great Gray Owl	r	e	r	r	r	r	r	r
Long-eared Owl	u	r	u	u	r	r	r	o
Short-eared Owl	u	o	u	u	r	r	r	o
Boreal Owl	r	–	r	r	r	r	r	r
Saw-whet Owl	r	r	r	r	r	r	r	o
ORDER CAPRIMULGIFORMES								
Chuck-will's-widow	o	o	o	–	–	–	–	–
Whip-poor-will	u	u	r	–	r	r	–	–
Common Nighthawk	f	c	c	–	f	c	c	–
ORDER APODIFORMES								
Chimney Swift	c	c	c	–	u	u	u	–
Ruby-throated Hummingbird	f	u	c	–	u	u	u	–
ORDER CORACIIFORMES								
Belted Kingfisher	c	c	c	r	c	c	c	–
ORDER PICIFORMES								
Common Flicker	c	c	c	r	c	c	c	–
Pileated Woodpecker	u	u	u	u	u	u	u	u
Red-bellied Woodpecker	r	r	r	r	–	–	e	–
Red-headed Woodpecker	f	f	f	r	r	r	r	–
Yellow-bellied Sapsucker	c	r	c	r	c	c	c	–
Hairy Woodpecker	f	f	f	f	c	c	c	c
Downy Woodpecker	a	a	a	a	a	a	a	c

	SOUTH				NORTH			
	S	Su	F	W	S	Su	F	W
Black-backed Three-toed Woodpecker	o	o	o	r	r	r	r	r
Northern Three-toed Woodpecker	o	e	o	o	r	r	r	r
ORDER PASSERIFORMES								
Eastern Kingbird	a	a	a	–	c	c	c	–
Western Kingbird	o	e	o	–	e	e	e	–
Scissor-tailed Flycatcher	e	e	e	–	e	e	e	–
Great Crested Flycatcher	c	c	c	e	r	r	r	–
Eastern Phoebe	f	f	f	o	u	u	u	–
Yellow-bellied Flycatcher	u	r	u	–	u	u	u	–
Acadian Flycatcher	r	r	r	–	–	–	–	–
Alder Flycatcher	c	u	c	–	c	c	c	–
Willow Flycatcher	f	f	f	–	–	–	–	–
Least Flycatcher	c	c	c	–	c	c	c	–
Eastern Wood Pewee	c	c	c	–	f	f	f	–
Olive-sided Flycatcher	u	r	u	–	u	u	u	–
Horned Lark	c	c	c	u	u	u	u	–
Tree Swallow	c	c	c	o	c	c	c	–
Bank Swallow	c	c	c	–	r	r	r	–
Rough-winged Swallow	f	f	f	e	o	o	o	–
Barn Swallow	a	a	a	o	c	c	c	–
Cliff Swallow	u	u	u	–	c	c	c	–
Purple Martin	f	f	f	–	r	r	r	–
Gray Jay	r	r	r	r	c	c	c	c
Blue Jay	c	c	c	f	c	c	c	f
Black-billed Magpie	e	e	e	e	r	r	r	r
Common Raven	r	r	r	r	a	a	a	a
Common Crow	a	a	a	f	c	c	c	e
Black-capped Chickadee	a	a	a	a	a	a	a	a
Boreal Chickadee	r	r	r	r	u	u	u	u
Tufted Titmouse	r	r	r	r	–	–	–	–
White-breasted Nuthatch	c	f	c	f	r	r	r	r
Red-breasted Nuthatch	c	u	c	u	c	c	c	f
Brown Creeper	c	f	c	u	c	f	c	r
House Wren	c	c	c	e	r	r	r	–

	SOUTH				NORTH			
	S	Su	F	W	S	Su	F	W
Winter Wren	c	u	c	r	c	c	c	–
Bewick's Wren	o	e	e	e	–	–	–	–
Carolina Wren	r	r	r	r	–	–	e	e
Marsh Wren	f	f	u	o	r	r	r	–
Sedge Wren	u	u	r	e	r	r	r	–
Mockingbird	r	r	r	r	o	o	o	–
Gray Catbird	c	c	c	e	r	r	r	–
Brown Thrasher	c	c	c	r	r	r	r	e
American Robin	a	a	a	u	a	a	a	r
Varied Thrush	r	–	r	r	o	–	o	o
Wood Thrush	c	c	c	e	r	r	r	–
Hermit Thrush	c	u	c	r	c	c	c	e
Swainson's Thrush	c	u	c	o	c	c	c	–
Gray-cheeked Thrush	u	e	u	e	r	r	r	–
Veery	c	c	c	–	u	u	u	–
Eastern Bluebird	u	u	u	r	r	r	r	–
Wheatear	e	–	o	–	–	e	o	–
Blue-gray Gnatcatcher	r	r	r	e	o	o	e	–
Golden-crowned Kinglet	a	r	a	u	a	c	a	e
Ruby-crowned Kinglet	a	u	a	r	a	a	a	–
Water Pipit	u	–	c	o	u	r	c	–
Bohemian Waxwing	r	e	r	r	r	o	r	r
Cedar Waxwing	c	c	c	u	c	c	c	r
Northern Shrike	u	–	u	u	u	o	u	u
Loggerhead Shrike	r	r	r	o	r	r	r	–
Starling	a	a	a	a	c	c	c	u
White-eyed Vireo	r	r	r	–	–	–	–	–
Bell's Vireo	e	e	–	–	–	–	–	–
Yellow-throated Vireo	u	u	u	–	r	r	r	–
Solitary Vireo	c	r	c	–	c	u	c	–
Red-eyed Vireo	c	c	c	–	c	c	c	–
Philadelphia Vireo	u	r	u	–	u	u	u	–
Warbling Vireo	c	c	c	–	r	r	r	–
Black-and-white Warbler	c	u	c	e	c	c	c	–
Prothonotary Warbler	r	r	r	–	e	–	–	–
Worm-eating Warbler	r	o	o	–	–	–	–	–
Golden-winged Warbler	u	r	r	–	o	o	–	–

	SOUTH				NORTH			
	S	Su	F	W	S	Su	F	W
Blue-winged Warbler	r	r	r	–	–	–	–	–
Tennessee Warbler	f	r	f	–	f	f	f	–
Orange-crowned Warbler	u	–	u	o	u	r	u	–
Nashville Warbler	c	r	c	o	c	c	c	–
Northern Parula Warbler	u	r	r	–	u	u	r	–
Yellow Warbler	c	c	c	e	f	f	f	–
Magnolia Warbler	c	r	c	e	c	c	c	–
Cape May Warbler	f	o	f	–	f	u	f	–
Black-throated Blue Warbler	f	u	f	e	u	u	u	–
Yellow-rumped Warbler	a	r	a	r	c	c	c	e
Black-throated Green Warbler	c	r	c	–	c	c	c	–
Cerulean Warbler	u	r	r	–	–	–	–	–
Blackburnian Warbler	c	r	c	e	c	c	c	–
Yellow-throated Warbler	o	–	e	–	–	–	–	–
Chestnut-sided Warbler	c	u	c	–	c	c	c	–
Bay-breasted Warbler	f	r	c	o	f	f	c	–
Blackpoll Warbler	f	e	c	–	f	r	c	–
Pine Warbler	u	u	u	o	r	r	r	–
Prairie Warbler	u	r	r	–	–	–	–	–
Palm Warbler	c	e	c	o	c	r	c	–
Ovenbird	c	c	c	e	c	c	c	–
Northern Waterthrush	c	u	c	e	c	c	c	–
Louisiana Waterthrush	r	r	r	–	–	–	–	–
Kentucky Warbler	r	e	o	–	–	–	–	–
Connecticut Warbler	r	e	r	–	r	r	r	–
Mourning Warbler	f	f	f	–	f	f	f	–
Common Yellowthroat	c	c	c	r	c	c	c	–
Yellow-breasted Chat	r	r	r	e	e	–	e	–
Hooded Warbler	r	r	r	–	–	–	–	–
Wilson's Warbler	c	e	c	–	c	f	c	–
Canada Warbler	c	u	c	–	c	c	c	–
American Redstart	c	c	c	–	c	c	c	–
House Sparrow	a	a	a	a	c	c	c	c
Bobolink	c	c	c	e	u	u	u	–
Eastern Meadowlark	c	c	c	r	r	r	r	–
Western Meadowlark	r	r	r	r	r	r	r	e
Yellow-headed Blackbird	r	r	r	r	r	r	r	–

	SOUTH				NORTH			
	S	Su	F	W	S	Su	F	W
Red-winged Blackbird	a	a	a	r	c	c	c	o
Orchard Oriole	r	r	r	e	–	–	–	–
Northern Oriole	c	c	c	o	r	r	r	–
Rusty Blackbird	c	r	c	r	c	c	c	e
Brewer's Blackbird	r	r	r	o	r	r	r	e
Common Grackle	a	a	a	r	c	c	c	o
Brown-headed Cowbird	a	a	a	r	c	c	c	o
Scarlet Tanager	c	f	c	e	r	r	r	–
Summer Tanager	r	e	o	–	e	–	e	–
Cardinal	c	c	c	c	o	o	o	o
Rose-breasted Grosbeak	c	c	c	o	c	c	c	–
Blue Grosbeak	e	e	e	–	e	–	–	–
Indigo Bunting	c	c	c	e	r	r	r	–
Dickcissel	o	e	o	e	e	–	e	–
Evening Grosbeak	c	r	c	c	c	c	c	c
Purple Finch	c	u	c	u	c	c	c	u
House Finch	r	r	r	r	e	–	–	–
Pine Grosbeak	r	o	r	r	u	r	u	u
Hoary Redpoll	o	–	o	r	r	–	r	r
Common Redpoll	u	–	u	f	c	r	c	c
Pine Siskin	f	r	f	c	c	c	c	c
American Goldfinch	c	c	c	c	c	c	c	r
Red Crossbill	r	r	r	r	r	r	r	r
White-winged Crossbill	r	o	r	r	r	r	r	r
Rufous-sided Towhee	f	f	f	r	r	r	r	e
Savannah Sparrow	a	a	a	o	c	c	c	–
Grasshopper Sparrow	u	u	r	e	r	r	r	–
Henslow's Sparrow	r	r	r	e	e	–	–	–
LeConte's Sparrow	r	o	r	–	r	r	r	–
Sharp-tailed Sparrow	o	e	r	–	r	r	r	–
Vesper Sparrow	c	c	c	o	r	r	r	–
Lark Sparrow	o	e	e	–	e	e	e	–
Dark-eyed Junco	c	r	c	c	c	c	c	r
Tree Sparrow	c	–	c	c	u	r	u	r
Chipping Sparrow	c	c	c	o	c	c	c	–
Clay-coloured Sparrow	r	r	r	–	r	r	r	–
Field Sparrow	c	f	c	r	e	e	e	e

	SOUTH				NORTH			
	S	Su	F	W	S	Su	F	W
Harris's Sparrow	o	e	o	o	r	e	r	e
White-crowned Sparrow	c	e	c	r	c	r	c	e
White-throated Sparrow	a	u	a	r	c	c	c	o
Fox Sparrow	u	–	u	o	u	r	u	–
Lincoln's Sparrow	f	r	f	o	f	u	f	–
Swamp Sparrow	c	c	c	r	c	c	c	–
Song Sparrow	c	c	c	r	c	c	c	o
Lapland Longspur	r	–	u	r	r	r	u	r
Smith's Longspur	e	–	e	–	e	r	e	–
Snow Bunting	f	e	f	f	c	r	c	u

CASUAL SPECIES

The following species have occurred on fewer than 15 occasions in the last 20 years.

ORDER GAVIIFORMES
Yellow-billed Loon

ORDER PODICIPEDIFORMES
Western Grebe

ORDER PROCELLARIIFORMES
Northern Fulmar
Audubon's Shearwater
Black-capped Petrel
Leach's Storm-Petrel
Harcourt's Storm-Petrel
Wilson's Storm-Petrel

ORDER PELECANIFORMES
Brown Pelican
Gannet
Great Cormorant
Anhinga

ORDER CICONIIFORMES
Wood Stork
White Ibis

ORDER ANSERIFORMES
Trumpeter Swan

Cinnamon Teal
Tufted Duck
Smew

ORDER FALCONIFORMES
Black Vulture
Swallow-tailed Kite
Mississippi Kite
Swainson's Hawk

ORDER GALLIFORMES
Rock Ptarmigan
Greater Prairie Chicken

ORDER GRUIFORMES
Whooping Crane
Purple Gallinule

ORDER CHARADRIIFORMES
American Oystercatcher
Snowy Plover
Eskimo Curlew
Spotted Redshank
Wandering Tattler

Sharp-tailed Sandpiper
Curlew Sandpiper
Little Stint
Rufous-necked Sandpiper
Black-necked Stilt
Long-tailed Jaeger
California Gull
Mew Gull
Ivory Gull
Least Tern
Sandwich Tern
Black Skimmer
Razorbill
Thick-billed Murre
Dovekie
Ancient Murrelet

ORDER COLUMBIFORMES
Band-tailed Pigeon
White-winged Dove
Passenger Pigeon
Ground Dove

ORDER CUCULIFORMES
Groove-billed Ani

ORDER STRIGIFORMES
Burrowing Owl

ORDER CAPRIMULGIFORMES
Lesser Nighthawk

ORDER APODIFORMES
Rufous Hummingbird

ORDER PICIFORMES
Lewis's Woodpecker

ORDER PASSERIFORMES
Cassin's Kingbird
Fork-tailed Flycatcher
Say's Phoebe
Gray Flycatcher
Vermilion Flycatcher
Clarke's Nutcracker
Rock Wren
Sage Thrasher
Fieldfare
Mountain Bluebird
Townsend's Solitaire
Sprague's Pipit
Phainopepla
Virginia's Warbler
Hermit Warbler
Black-throated Gray Warbler
Townsend's Warbler
Kirtland's Warbler
MacGillivray's Warbler
Painted Redstart
Scott's Oriole
Western Tanager
Black-headed Grosbeak
Lazuli Bunting
Painted Bunting
Gray-crowned Rosy Finch
Green-tailed Towhee
Lark Bunting
Bachman's Sparrow
Cassin's Sparrow
Golden-crowned Sparrow
Chestnut-collared Longspur

Index

This is an index of major localities and bird names, including cross-references for anticipated name changes in the 6th Edition of the American Ornithologists Union Check List.